ESSAYS ON
MIDDLE ENGLISH
LITERATURE

ESSAYS ON
MIDDLE ENGLISH
LITERATURE

BY

DOROTHY EVERETT

EDITED BY
PATRICIA KEAN

OXFORD
AT THE CLARENDON PRESS

Oxford University Press, Amen House, London E.C.4

GLASGOW NEW YORK TORONTO MELBOURNE WELLINGTON
BOMBAY CALCUTTA MADRAS KARACHI LAHORE DACCA
CAPE TOWN SALISBURY NAIROBI IBADAN ACCRA
KUALA LUMPUR HONG KONG

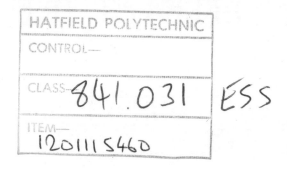
FIRST PUBLISHED 1955
REPRINTED LITHOGRAPHICALLY IN GREAT BRITAIN
AT THE UNIVERSITY PRESS, OXFORD
FROM CORRECTED SHEETS OF THE FIRST EDITION
1959, 1964

EDITOR'S PREFACE

THE papers which make up this volume were left by their author at very different stages of revision. I, 'A Characterization of the English Medieval Romances'; VI, 'Chaucer's "Good Ear" '; and VII, 'Some Reflections on Chaucer's "Art Poetical" ', were printed in her lifetime and show her work in a state in which she herself passed it for the printer. These three vary greatly in style and purpose. The first is the nearest to a true essay: it is a general treatment of a general subject originally written for the fifteenth volume of *Essays and Studies by Members of the English Association* and printed in 1929. It belongs to the period in Miss Everett's career just before Chaucer became her main interest. She originally planned to write a book on the Middle English Romances, and, though this was never finished, she never lost her interest in them. The second, 'Chaucer's "Good Ear" ', is an extended note on a point of detail, originally written for a specialist periodical, *Review of English Studies*, in 1947. It is the most specialized paper in the present volume, but it is reprinted here because it is a companion piece to the more general 'Some Reflections on Chaucer's "Art Poetical" ', and because of the light that it casts on Chaucer's style and technique. The third, 'Chaucer's "Art Poetical" ', was delivered as the *Sir Israel Gollancz Memorial Lecture* for the British Academy in 1950.

'Laȝamon and the earliest Middle English Alliterative Verse', and the three papers on the poetry of the Alliterative Revival were written for the *Oxford History of English Literature* for the volume on Middle English Literature before Chaucer. They were not far from being finished when Miss Everett died, though there is no doubt that she would have given them a final revision before sending them to the printer. But except in a few passages this revision would only have affected minor details. In the few cases where she noted her dissatisfaction over more important issues, the passage has either been omitted or an attempt has been made to carry out her evident intention.

The plan of the *O.H.E.L.* excluded references to secondary sources, except in very rare cases. These chapters, therefore, are in sharp contrast to the carefully documented 'Chaucer's "Good Ear" ' and 'Chaucer's "Art Poetical" '. The translations of quotations were also required by the editors of the *O.H.E.L.* The chapters are printed here as Miss Everett wrote them, except for minor revisions and the deletion of some pages in which very brief reference was made to a number of minor alliterative poems. These would necessarily have been included in a textbook, but disturbed the unity of the chapters as they stand by themselves.

'Chaucer's Love Visions' and '*Troilus and Criseyde*' were given as lectures in Oxford during the summer of 1953. Miss Everett's published work on Chaucer bore no proportion to her interest in and knowledge of the subject. She did, however, intend ultimately to write a book on Chaucer, of which such lectures as these would have been the basis. These two were chosen to represent this side of her work as the most complete in themselves. They also showed signs of having been recently and carefully worked over. It must be remembered, however, that they were never prepared, or even intended, for publication. The style is deliberately adapted to the hearer rather than the reader. Those who heard them delivered may miss a certain tentativeness; a care to qualify statements and to rouse a primarily undergraduate audience to think for itself, rather than merely accept a lecturer's dictum. In this respect these two lectures have been freely revised to remove a looseness appropriate to the lecture-room, but which could only irritate and delay the reader.

In these ways I have tried to bring these unpublished papers as nearly as possible into the form in which Miss Everett herself would have passed them for the printer. My thanks are due to Mr. K. Sisam and Miss Mary Lascelles for generous help in this task. Thanks are also due to the English Association, *The Review of English Studies*, and the British Academy for permission to reprint the articles originally published by them, and to the Editors of the *O.H.E.L.* for their generosity in giving up their claim to the papers on Alliterative Verse.

P. M. KEAN

CONTENTS

MEMOIR BY MARY LASCELLES   ix

I. A CHARACTERIZATION OF THE ENGLISH MEDIEVAL ROMANCES   I

II. LAƷAMON AND THE EARLIEST MIDDLE ENGLISH ALLITERATIVE VERSE   23

III. THE ALLITERATIVE REVIVAL
(i) The Alliterative *Morte Arthure* and other poems   46
(ii) *Patience, Purity,* and *Sir Gawain and the Green Knight*   68
(iii) *Pearl*   85

IV. CHAUCER'S LOVE VISIONS, WITH PARTICULAR REFERENCE TO THE *Parlement of Foules*   97

V. *Troilus and Criseyde*   115

VI. CHAUCER'S 'GOOD EAR'   139

VII. SOME REFLECTIONS ON CHAUCER'S 'ART POETICAL'   149

BIBLIOGRAPHY OF WRITINGS BY DOROTHY EVERETT   175

INDEX   177

MEMOIR

THE death of Dorothy Everett on 22 June 1953 brought to her friends the sense of irreparable loss and hopes unfulfilled. It came besides as a shock even to those who had some idea how ill she was: her health, long precarious, had weathered several storms, and she seemed inseparable from the activities and interests with which her life was bound up.

Dorothy Everett was born at King's Lynn in 1894. She came of an East Anglian family and liked to boast that she was of purely English descent. She might likewise have claimed for herself the traditional English virtues of a strong sense of practical justice and a keen eye for a constitutional issue. She went up to Girton as an exhibitioner in 1913, and took a first class in the Medieval and Modern Languages Tripos in 1916. The following year she spent at Bryn Mawr with a British Scholarship; the beginning of friendly relations with many American scholars. Her love of medieval studies grew, and, while Assistant Lecturer at Royal Holloway College, she submitted for her London M.A. a thesis on the English Psalter of Richard Rolle. Her first appointment in Oxford, to a tutorship at St. Hugh's, was a fortunate event for all the women's societies there. She was lecturer in English for a year at Somerville, and in 1926 was appointed tutor in English Language and Literature at Lady Margaret Hall, becoming a Fellow in 1928. A University Lecturership in Middle English meant the beginning, in 1930, of wider responsibilities, which seemed always to increase. As a member of the Board of the English Faculty she was concerned in the adjustments which conscription called for; and as a recognized authority in her own field she examined not only in Oxford but also for the Universities of London and of Wales, enjoying the new opportunities for friendship which this external examining brought. Indeed, though the burden she carried was heavy, it should not be thought of as a dead weight: she liked taking her share in decisions, just as she liked being consulted about problems of divers kinds. The wide range of her obligations could not diminish her practical concern with the business of Lady Margaret Hall and its growing and changing needs. Intent on composing differences, she had yet no use for the merely convenient compromise, and would allow nothing ill-conceived nor inexactly defined to pass unchallenged. She was an alert and wary member of committees and such bodies, and a wise and forbearing chairman.

These administrative offices, however, were not performed at the expense of her proper function: the furtherance of medieval studies, through her own work and the work she taught others to do. She laboured in her vocation with wholly unselfish absorption, indefatigable in her regular contribution to the *Year's Work in English Studies* and in her reviewing for the *Modern Language Review*, the *Review of English Studies* and *Medium Aevum*. These and the Early English Text Society and the Modern Humanities Research Association likewise are deeply in her debt. Her election to the Readership in English Language of which, in 1948, she became the first holder, freed her from the weight of tutorials but brought its own obligations: to break ever fresh ground in her lectures. She was, besides, increasingly occupied with the supervision of others' research.

Mere enumeration of these activities is, of course, a reflection of Dorothy Everett's eminence in the field of medieval literature: she was an acknowledged authority on Chaucer. Praise of her scholarship would be an impertinence, but it must be said that her collation of the Ellesmere Manuscript of the *Canterbury Tales* is a reminder of what we have lost in the edition of Chaucer that should have been hers, just as her article on 'Chaucer's "Good Ear"' and her lecture on his 'Art Poetical' sharpen the wish that we might have had a book of Chaucerian criticism from her. After Chaucer, she delighted in other poets and story-tellers of his age, especially the author of *Pearl*; and her 'Characterization of the English Medieval Romances' in the 1929 volume of *Essays and Studies* led to work on *Sir Launfal*, of which she was preparing an edition for the Clarendon Press.

To do so much, give so much, set herself so exacting a standard, and die at fifty-nine meant that work must be left uncompleted. Her volume for the *Oxford History of English Literature* was begun only after her health had seriously worsened. Even this was well on its way. Yet the best memorial to her tireless and unselfish work (apart from these gathered papers) must be the achievements of her pupils and the recollections of those friends who were steadied and encouraged by the experience of working with her. It was impossible not to turn to her, in moments of perplexity or when there was something to be shared. Her wise advice might be astringent, just as the criticism in her reviews might be severe. She owed no less to the truth. But there was never any rigour to repel. She was touched and pleased when simple people took her for one of themselves, and she was proud of her skill in the simpler arts of life, in household affairs and gardening: she dealt with plants on her own terms. It amused her to obtain her ends by the simplest means. Her sense of fun was always delighted by the inopportune event which confounds ceremony.

Towards the end she had to curtail many activities and say no to invitations which it had been in her to welcome and enjoy. She did not attempt to conceal the state of health which made these denials necessary, preferring to flaunt it and defy it as a matter of no account. Friendship, and the fortitude of the friend who shared everything, made this fighting retreat possible.

MARY LASCELLES

I

A CHARACTERIZATION OF THE ENGLISH
MEDIEVAL ROMANCES

'NO one can go far in the history of poetry', says Professor Ker, speaking of the seventeenth century, 'without recognizing the power of formal and abstract ideals, especially in the age of the Renaissance. Of the empty patterns that fascinate the minds of poets there were two pre-eminent: the Heroic Poem and the Classical Tragedy.'[1] The fascination of 'empty patterns' was felt strongly by the English poets of an earlier time—not least by Chaucer, the greatest of them—and this must be the excuse for studying the nature of a poetic form popular in the thirteenth and fourteenth centuries—the romance.

In the course of centuries the appeal made by any piece of written matter rarely remains unchanged. What the reader finds in any work must to some extent depend on his own mental and emotional equipment, and this, in its turn, depends partly on the mental and emotional characteristics of his age. It has been noticed that until the middle of the eighteenth century some writers on Chaucer disparage, but more ignore, the quality in him which seems to the modern reader most obvious and excellent—his humour.[2] This particular appeal of his work, though the discovery of it was belated, seems legitimate and in accordance with a true understanding of it. But it is possible for literature belonging to a past age to make an appeal to a later public which is not in accordance with the spirit of the writer, or of his work as it was originally conceived.[3] However the scholar may sympathize with the natural reactions of his contemporaries to any work of art, it is

[1] See *The Art of Poetry*, by W. P. Ker (Oxford, 1923), p. 53.
[2] See *Five Hundred Years of Chaucer Criticism and Allusion*, by C. E. F. Spurgeon (Cambridge, 1925), pp. cxxxviii–cxxxix.
[3] Perhaps the modern tendency to stress the pathos of Malvolio's or Shylock's situation is an instance.

part of his business to make clear its significance for the time in which it was created and not to confuse the appeal it makes at the present time with that which it made at first.

The medieval romances seem particularly in danger of being misinterpreted in the manner suggested, possibly partly because the word 'romance' inevitably calls to the mind the general vague term 'romance' or the adjective 'romantic'. But it is obviously unsafe to conclude that the peculiar modern connotations of these words necessarily express the nature of the medieval romance. This study will attempt, among other things, to characterize the romances as they appeared to the writers of them and their contemporary public, and it may be well to begin it by considering the meaning of the word 'romance' in medieval England.

In a passage in Chaucer's *Troilus and Criseyde*, Pandarus comes to see his niece Criseyde and finds her sitting with two other ladies in a 'paved parlour' while a maiden reads aloud to them. We learn what the book is about. 'This romance is of Thebes, that we rede', says Criseyde. The use of the word to describe a medieval story of the Siege of Thebes is one that does not strike the modern student as peculiar. A list of English medieval romances compiled at the present day would undoubtedly contain a *Siege of Thebes*, though, for reasons of chronology, it could not be the one that Chaucer's characters read.[1] On the other hand Chaucer uses the word elsewhere of a book to which we would not apply it. In *The Book of the Duchess*, he tells how, unable to sleep, he chose to 'dryve the night away' by reading a romance and he relates one of the stories he read. From this story it is possible to identify the book as Ovid's *Metamorphoses*.

In both French and English the history of the word 'romance' is a similar one. It originally denoted the vernacular language of France as distinct from the Latin from which it was derived, but it soon extended its meaning to cover works written in French, so that the medieval English word can often be translated into modern English as 'the French book'. Very gradually there is a further

---

[1] In *A Manual of the Writings in Middle English*, by J. E. Wells, two are mentioned in the section headed 'Romances'. Both were written in the fifteenth century.

alteration of its meaning and it comes to be used for those tales of knights and their doings for which the French were first famous, without regard to the language in which they were written. But owing to its previous wider connotation, there is always a tendency to use it to mean any kind of fictitious narrative, and even books of other kinds in the French tongue.[1] In speaking of medieval romance, I shall ignore its wider meaning and confine myself to what we still call 'romances of chivalry'. Exactly what is implied by that term will, I hope, become clear in the course of the following characterization.

The medieval romance is of course incapable of such exact definition as some literary types, but it is not impossible to describe it so that its nature and limits are comparatively clear. In attempting to do so, I shall necessarily be led to make generalizations to which particular instances may be exceptions. I can only hope to describe the majority of romances.[2]

Medieval romances are stories of adventure in which the chief parts are played by knights, famous kings, or distressed ladies, acting most often under the impulse of love, religious faith, or, in many, mere desire for adventure. The stories were first told in verse, but when, later, prose versions were made, they were also called romances. In length the verse romances may vary from a few hundred lines to tens of thousands (*Guy of Warwick*, Lydgate's *Troy Book*); the prose ones are mostly very long.

The material for the stories could be drawn from any source, from Greek or Latin history or legend (*The Lyfe of Alisaunder*), from tales brought by travellers from the East (*Floris and Blaunche-flur*), from legends which had collected round the figures of English, French, or British history (*The Lay of Havelok, Sir Ferumbras, Morte Arthure*). The chief thing needed to turn any story into a romance of chivalry was conformance to a certain set of literary and social conventions. Something of the nature of these conventions is revealed by comparing the first mention of Priam's sons in

[1] After this essay was completed the writer discovered that in Nathaniel E. Griffin's 'The Definition of Romance' (*P.M.L.A.* xxxviii, pp. 50 ff.) a similar account of the development of the word is given.

[2] My remarks will be applicable primarily to the English romances and may or may not be true of the French.

Lydgate's *Troy Book* with the same passage in its source, the
Latin *Historia Troiana* written by Guido delle Colonne, which,
though a medieval compilation, is not a romance. In the latter,
Hector is described as 'inaudite strenuitatis miles virtute maxima
bellicosus cuius gesta virtute multa vigent in longa memoria
longum non sine causa recensenda per euum'.[1] Lydgate, who
professes to follow Guido 'as nyȝe as euer' he may, has the following version of this:

> . . . also fer as Phebus in compas
> A natural day goth his cercle aboute,
> So fer of hym, with-outen any doute,
> Reported was þe renoun and þe name,
> Þe worþines and þe noble fame.
> For liche as bokis of him specefye,
> He was þe Rote and stok of cheualrie,
> And of knyȝthod verray souereyn flour,
> Þe sowrs and welle of worship and honour;
> And of manhod, I dar it wel expresse,
> Example and merour . . .

There are a good many more lines of the description ending
with:

> In olde auctours rede and ȝe may fynde
> Of his knyȝthood how ȝit þei make mynde.[2]

In the *Lyfe of Alisaunder*, at the outset of Alexander's career,
Philip of Macedon girds him with a sword and tells him to be a
good knight. Whatever the original home of the romance hero, he
is transformed into a knight and conforms to the medieval ideas
of knightly behaviour. The qualities that Chaucer notes in his
knight—a pattern of chivalric virtue—are

> Trouthe and honour, fredom and courtesy,

and later he comments on his gentleness:

> And of his port as meke as is a mayde,
> He never yet no vileinye ne sayde
> In al his lyf, unto no maner wight.

---

[1] Quoted from edition of 1486 'in ciuitate Argentina impressa'.
[2] Lydgate's *Troy Book*, ii. 238–56.

Accordingly, Lydgate's description of Hector speaks of his being

Wonder benigne and lawly of his chere,
Discret also, prudent and vertuous,

and we read of Alexander that, at his death, his knights lamented him for his 'hardynesse, his gentryse and his courtesye'.

One qualification must be made with regard to the statement that all romance heroes conform to medieval ideas of chivalric conduct. In different periods and in the hands of different writers these ideas are naturally not precisely the same. Hence in *King Horn*, for instance, there is a cruder conception of knightly duty than in *Sir Gawain and the Green Knight*. But the common ideas at the basis of all variations are important enough to prevent the statement from being meaningless.[1]

Not only are the heroes medieval in their ideals and behaviour, but the setting which forms their background is medievalized too. The armour, dresses, and jewels which romance writers eagerly describe are those that were fashionable at the time when the descriptions were written.

At the feasts, which are frequent in the romances, the favourite medieval dishes are served. The author of *Morte Arthure*, whose story begins with a feast, mentions boars' heads, wild and specially fatted venison, peacocks, plovers, sucking pigs, herons in sauce, swans, 'frumentee' (furmenty), 'tartes of Turky', and many other delicacies, served on gold and silver dishes. Often the account of the dishes is followed by a list of well-known wines. We read of

rumney and malmesyne,
Both ypocrasse and vernage wyne,
Mount rose and wyne of Greke;
Both Algrade and respice eke,
Antioche and bastarde,
Pyment, also, and garnade;
Wyne of Greke and muscadell,
Both claré, pyment and Rochell.[2]

This second quotation is taken from a passage in the *Squyr of*

[1] The Charlemagne romances probably have least of the spirit of chivalry, being affected by their origin in the *chansons de geste*.
[2] *Squyr of Lowe Degré*, 753 ff. Ed. Ritson, *Ancient Engleish Metrical Romanceēs*, iii.

Lowe Degré in which a king, obliged to prevent his daughter from marrying beneath her, attempts to console her by offering her everything in his power. The passage is a long catalogue of all medieval delights. Conspicuous among the amusements he suggests is hunting, and a cursory glance at the romances shows that this was as common a form of amusement for the heroes of all romances as it was in reality for the high-born of medieval France and England. Even the king of the Fairies goes hunting (*Sir Orfeo*). In *Sir Gawain and the Green Knight*, the poet describes minutely a deer-hunt, a boar-hunt, and a fox-hunt, using a number of technical terms such as *quest, querré, rechated, mute*, and even going into detail over the breaking up of the deer and the 'unlacing' of the boar—accomplishments expected of a gentleman.[1] The author of this poem clearly intended to appeal to the fashionable world by his mention of the very latest fashions in shoes, in ladies' head-dresses, in architecture, and other things.[2]

In fact, the romances were partly popular, because, unlike so much of the Latin literature known to medieval readers, they were up to date in their ideas and their properties. This has been recognized by some scholars, notably Professor W. P. Ker and Sir Walter Raleigh.[3] W. P. Ker is, however, writing of the French romances[4] and Sir Walter Raleigh's remarks are introductory to a discussion of romance in later English literature, and neither of them shows in any detail how the English romances illustrate the point.

It is partly by reason of the 'modernity' of their settings that discussion of the general term 'romance' is mostly irrelevant in

[1] See 1325 ff. and 1606 ff., *Sir Gawain and the Green Knight*, ed. by J. R. R. Tolkien and E. V. Gordon. See also the note in this edition on l. 1325.
[2] See ibid., pp. xx, xxi.
[3] See *Romance. Two Lectures*, by Sir Walter Raleigh (1916), pp. 25 ff. Of the romances, he says, 'The note of this Romance literature is that it was actual, modern, realistic at a time when classical literature had become a remote convention of bookish culture.' Cf. also p. 29. Cf. W. P. Ker, *Epic and Romance* (1908), pp. 324 ff.; *English Literature: Medieval*, p. 112; *Cambridge History of English Literature*, i, p. 280.
[4] Except in the second reference given; but even here he does not work out in any detail the applications of his remark. Sarah F. Barrow's book, *The Medieval Society Romances* (1925), which points out the 'modernity' of romances, also deals chiefly with French romances.

connexion with them, if romance is, in the words of Professor Ker, 'the name for the sort of imagination that possesses the mystery and the spell of everything remote and unattainable.'[1] Yet several recent critics use somewhat similar definitions to explain a quality they claim to find there. Miss Rickert[2] finds that widely different romances 'agree in being as far as possible removed from the facts of daily experience', and concludes: 'Briefly the essential implication seems to me to be that of the soul leaving its customary habitations and wandering in strange places, and essaying to bring into literature the fruits of its adventures.' W. M. Dixon[3] and G. Wyndham[4] seem to hold the same view. Professor H. R. Patch, in his discussion of *Chaucer and Mediaeval Romance*,[5] thinks that, though the twelfth-century French romances of Chrétien de Troyes may have been to some extent realistic, 'in the fourteenth century it was rather to the imagination which found special glamour in the remote or impossible that these stories offered an appeal'. The aim of his paper is to answer the question 'To what extent does the romantic quality (or the quality of the romances) appear in Chaucer's work?' But in this sentence with its parenthesis he begs a question to which the answer must be sought before his own can be asked; namely, is 'romantic quality' the same thing as 'the quality of the romances'?

It has already been suggested here that such interpretations of the romances have arisen because it is too easily assumed that they have made the same kind of appeal in all ages. It is certainly clear from a recent discussion of the meaning of the word 'romantic'[6] that when it was first used in the seventeenth century to denote that which was 'like the old romances', the qualities that these romances were believed to possess were unreality and remoteness. If this is what the seventeenth-century readers saw in them, for us, separated

---

[1] *Epic and Romance* (1908), p. 321.
[2] *Early English Romances in Verse, Romances of Love*, pp. xiv ff.
[3] *English Epic and Heroic Poetry*, pp. 98 ff.
[4] *Springs of Romance in the Literature of Europe*.
[5] *Essays in Memory of Barrett Wendell*, by his Assistants. Cambridge: Harvard University Press (1926).
[6] Cf. *Words and Idioms*, by Logan Pearsall Smith (1925). The author had previously made some study of the use of the word 'romantic' in a *S.P.E. Tract* for 1924.

from all things medieval by the 'dark backward and abysm of time',
distance lends mysterious charm to the heroes and heroines of the
romances and to their surroundings; but to those who lived when
they were written, the settings at least were not, in this sense,
romantic.

At the same time, he who looked to them for realistic pictures of
medieval manners and properties would be disappointed, except
in a few noteworthy instances, among which are *Havelok* and *Sir
Gawain and the Green Knight*. Generally speaking, there is in
them nothing of the realism of the Prologue to *The Canterbury
Tales*, still less of that of the *Vision of Piers the Plowman*. The
pleasure they afforded in their own time has nothing in common
with that given by some of the novels of Arnold Bennett in ours;
rather they pleased as modern novels of 'high life' do. One of their
merits in the eyes of those for whom they were written must have
been that they provided an escape from the failures or partial
successes of life as it was lived by showing them that life idealized.[1]
The dresses and armour, the feasts and hunts, were cut to the
pattern of things known, but on those patterns the romancer
embroidered every splendour his imagination could conjure up.
In the romances, everything must be of a gorgeousness to which
real life could not attain. Hence the length and monotony of some
of the descriptions. When a hero of romance gave a feast, he provided all the fine dishes of which the writer had heard; if the
heroine's mantle is described, it is covered so thick with embroidery
and precious stones that the account of it wearies the mind (*Emaré*).
This idealization of ordinary life is found in other than material
things. Doubtless, in fact, knights did not always act in accordance
with the highest conceptions of chivalric conduct. In the Middle
Ages, wife-beating was not unknown, even among the nobler
classes of society. But in the romances, the hero is a superman. He
does his duty whatever it may cost him (*Lybeaus Desconus*), and
should he fail to do it, he only recovers self-respect and the esteem
of his fellows after a long-drawn-out period of misery and penance

[1] Just as in Restoration Comedy the wit and immorality reflect the fashion
of the time, but there can be little doubt that in the plays the wit was more
sparkling and the immorality more outrageous and less frequently attended by
unpleasant consequences than in real life.

(*Ywain and Gawain*). The romance writers believed in that 'heightening' of the characters and the action once admired by Dryden and exemplified in the *Conquest of Granada* and its hero Almanzor; and with them, as with him, this heightening was accompanied, perhaps inevitably, by simplified character-drawing. The half-tones of ordinary human nature are not for the romance writers; every man is either a hero and a good man, or a villain. The man who disregards knightly duty has the latter label attached to him from the outset and is, in due time, disgraced or killed.[1] Poetic justice reigns supreme throughout the romances. The great majority of them end happily, with a wedding or perhaps a reunion or a reconciliation. It is typical of them, that in *Sir Orfeo*, the conclusion of the classical story of Orpheus is changed; the hero wins back his wife and 'they lyved gode lyfe afterwarde'. At the end of a romance innocence is always vindicated and triumphant, however violent may have been the trials by which it was beset (*Athelston, Chevalere Assigne, Emaré, Havelok*). The true Christian gets the better of all villains, slanderers, magicians, and Saracens (*King Horn, Roland and Vernagu, Lybeaus Desconus, Guy of Warwick*). The few exceptions are due to the occasional intractability of historic or legendary material (*Lyfe of Alisaunder, Morte Arthure, Knight of Courtesy*), or to the fact that the French original, not a romance proper, is too well known to be tampered with (*Song of Roland*).[2] On the whole the ordinary limitations of human life do not exist. At the end of *Amis and Amiloun*, a story of the complete devotion of two friends, Amiloun is brought to Amis suffering from leprosy. It is revealed to both the friends in dreams that a cure could be wrought if Amiloun were bathed in the blood of Amis's two children. Thereupon Amis cuts the children's throats and effects the cure. Soon he is forced to break the news of his deed to his wife, but when they both go to look at the children's bodies, they find them alive and quite sound.

[1] *Sir Gawain and the Green Knight* is an obvious exception; but it is not in all ways a typical romance, being a work of art in a greater degree than most romances.

[2] Actually the surviving English version of this is a fragment, but its likeness to the course of the French *Chanson de Roland* is too great for us to suppose its end would have differed from that of the *Chanson*.

Miracles as wonderful as this are of constant occurrence in the romances, and though, to some extent, they can be regarded as further examples of the idealization of ordinary life, they are also connected with another feature of the romances which is not to be explained so simply—the use of the marvellous in all its aspects. It is perhaps employed most constantly by the writers of Arthurian romances, but it is obvious that it is not confined either to them or to the romances as a whole. Dragons, giants, monsters of all kinds, hauntings, shape-changings, and sorcery are to be found in all medieval tales; *Beowulf* and the Old Norse sagas use them as much as the romances. But the romance writers probably exploit the marvellous more untiringly than any other medieval writers, and, to those wonders used also by the Old English and Old Norse writers, they add new ones less terrifying, and, when well treated, more subtle—stories of fairyland (*Sir Orfeo, Sir Launfal*), of magic castles and enchanted ladies (*The Weddynge of Sir Gawen*), and the mystical wonders of the Holy Grail.

At this point it is necessary to reconsider the statement that the romances are not 'romantic'. Do not these marvels contain the essence of 'romance' in the meaning in which Professor Ker used the word? The answer to this question is not a simple one. Undoubtedly in a sense they do; they are so remote from human life in any period or country that they would seem to be necessarily invested with the charm of mystery. Whatever has been said of the unromantic nature of the details and background of the romances, it must be admitted that many of the stories told in them are to the modern mind essentially romantic stories, many of the adventures through which the heroes pass are romantic. But it appears that remoteness from real life is not enough. If an incident is to be 'romantic' in this sense in literature, the writer who uses it must regard it in a particular way. It would perhaps be difficult for a modern possessing any imagination to write of the marvels described in the romances in other than a 'romantic' manner. But, because he did not make as definite a dividing line between the possible and the impossible as most of us do, the medieval romance writer in France and England looked upon his marvels with so unmoved and matter-of-fact an air that the glamour and mystery which should surround them is, in the majority of romances, completely lacking. We are told in the *King of Tars*, that on being baptized the Saracen Sultan changed his colour from black to white, but this startling change seems quite dull because of the manner of its telling:

> The Preste hihte sire Cleophas
> And nempnede so the soudan of Damas,
> After his own name.
> His colour that lodlich and blak was
> Hit bicom feir thorw godes gras
> And cler withoute blame.[1]

The Rime of the Ancient Mariner shows us that there must be a preparation for a mystery; the right setting must be created, the imagination of the reader must be stimulated in the right way; and this is not done in the romances, with a very few exceptions. It is one of the failures at which Chaucer mocks in *Sir Thopas* when he makes his hero suddenly, for no particular reason, announce his determination to have a fairy mistress:

> O seinte Marie, benedicite!
> What eyleth this love at me
> To binde me so sore?
> Me dremed al this night, pardee,
> An elf-quene shal my lemman be,
> And slepe under my gore.
>
> An elf-quene wol I love, y-wis,
> For in this world no womman is
> Worthy to be my make
> In toune;
> All othere wommen I forsake,
> And to an elf-quene I me take
> By dale and eek by doune![2]

Elsewhere Chaucer shows that he knew how a fairy should be introduced:

> And in his way it happed him to ryde,
> In all this care, under a forest-syde,

[1] *The King of Tars*, 851–6. Ed. Ritson, ii.
[2] *Canterbury Tales*, B 1974 ff.

Whereas he saugh upon a daunce go
Of ladies foure and twenty, and yet mo;
Toward the whiche daunce he drow ful yerne,
In hope that som wisdom sholde he lerne.
But certainly, er he came fully there,
Vanisshed was this daunce, he niste where.
No creature saugh he that bar lyf,
Save on the grene he saugh sitting a wyf . . .[1]

The very lavishness of the display of marvels in the romances breeds contempt in the reader. Who could be moved by three giants, two magicians, one sorceress, a magic hall, and an enchanted lady all in the course of one fairly short story (*Lybeaus Desconus*)? The baldness of treatment of the marvellous and the abundant supply of it destroy the sense of remoteness and once again 'romance' is not to be found. It is impossible to say with absolute certainty that this use of the marvellous never gave medieval readers the thrill of the remote and mysterious, but so infrequently do we find any obvious attempt to exploit the sensations of surprise and horror that might be expected to arise from them,[2] that it seems likely that this was not what they sought in the romances. What is certain is that medieval readers and hearers thirsted for tales of all kinds, enjoyed the mere narration of a series of events. Only by this supposition can we explain the duplication of incident in the romances such as is found when, in *King Horn*, the hero twice returns in disguise at a crucial moment. The length of romances like *Guy of Warwick* is due to the same cause. In order to satisfy this thirst it was natural for the romance writer to ransack all possible sources for stories, and this by itself accounts in part for the use of the marvellous. A crude romance like *Sir Perceval of Galles*, in which marvellous incidents abound, is clearly meant primarily to appease the demand for stories. Though references to rich feasts, castles, and other medieval properties are to be

---

[1] *Canterbury Tales* D 989 ff. I am glad to find myself so far in agreement with Professor Patch that we have both, independently, chosen this passage for the same purpose. See p. 108 of his essay.

[2] As, for instance, in the horror-novel of the late eighteenth and early nineteenth centuries. These by themselves, apart from any other evidence, bear witness to a taste for the 'romantic' in the contemporary public.

found, there are none of the fashionable details which have been noticed in other romances, and it is possible that it was written for a popular rather than a fashionable audience. *Lybeaus Desconus* shows the same heaping together of adventures, this time by so undiscriminating a hand that the story has little coherence. Unlike *Sir Perceval*, it contains much descriptive detail, but it is used without any art. The writer is copying fashionable romances without possessing the training and culture necessary to appreciate the best that could be done with such material. It is significant that this 'marvellous' story is one of those at which Chaucer mocks.

To sum up what has been said of the unromantic nature of the majority of these poems: it would seem that some critics of the romances have not made a necessary distinction between the 'properties' used by romance writers and the actual treatment of them in the romances themselves. These 'properties' may be con sidered in two groups—the details of setting, and the marvellous happenings. Both of these, if they are considered apart from any particular treatment of them, spell 'romance' to the modern; to the medieval reader the first did not, and the second may or may not have done so. But when we come to look at the treatment of these 'properties' in the romances themselves we find that it is 'romantic' in the sense that some modern poetry[1] is romantic in a few only, and those the greatest of them.

Two such widely different poems as *Sir Orfeo* and *Sir Gawain and the Green Knight* will serve as examples of romances in which something of the glamour of 'romance', as the modern understands it, is to be found. In the first, the other-world of fairyland is as truly created in the lines:

> He miʒt se him bisides
> Oft in hot undertides
> Þe king o fairy wiþ his rout
> Com to hunt him al about,
> Wiþ dim cri and bloweing;
> And houndes also wiþ him berking;

[1] For instance, *The Ancient Mariner* and some of Keats's poetry.

Ac no best þai no nome,
No neuer he nist whider þai bicome![1]
(281 ff.)

as in Prospero's speech to those who

. . . on the sands with printless foot
Do chase the ebbing Neptune and do fly him
When he comes back . . .

In *Sir Gawain and the Green Knight* the 'romance' is of a robuster, and at the same time subtler kind. The poet throws the 'modifying colours of imagination' over the familiar so that it lives with a new life. Wintry weather in the mountainous country where Sir Gawain finds the Green Chapel, a castle with its battlements standing clearly outlined against the sky as though 'pared out of papure', the pleasure of a glowing fire and fresh clothes after a journey—these must have been familiar things to him, but he transforms what is familiar and topical into the unique and permanent. At times, too, he displays the other power used by Coleridge with such skill in the *Ancient Mariner*. The Green Knight himself is of the other world, but he can mingle with men without arousing incredulity because of the 'dramatic truth' of his behaviour when, for instance,

Wyth sturne schere þer he stod he stroked his berde,
And wyth countenance dryȝe he droȝ doun his cote.

(334–5.)

But if these two poems are exceptions to the general statement that the romances are not 'romantic', it is by virtue of one quality alone—the imagination of their writers. Everything in the stories might be found in other romances that lack the quality of 'romance'. Comparison of these poems with other romances reveals the fact that 'romance' is not inherent in any kind of subject-matter, nor is it found by nature in any literary form; it is the gift of the artist, the result of a peculiar and individual way of seeing things. The majority of English romance writers are not imaginative enough to possess it.

[1] Quoted from the edition of the poem in *Fourteenth-Century Verse and Prose*, ed. by K. Sisam. It is probably true to say that this kind of 'romance' is more often found in the 'Breton *lais*' than in the other romances.

Up to this point it is the contents and the spirit of the romances that have been considered, and any student of medieval literature will know that a good deal of what has been said of these characteristics is true of other forms of vernacular literature at the time. The expression of the unknown in terms of the familiar and the medieval is a feature of all story-telling in the period, whether it be in narrative or dramatic form. In the poem known as *Cleanness*, Nebuzaradan, captain of Nebuchadnezzar's guard[1] is a 'gentyle duc' and the 'chef of his cheualrye', and in the *Second Shepherds' Play*, belonging to the *Towneley Cycle*, the shepherds at Nazareth grumble at weather that is unmistakably English and bring as offerings to the child Christ a 'bob of cherys' and a ball with which to 'go to the tenys'. The matter-of-fact attitude towards the marvellous is perhaps even more striking in the legends of the saints than in the romances, and so is the idealization of ordinary life, though, on the whole, sides of life different from those found in the romances are treated. Nor is the type of story used a distinguishing sign of the romance. Several instances exist of the treatment of the same story in a romance and in another literary form. It is therefore clearly necessary to mark out more definitely the boundaries of the romance species, particularly in regard to literary treatment and form. It is, of course, only possible to do this on broad lines.

I propose to begin with those distinctions which are easiest to make. The similarity between the saint's legend and the romance has already been indicated,[2] but the differences between the two are really obvious enough. The legend is written with didactic intent, the romance chiefly to give pleasure; even when a didactic element enters into the romance the other object is predominant. On the whole, therefore, the two forms make use of different stories, though some motives are found in both.[3] Very rarely in the

[1] 2 Kings xxv. 8.
[2] Cf. Saintsbury, *History of the French Novel*, i, p. 9, where the view that the saints' lives gave birth to the romances is put forward.
[3] The romances which use the theme of Chaucer's story of Constance (see Wells's *Manual*, pp. 112 ff.) share several of their incidents with the legends. For instance, the separation of members of a family through divers accidents and their subsequent reunion is found in most of them as well as in the legend of St. Eustace or of St. Clement in the *South-English Legendary*. Several of them have stories of the persecution of an innocent woman similar to those of some Christian martyrs.

saints' lives is there that attention paid to descriptive detail which is such a feature of the romance. *Sir Isumbras*, which tells a story very near in many ways to the legend of St. Eustace, has descriptions of the great stature of the knight; of his wrapping his wife and children in his 'mantille of palle' and his 'riche surcoat'; of the fine ships of the Sultan 'with toppe-castelles set one lofte . . .' which are entirely lacking in the Eustace legend in the *South-English Legendary*. It is characteristic, too, that in *Sir Isumbras* the reunion is followed by a long and happy life:

> Thay lyffede and dyed with gud content,
> And sythen alle till hevene thay went,
> When that they dede ware[1]—

whereas in the legend of Eustace the reunion is followed by a further trial of faith and eventually by martyrdom for the whole family.

Another distinction to be made is that between the romance and the ballad. If one considers a typical ballad and a typical romance, the distinction between the two seems so obvious as to be hardly worth making, but the apparent ease with which it can be made is a little misleading. A more careful examination of the two forms reveals that there are ballads using the same kind of story as is commonly found in a romance. An example is *Sir Aldingar* from the *Percy Folio Manuscript*.[2] At other times we find the same story appearing in a ballad form and in a Breton *lai* or romance. The *lai*, *Sir Orfeo*, has a counterpart in *King Orfeo*, a ballad preserved till the nineteenth century in the Shetlands;[3] *Hind Horn* is a ballad on the same subject as *King Horn* and *Horn Childe and Maiden Rimnild*; and the same story is at the back of the ballad *Fair Annie* and the Breton *lai*, *Lai le Freine*. It is, however, precisely these ballads that approach closest to the romances and *lais* that give away most completely the secret of the difference between the forms.[4] In *Lai le Freine* the events of the story are told in the

---

[1] 789–91. Ed. Halliwell, *Thornton Romances*.   [2] i, pp. 166 ff.
[3] The version in Child's *English and Scottish Popular Ballads*, i, pp. 217 ff., was taken down in the nineteenth century from the lips of an old man in Unst, Shetland.
[4] On pp. 21–22, the difference between some of the 'Breton *lais*', of which *Lai le Freine* is an example, and romances proper is discussed. But both 'Breton *lais*'

following sequence: two knights, who are great friends, live in the west country. The wife of one of them gives birth to twin sons. Thereupon the wife of the other, an envious and spiteful woman, declares that to bear twins is a sign of infidelity. Soon after she herself bears twin girls and, afraid that what she has said will recoil on her own head, she plots to get rid of one of the children. A maid takes the child away, and, after wandering over a wild heath throughout the night, at dawn hides her in an ash-tree near a 'hous of religion', and makes off. There the child is found by the porter and taken to the abbess. She is called Le Frain (= ash-tree) after her hiding-place, and is brought up by the abbess till she is twelve years old. Then a young knight persuades her to run away with him and be his mistress. So she lives until his knights urge him to forsake her for 'sum lordes douhter'. The lady he decides to marry is the twin sister of Le Frain and he brings her as a bride to his house. . . . Here the English version, which is a fragment, ends, but the conclusion of the tale can be supplied from the original version, the French *lai* of Marie de France. Le Frain sets herself to help and serve all she can and her behaviour wins the love of the lady's mother, who is Le Frain's own mother too. Thinking the bridal bed is not fair enough, Le Frain spreads over it the rich mantle in which she had been wrapped as a baby when she was carried away by the maid, and which has never left her. The mother of course recognizes it and the whole story comes out. The marriage is annulled and Le Frain weds her lover. After a time the sister is married to another knight.

The ballad *Fair Annie* begins thus:

> It's narrow, narrow make your bed
> And learn to lie your lane;
> For I'm ga'n o'er the sea, Fair Annie,
> A braw bride to bring hame.
> Wi her I will get gowd and gear;
> Wi you I neer got nane.[1]

At once a most important difference between the two versions

and romances have in common the points of difference from the ballads which are under consideration and it is therefore legitimate, as it is convenient, to take a *lai* as illustration here.

[1] *English and Scottish Popular Ballads*, ii, p. 69, Version A.

leaps to the eye. The ballad deals with a story, but its method is quite different from that of a narrative poem; it does not tell the story, but alludes to it as to something that is already known. The explanations, motivations of actions, and other things that make the links in a connected narrative are omitted. Only the salient points in the story appear at all and they are not presented with the detachment of a narrator but coloured by the passion aroused in an actor in the story.[1] This is how the arrival of the bride is told in the ballad:

> 'Come up, come up, my eldest son,
>   And look o'er yon sea-strand,
> And see your father's new-come bride,
>   Before she comes to land.'

> 'Come down, come down, my mother dear,
>   Come frae the castle wa.
> I fear, if langer ye stand there,
>   Ye'll let yoursell down fa.'

The last quotation shows another feature that differentiates the two, the distinctive ballad manner, which partly consists in the repetition of the same phrase or similar phrases. In the ballad *Hind Horn*, Horn is recognized by his lover by means of a ring which she gave him long ago, and she asks:

> 'O got ye this by sea or land?
> Or got ye it off a dead man's hand?'

> 'I got it not by sea, I got it by land,
> And I got it, madam, out of your own hand.'

> 'O I'll cast off my gowns of brown
> And beg wi you frae town to town.

> 'O I'll cast off my gowns of red,
> And I'll beg wi you to win my bread.'

> 'Ye needna cast off your gowns of brown,
> For I'll make you lady o many a town.

> 'Ye needna cast off your gowns of red,
> It's only a sham, the begging o my bread.'[2]

---

[1] Of course these remarks are not so applicable to all ballads as to *Fair Annie*. *Sir Aldingar*, for instance, comes much nearer to being a simple narrative poem than this.   [2] *English and Scottish Popular Ballads*, i, p. 202, Version A.

There are no mannerisms of this kind in *King Horn*, or *Horn Childe and Maiden Rimnild*. Comparatively, they are straightforward narrative.

It is unnecessary to give here a complete account of the ballad manner. What is abundantly clear is that, though there may be no difference between the story used by the writer of a *lai* or romance and of a ballad, there is a great difference in treatment.

It is more difficult to draw the distinction between the French epics (the *chansons de geste*) and the romances. Historically the two forms of narrative poetry influenced one another. Those epics which survive in late forms show sometimes a complete remodelling in order to make them more like the stories of adventure popular in the romances; the *Quatre Fils d'Aymon* is an example. Sometimes, as in *Huon de Bordeaux*, to the epic story is added a 'romantic' ending. But the distinction between the two forms is clear enough when the earliest extant *chanson de geste* is considered side by side with a typical romance. The differences in conception and treatment have been more fully discussed by Professor Ker in *Epic and Romance* than is possible or necessary here. The earliest *chansons de geste* are heroic poems, real epics; that is, as Professor Ker indicates, they have a dramatic variety which the romances have not. The characters speak for themselves, whereas in the romances we are always conscious of the story-teller and his manipulation of episode and character. In the *chansons de geste*, as in other national epics, man is chiefly concerned with one activity—that of fighting: and in *Roland*, the greatest of them, the poet's theme is 'essentially the old story of the heroic age—no knight-errantry, but the resistance of a man driven in a corner'. The romance, as we have seen, has no concern with tragedy and the romancer is interested in other activities than fighting, particularly in activities resulting from the passion of love. Instead of the heroic sentiments and actions of the tragic hero, there is the sensibility of the lover and the well-regulated behaviour of the follower of the ideals of chivalry.

The earliest of these French epics are further distinguished from romances by being written in a metrical form of their own—in those groups of decasyllabic lines, linked together by assonance, to which the French have given the name *laisses*.

These differences between the forms are chiefly of use to students of French literature. English romance writers sometimes took French epics for their sources[1] and dealt with them as far as possible as they did with other narrative material. There is never, it is true, the same sophistication as in the Arthurian romances. Descriptions are fewer and shorter and not concerned much with fashionable contemporary life. The stories are mainly about fighting, and ladies and love-making mostly play a small part; *Duke Rowlande and Sir Ottuell of Spayne* is a fair example. When ladies do appear, they have not the good manners that one expects of a romance heroine. Floripas, in *Sir Ferumbras*, takes the law into her own hands and kills Oliver's jailer by hitting him over the head in order that she may see Oliver.[2] In these ways the English Charlemagne romances bear the traces of their origin; but apart from these things there is no difference between these romances and others. The 'dramatic variety' of the original epics is gone. The power to convey lofty sentiments and a tragic atmosphere—to create an epic hero, in fact—is gone too; the bare events are left without the heroic spirit which originally informed them. The English fragmentary *Song of Roland* is so poor a poem that it is hardly a fair illustration, but it does show how an epic can be turned into a narrative poem that is not an epic, even when the main course of events remains unchanged. One has only to compare ll. 511–54 of the English poem (E.E.T.S. edition) with ll. 1017–81 of the *Chanson* (ed. Bédier) to see how the vigour and strength, the intense and dramatic expectation, the grandeur of Roland and Oliver and of their situation—all that makes the epic quality of the *Chanson*— have gone out of the story. The English poet has not even the sense to keep the stirring repetition, 'Cumpainz Rollanz, l'olifan car sunez'—'Cumpainz Rollanz, sunez vostre olifan'.

It is owing to this use and transformation of the French epics in English that the distinction in form between *chanson de geste*

---

[1] For instance, *The Sowdone of Babylone* and *Sir Ferumbras* go back to French versions of the Fierabras story, *Otuel* to a version of the Otinel story.

[2] The English Charlemagne romances, many of which are late, give the impression that they were written for a popular, not a fashionable, audience, or by writers who were driven to this somewhat uncongenial material by the insatiable demand for romances.

and romance has no relevance for English criticism. The distinction which needs to be made in considering English romances is rather between the romance and epic poetry in general than between the former and the particular branch of epic represented by the *chanson de geste*. Generally speaking, the English romance form differs from the epic form in the same ways as the French romances differ from the *chansons de geste*,[1] but detailed study of individual romances would show that the degree to which they differ varies greatly. One romance, the alliterative *Morte Arthure*, on a theme which roused more patriotic enthusiasm in an English poet than the doings of Charlemagne and his peers ever could, comes very near to claiming a place among heroic poems in English.

The last distinction to be made is that between the romance and what is usually called nowadays a tale. It is far the hardest to draw and is one that some critics would not admit except in certain obvious instances. The romance is distinct enough in subject-matter from the kind of medieval tale known as a *fabliau*, a tale, such as those which Chaucer puts into the mouths of the Miller and the Reeve, which deals essentially with middle-class or lower-class life and is full of broad fun. But in Gower's *Confessio Amantis* there are a number of tales, linked together by a thin thread of narrative, many of which are on the same subjects as the romances. The Tale of Constance,[2] besides being the same as Chaucer's *Man of Law's Tale*, has episodes in common with a number of romances, among which are *Emaré*, *Sir Eglamour of Artois*, and *Sir Torrent of Portyngale*. The Tale of Jason and Medea,[3] has some of the characteristics that we have noted in the romances. Jason is a duke and Medea a witch who gathers herbs and mutters spells.[4] Is there any essential difference in form between one of the tales in Gower's *Confessio Amantis* and a short romance? I think there is, but that the difference is obscured by the existence of the Breton

[1] Nathaniel E. Griffin in *The Definition of Romance* argues that the essential difference between the romance and the epic is that the former is an incredible tale, while the latter, at least for those for whom it is written, is credible. The epic presupposes a 'perfect accord between the poet and his hearer'; the romance is a story which needs interpretation on the part of the story-teller to be significant to the hearer. It must be interpreted in the light of ideas with which both poet and hearer are familiar.

[2] ii. 587 ff.

[3] v. 3247 ff.

[4] Cf. Ker, *Epic and Romance*, p. 334.

lais, some of which (notably some of those of Marie de France, the earliest known) are really tales[1] but are usually and naturally classified as romances because of the close connexion of their subject-matter with that of the romances. It must be admitted, however, that it is impossible to lay down detailed rules for differentiating the two. Following a suggestion of Ten Brink,[2] the distinction I would make is that in the tale the chief concern is with the story and 'with the characters of its heroes only so far as this is revealed in the plot'. The tale is pure narrative art, at its simplest and barest, stripped of all else. Nowadays it is not often that pure narrative holds the attention of a reader. His interest is rather in some accessory—character drawing, description, or even a lesson or a moral. But children can always be held by this art and this probably explains the perennial popularity of *Robinson Crusoe*. In this matter the medieval reader was like a child and the tale fed his desire for pure narrative. As a result of its limitations, in the medieval tale the plot is closely knit and clear in outline, and the whole has a simplicity and brevity that in the hands of the best writers gives it a real charm. This is the characteristic of the best of Gower's tales, and of the Breton *lais* of Marie de France. In the romance, the plot may be elaborate and complicated, is often rambling and often interrupted by long descriptive passages or accounts of the hero's feelings (particularly in the French romances of Chrétien de Troyes). 'The unity rests in the person of the hero . . . in the combination of motives, in the idea.'[3] Compared with the tale, the romance can be clumsy, vague, and discursive, but at its best there is a breadth of view about it. Whereas the teller of a tale goes straight forward, looking neither to right nor left, the romance writer 'dwells on the circumstantial'.[3] Hence, in the worst of them, wearisome catalogues of irrelevant details; in the best, a gorgeous and thrilling setting for action. The romance offers a more difficult and dangerous road to success than the tale.

---

[1] Some are really romances, I think, e.g. *Emaré*, Chaucer's *Franklin's Tale*.
[2] *Early English Literature* (1887), pp. 253 ff.
[3] Ten Brink, op. cit.

II

LA3AMON AND THE EARLIEST MIDDLE
ENGLISH ALLITERATIVE VERSE

A GREAT deal of Middle English poetry, and some of the best of it, witnesses to the vitality of a poetic tradition which begins, for us, in the eighth century, but which, to judge from *Beowulf*, was even then well established. This tradition is rooted in the kind of blank verse usually known today as 'alliterative verse', the verse which the fourteenth-century poet of *Sir Gawain and the Green Knight* described as 'linked with true letters, as has long been the custom in the land'. To Middle English poets, however, the tradition meant more than the verse form. Even in Old English poetry it is clear that there existed a stock of alliterating words and phrases on which poets were accustomed to draw. There were, too, certain fixed habits of composition, intimately connected with the nature of the alliterative line; notably a cumulative method of description, the piling up of phrases, usually a half-line in length and often similar in construction, each of which makes its contribution to the total impression. When, therefore, the rhythm of alliterative verse beat in a poet's mind, it brought with it a manner to some extent predetermined and a store of words and phrases, some of them age-old and many not known outside alliterative verse.

There are other things too, less easy to define, which the tradition meant to the Middle English poet. The verse, largely perhaps through its special diction, seems to have carried with it memories of the subjects and scenes that had most interested its earlier users —some memory, however blurred, of the ancient heroic system centring in the Lord and his hall which is pictured in *Beowulf*, and a clearer memory of certain kinds of descriptions—of battles, of scenes of revelry in the hall, of voyages and storms at sea, of terrors natural and supernatural. Hence Middle English poets often write as if they had an inherited knowledge of how such things could be effectively presented.

The marks of this tradition appear in alliterative poetry of the whole of the Middle English period, though naturally one poet differs greatly from another in what he takes and what he leaves.

We know very little about alliterative verse in the first century after the Norman Conquest. Several scraps survive in manuscripts of that time or a little later; but the date of their composition is usually hard to determine. Two which are sometimes claimed as early Middle English, the charm *Against a Wen* ('Wenne, wenne, wenchichenne[1]'), and the impressive fragment known as *The Grave*, were almost certainly composed in the Old English period, though in their extant form they have been partially modernized. The earliest post-Conquest verse which has come down to us is probably the so-called *First Worcester Fragment*, preserved in a manuscript in Worcester Cathedral Library. This opens with the words 'Sanctus Beda was iboren her on Breotene mid us',[2] and it goes on to name famous Englishmen—Abbot Ælfric, the bishops Aidan, Cuthbert, Dunstan, and Ælfeah (Alphege) among them— who once taught 'our people in English', and to lament that now others 'teach our folk and many of the [English] teachers perish and the folk with them'. This complaint would seem to be directed against the appointment, shortly after the Conquest, of foreign bishops to almost every bishopric in England; and, if so, the piece is likely to have been composed a good deal earlier than the date of the manuscript (*c.* 1180) in which it survives. The same may be true of the other passages of alliterative verse in this manuscript. These are fragments of a poem, sometimes called *The Departing Soul's Address to the Body*, on a theme which was treated by many English writers, both poets and homilists, before and after the Conquest. The fragments describe the 'painful parting' of body and soul, and the failing powers of the dying man. The soul reproaches the body for its love of material things and neglect of spiritual and it points the contrast between past delights and the misery and horror of the grave—'low are the end-walls, unlofty the

---

[1] 'little wen'.   [2] 'St. Bede was born among us here in Britain.'

side-walls; your roof lies very near upon your breast. . . . Now you are hateful and vile to all your friends'. Many of the ideas and images in these fragments are also found in other versions of the theme and, though they are sometimes presented forcefully here, the best things are better done in the closely related but more compact lines of *The Grave* where, for instance, two phrases unrelated in the Worcester fragments ('on durelease huse' and 'deað haueð þe kei3e') appear united in the grimly suggestive lines,

Dureleas is þet hus and dearc hit is wiðinnen:
Ðær þu bist feste bidytt and dæð hefð þa cæ3e.[1]

To lament what is passed, to dwell on death and decay, is natural enough to a people suffering from defeat and foreign domination, and these Worcester fragments may well represent kinds of verse which were popular among the English after the Conquest. But other kinds must also have been known. The twelfth-century chroniclers William of Malmesbury and Henry of Huntingdon seem to have used as sources old poems on historical subjects and there are special reasons for thinking that what Henry knew was in alliterative verse. Giraldus Cambrensis, writing in the late twelfth century, remarks that the English, like the Welsh, employ alliteration *in omni sermone exquisito*,[2] and he quotes three English alliterative lines which are proverbial in character, the last of which ('Betere is red thene rap and liste thene lither streingthe')[3] is echoed in part in La3amon's *Brut*, the *Ancrene Riwle*, and *The Proverbs of Hendyng*. The nature of La3amon's *Brut* (dating in all probability from the last years of the twelfth century) suggests that its author knew earlier verse which, in subject, had things in common with Old English heroic poems; and more certain evidence of the existence of such verse is provided by a few rough alliterative lines belonging to a version of the story of Wade which are included in a thirteenth-century Latin sermon. Some of the verse known to these twelfth- and thirteenth-century writers may have been composed near to their own time, but much of it could have been, and some of it must have been, Old English verse orally transmitted,

[1] 'Doorless is that house where you are fast shut and dark it is within; and Death has the key.' [2] *Descriptio Cambriae*, I. xii.
[3] 'A plan of action is better than violence and cunning than brute force.'

sometimes over a long period of time, and more or less modernized in language and metre in the course of transmission—a process which would explain some of the characteristics of the verse and diction of Middle English alliterative poetry.

The existing scraps of Middle English verse throw some light on what happened and was happening to the structure of the alliterative line. Verse of the kind which we know in the best Old English poems ('classical' verse) survives only in one piece, *The Description of Durham* (1104–9). This is an example of a literary exercise, the *encomium urbis*, inherited by the Middle Ages from the Latin schools of rhetoric, and is obviously the work of a learned author. It is possible, therefore, that his correct use of 'classical' verse may have been a deliberate piece of antiquarianism. If, as has been suggested, the writer of the *First Worcester Fragment* was trying to compose in this kind of verse, he evidently understood much less about it.

The other Worcester fragments (*The Departing Soul's Address to the Body*) are certainly in another kind of verse, similar to the so-called 'popular' verse of the lines on the death of Edgar (975) in the D and E versions of the *Anglo-Saxon Chronicle*, or those on Alfred and Godwin (1036) in the C and D versions. This 'popular' verse developed in oral poetry and was to be the fruitful type in Middle English. All the more important earlier poems, La3amon's *Brut*, the *Proverbs of Alfred*, and parts of the *Bestiary* are composed in some variety of it, and some, though not all, of its characteristics persist in later Middle English.

The two kinds of verse, 'popular' and 'classical', have some fundamental features in common, and their likenesses as well as their differences are important for the understanding of Middle English alliterative verse. In both the line is made up of two half-lines, each of which is a complete rhythmic unit usually containing two primary stresses. But, while in 'classical' verse the alliteration is the sole means of linking the half-lines, in 'popular' verse, rhyme or assonance can be used, either with alliteration or without it. This occasional use of rhyme or assonance is peculiar to the verse of the late Old English and early Middle English periods; it is not a feature of the fourteenth-century long line. When alliteration is used (as it is in the majority of lines), its placing does not conform to the strict rules of 'classical' verse. It is common to find the last stressed syllable of a line bearing the alliteration, as in 'faren mid feondes in eche fur' in the *Departing Soul's Address to the Body*; and there are a number of other irregularities.

A basic condition of all Old English verse is that the metrical stresses fall on the first or stem syllable of a word, and it is because this continues to be so in Middle English that the same alliterative phrases could survive as rhythmic units for centuries, in spite of the many metrical and linguistic changes that took place. 'Classical' and 'popular' verse differ, however, in regard to the arrangement of the stresses within the half-line. Composers of 'popular' verse were not fully acquainted with (or they chose to ignore) the rhythmic patterns characteristic of Old English 'classical' verse— patterns probably still best known, in their basic forms, as 'Sievers's five types'. Some of these they do use, often in modified forms, but others never; and many of their half-lines are of other types. It may be that the reason for this difference in the structure of the half-lines is that composers of 'popular' verse ignored the distinctions of quantity which were vital to the 'classical' patterns, but since the part which was played by these distinctions in 'classical' rhythms is now in dispute, this explanation can only be tentatively advanced. What is certain is that in early Middle English verse, as illustrated by the *Departing Soul's Address*, the rhythm depends purely on stress, and the half-lines show much less variety of movement than Old English 'classical' verse. One movement, the rising– falling rhythm $(x' \, x' \, x)$ predominates over all others. This is still so in the fourteenth century, and this later verse also shares with the earlier two other features—an increase in the number of unstressed syllables and a more frequent use of three-stressed half-lines—both of which make the Middle English line longer as well as looser in structure than Old English 'classical' lines. At the same time Middle English lines are much more often self-contained, a single line usually expressing a complete sense unit.

Early Middle English verse has one peculiarity of its own, which seems to have accompanied, and was perhaps caused by, the use of rhyme or assonance to link the half-lines. In many of the rhyming lines there is a more or less regular alternation of stressed and unstressed syllables, so that they sound like rough couplets, as in the following line from Laƹamon's *Brut*:

> Leófe fǽder dúre swa bíde ich gódes áre,[1]

or in

> Hire fáder héo wolde súge seóþ, wére him léf wére him láþ.[2]

Such lines can have alliteration or not, and the half-lines can have two, three, or four stresses, three being the most usual number. Their appearance in alliterative verse has been taken to mean that poets of this period found it hard to keep the rhythms of alliterative verse unaffected by that of Middle English couplet metres derived from French; but, since a similar tendency appears in the late Old English lines on Alfred and Godwin, it is likely that it was a natural development in 'popular' verse. In any case, the fact that fourteenth-century alliterative verse is free from it may suggest that, in the early period too, there was some verse that was more correct.

Obviously Middle English alliterative metre was essentially a poorer vehicle of expression than Old English 'classical' metre. Middle English poets found it harder to avoid monotony and to achieve subtle effects. In addition, in the early period, they were hampered by the uncertainty of rhythms resulting from the tendency just described.

Laƹamon's[3] *Brut*, the most important alliterative poem of the early period, does not escape these dangers. Its rhythms are, for the most part, rough and insecure; and when they appear more settled, as occasionally in passages that are strongly reminiscent of Old English poetry, they are monotonous. The following passage has the merit of vigour, but if it is set beside comparable lines in Old English (for instance *The Fight at Finnsburuh*, 28–30), it is clear what the later form of verse has lost in variety and flexibility:

> Heven here-marken, halden to-gadere,
> Luken sweord longe, leiden o þe helmen,

---

[1] *Brut*, ed. Madden (London, 1847), i, p. 126.
[2] *Brut*, i, pp. 128–9.
[3] This is the earliest form of the poet's name. The 'Ʒ' implies a sound, now non-existent in English, but fairly close to the 'g' in North German 'sagen'.

Fur ut sprengen. Speren brastlien,
Sceldes gonnen scanen, scaftes to-breken.[1]

Yet, in spite of the deficiencies of his metre, Laȝamon can describe the passing of Arthur so that his readers are compelled to feel its mystery:

Aefne þan worden, þer com of see wenden,
Þat wes an sceort bat liðen, sceoven mid vðen;
And twa wimmen þerinne, wunderliche idihte.
And heo neomen Arður anan, and aneouste hine uereden,
And softe hine adun leiden, and forð gunnen heo liðen.
Þa wes hit iwurðen þat Merlin seide whilen,
Þat weore unimete care of Arthures forð-fare.
Bruttes ileueð ȝete þat he bon on live,
And wunnien in Aualun mid fairest alre aluen.
And lokieð euere Bruttes ȝete whan Arthur cumen liðe.[2]

Or, in a different vein, he can present Arthur as the ferocious warrior rushing upon his foes:

Up bræid Arður his sceld foren to his breosten,
And he gon to rusien swa þe rimie wulf
Þenne he cumeð of holte, bihonged mid snawe,
And þencheð to-biten swulc deor swa him likeð.
Arður þa cleopede to leofe his cnihten,
'Forð we bilive, þeines ohte!
Alle somed heom to! Alle we sculleð wel don!'
And heo forð hælden, swa þe hæȝe wude
Þenne wind wode weieð hine mid mæine.[3]

[1] 'They raised their battle-standards, kept together, drew their long swords and smote upon helmets, they made sparks spring forth. Spears were splintered, shields shattered, shafts broke' (iii, p. 141).
[2] 'Even with these words there came moving from the sea a small boat journeying, driven by the waves; and two women in it, wondrously arrayed. They took Arthur at once and quickly bore him and laid him softly down and forth they went. Then had come to pass what Merlin once said, that there should be exceeding sorrow at Arthur's departure. The Britons still believe that he is alive and dwells in Avalon with the loveliest of all the fairies. And still the Britons ever look for the time when Arthur will come' (iii, pp. 144–5).
[3] 'Arthur caught up his shield before his breast and rushed forward like the frosty wolf when he comes from the wood, hung with snow, meaning to tear to pieces what beasts he pleases. Then Arthur called to his loved knights, "Go we forth quickly, brave warriors! At them, all together! We must all do great deeds!" And they went forth like the high wood when a wild wind tosses it mightily' (ii, p. 421).

Such passages will indicate that La3amon's poem has an interest of its own in addition to its historic interest as the first English work to tell the story of Arthur.

La3amon's subject, as he announces it at the beginning of his poem, is the history of the people 'who first possessed the land of the English'. It is, in fact, the history of the Britons as told by Geoffrey of Monmouth some time between 1130 and 1138 in his *Historia Regum Britanniae*. For the most part, however, La3amon was not directly indebted to Geoffrey, but to the Norman poet Wace who, some twenty years later, retold Geoffrey's history in verse in his *Roman de Brut*, completed in 1155. La3amon mentions Wace as one of his sources, adding a detail unknown elsewhere, that Wace gave his book 'to the noble Eleanor who was queen of Henry the mighty king (Henry II)'; but he also speaks of two other sources, 'the English book which Bede made' and another in Latin made by 'St. Albin and the fair Austin who brought baptism hither'. He is undoubtedly referring to the Old English and the Latin versions of Bede's *Ecclesiastical History*; but he does not appear to have made much use of these books, and the manner in which he refers to them suggests that he wished to lend the authority of great names to his own work rather than that he was familiar with the books he supposed they had written. The latest opinion is that, apart from some echoes of Geoffrey's Book vii (which contains the Prophecies of Merlin) almost everything in La3amon's story comes from Wace (as we know him), supplemented constantly by his own imagination. The views of earlier scholars, that he drew upon Welsh tradition, or that he knew an expanded, and now lost, version of Wace's *Brut*, have little to support them.

The history of the Britons, as related by La3amon, Wace, and Geoffrey, opens with a reference to the flight of Aeneas from Troy and a brief record of his descendants in Italy. So the high lineage of the British kings is established; for Brutus, the great-grandson of Aeneas, will be the founder of their dynasty and the Britons can claim a common Trojan ancestry with the Romans. Later in the history, the kinship of the two races is recognized by Julius Caesar, who says—in La3amon's words—'alle we comen of ane kunne'. We are told much of Brutus, of his exile after he had accidentally killed his father, and how, after many adventures, he came at last, by the advice of the goddess Diana, to the fair land of Albion which, when he had taken possession of it, he called Britain after his own name.[1]

In the long story of Brutus's successors, some reigns are passed over rapidly, but matters of real significance in the history of the British race are treated at length. The more fully developed narratives are concerned with the conflict between Belinus (Belin) and his brother Brennius (Brenne), their reconciliation and their conquest of France and Rome; Caesar's invasion of Britain, the resistance of Cassibellanus and various later conflicts of the Romans and the Britons; the first coming of the Saxons under Hengest and Horsa; the life of Arthur. Even in Geoffrey, however, the tale of Lear and his three daughters seems to have been elaborated for its own sake, and a few more—the story of St. Ursula and her virgins, for instance—are developed by Wace or by Laȝamon simply because they are good stories or, in the case of St. Ursula, already famous.

Arthur is of first importance in all three versions. The story of his life is told in great detail—particularly his wars and conquests and his last fight against Modred. In addition, his reign is introduced by a very full account of his ill-fated family; of the treacherous killing of the monk-king Constans (Constance), the vengeance taken by his brothers Aurelius and Uther, the reign of Aurelius and his death by poison, the succession of Uther, his love for Ygerna (Ygerne), wife of Gorlois, Duke of Cornwall, the begetting of Arthur, and finally Uther's death, again treacherously contrived. Throughout this section one is aware of the mysterious figure of Merlin, mostly retired and unseen, but emerging at critical moments to give help by advice, by practising strange arts and by his knowledge of the future. More than once he prophesies the coming of Arthur. If, as has been recently argued, Geoffrey is careful not to describe Merlin as a magician, there seems little doubt that Wace and Laȝamon believed him to be one.

[1] Similar etymologies of the place-names of Britain are frequent in the history—King Lud causes his chief city to be known as Kaerlud, later corrupted to Kaerlundem, and by the Saxons called Lundene; the gates which Belinus put up in London caused the place to be known as Billingsgate.

The history of the Britons does not end with Arthur, but continues, on a less exciting level, till the time of Cadwallader, when the Britons had become worn out with incessant war and with famine. Cadwallader, warned by God that the Britons shall no longer reign in Britain, went to Rome and died there (689). The Saxon Athelstan then ruled all England, and the Britons—in Laȝamon's words—came to Wales and lived 'dispersed among the rocks and cliffs, the churches and monasteries, the woods and mountains', henceforth to be called, not Britons, but Welsh.

This is a long story as Geoffrey tells it; it becomes longer in Wace, and much longer still in Laȝamon. Each successive writer, besides expanding the statements in his original, also adds completely new matter—Laȝamon much more often than Wace. Some of the most interesting additions are concerned with Arthur. Wace is the first writer ever to speak of the Round Table; Laȝamon alone tells how the fairies took Arthur at his birth and bestowed many gifts upon him and how in the end they carried him to Avalon to their queen Argante. But interesting as these additions are, they are less important when the two later versions are judged as poetry, than the transformation which the history undergoes with each retelling. Wace evidently wished to make the 'history' intelligible and attractive to sophisticated and more or less cultured readers by interpreting it in terms which they could appreciate. So, for instance, he begins his account of the qualities of Arthur with the statement,

> Chevaliers fu mult vertuus,
> Mult fu preisanz, mult glorius,[1]

and he proceeds to endow him with the virtues of a chivalric knight who surpassed all other princes in 'curteisie', 'noblesse', 'vertu', and 'largesce'. Wace makes the most of the first meeting between Uther and Ygerne, describing Uther sitting at the feast with his thoughts constantly upon her, looking sideways at her, smiling, making 'signs of love', while Ygerne behaves in a manner neither encouraging nor disdainful—a scene likely to interest those who, a very little later, were to be delighted by the love-romances of

[1] He was a very valiant knight, full of honour and renown', Wace's *Brut* (ed. Arnold), 9017-18.

Chrétien de Troyes. Wace took pains, too, to write in a style calculated to please his readers, a style 'sobre, net sans grand éclat, mais toujours assez vif', as Gaston Paris describes it, marked by a discriminating use of simple rhetorical devices, notably some forms of verbal repetition. His verse is smooth and careful and he uses the literary French of his day, which would have been familiar to the Norman court in England and in Paris.

Laȝamon was in many ways the antithesis of Wace. What he tells of himself at the beginning of his poem implies a man living a simple life, remote from the world which Wace knew. There was, he says, a priest called Laȝamon who lived

> at Ernleȝe, æt æðelen are chirechen,
> Vppen Seuarne staþe—sel þar him þuhte—
> Onfest Radestone, þer he bock radde.[1]

The suggestion of provincialism, rusticity almost, derived from Laȝamon's own statement seems to be confirmed by several facts. He writes in a dialect which is likely to have been that of the county he lived in, in a verse form peculiar to the conquered English. His diction includes words and phrases traditional in such verse and it is almost free from French words, a fact the more remarkable when it is remembered that he must have pored long over Wace's French. He shows no knowledge of French literature other than Wace's poem, though by his time some famous French Arthurian romances had been written. Yet he cannot have been completely provincial and inexperienced. He himself tells us that he had travelled widely through England to obtain books to help him with his poem; he succeeded in getting Wace's book, and, by some means or other, he learnt that Wace had given a copy of it to Queen Eleanor. If he had not read widely in French, he had at least, to judge by his understanding of Wace, a good knowledge of the language. There are even signs that he had some knowledge of the technique of poetic composition as understood by educated writers, or at least that he was capable of learning something about it from his study of Wace.

[1] 'At a noble church at Areley, near Redstone, upon the banks of the Severn where he read the Bible—pleasant it seemed to him there' (i, p. 1). Areley Kings or Lower Areley in north Worcestershire, with which 'Ernleȝe' has been iden-tified, is on the west of the Severn opposite Stourport.

It is possible, therefore, that his verse form and diction are the result, not of inability to write otherwise, but of a conscious preference for what was traditional among the English. A clear statement of this cannot be found in his poem, but this is not surprising for the nature of his history did not allow him to express partiality for his own people. It does give him an opportunity to praise his country, and this he does in lines, which while agreeing with Wace's in their main substance, are fuller and more appreciative.[1] Two of his additions to Wace are possibly significant. Immediately after he has recorded (following Wace) that Gurmund gave land to the English and for over a hundred years Christianity was not known there, he interpolates the story of Gregory and the English slaves ('Truly you are English, most like to angels; of all people who live on earth, your race is the fairest'[2]); and on one occasion he goes out of his way to disparage the Normans who 'destroyed this people'.[3] If it seems incongruous that he should have chosen to retell the history of the Britons, including their long struggle against the invading Saxons or English—Laȝamon sometimes uses the terms interchangeably—the lines which follow his remarks about the Normans provide a hint of the attraction it held for him. He is speaking of London and of the various names it has had under its various conquerors, and he remarks:

> Swa is al þis lond iuaren for uncuðe leoden
> Þeo þis londe habbeð biwunnen, and eft beoð idriuen hennene;
> And eft hit biȝetten oðeræ, þe uncuðe weoren.[4]

This seems to show that the Saxon conquest of Britain interested him as a parallel to the Norman conquest of which he and his countrymen were still conscious. However, the most compelling reason for his interest in British history was in all probability that it made abundantly clear that his country, whatever its misfortunes, had had a long and often glorious past.

Certain it is that, whether by deliberate choice or not, Laȝamon converted the French *Brut* into a poem that is astonishingly English

---

[1] *Brut*, i, p. 85; cf. Wace, 1209 ff.
[2] *Brut*, iii, pp. 181–2.   [3] *Brut*, i, p. 303.
[4] 'So has all this land fared because of foreigners who have conquered this land, and then are driven hence; and then others won it who were foreigners' (i, pp. 303–4).

—English, that is, in the sense that its conceptions and its manner constantly reflect the earlier poetry of England. The passage corresponding to Wace's description of Arthur is significant. Of the qualities which Wace attributes to him, Laȝamon mentions only his bravery and his liberality. He evidently felt that thè best indication of Arthur's greatness was the wealth and standing of his household, for he tells us that each of his cup-bearers, and his chamberlains ('bur-þæinen') and his porters had gold for their backs and their beds; he then adds 'He had never a cook who was not a very good warrior, nor ever a knight's servant who was not a bold thane'.[1] These lines, for which there is no hint in Wace, convert Arthur into the kind of lord (*hlaford*) described in *Beowulf*, whose household consists of thanes of noble birth, his equals in rank.

What Laȝamon tells us of the doings of kings and their warriors also reminds us of the earlier poetry. Warriors vow to do great deeds in battle and are bound by their vaunts. Frollo has to face Arthur in single combat because 'he had made his vaunt [his *beot*, the same word as in Old English] before his whole host'.[2] A brief reference in Wace to a banquet is developed into the lines:

> He wende into halle and his haleðes mid him alle.
> Bemen heo bleowen, gomen men gunnen cleopien.
> Bord heo hetten breden, cnihtes setten þerto;
> Heo æten, heo drunken; dræm wes i burȝhen.[3]

Laȝamon's description of the arming of Arthur is of special interest because, while his list of arms agrees fairly closely with Wace's and he even includes some of the same details about them, yet his conception of them is markedly different:

> Þa dude he on his burne ibroide of stele,
> Þe makede on aluisc smið mid aðelen his crafte;
> He wes ihaten Wygar, þe Witeȝe wurhte . . .
> Calibeorne his sweord he sweinde bi his side,
> Hit wes iworht in Aualun mið wiȝelefulle craften.

---

[1] *Brut*, ii, p. 413.   [2] *Brut*, ii, p. 572.
[3] 'He went into the hall and all his warriors with him. Trumpets were blown, merriment proclaimed. They ordered tables to be set up. Knights sat at them; they ate and drank. There was revelry in the castle' (ii, p. 173).

Halm he set on hafde, hæh of stele;
Þeron wes moni 3imston, al mid golde bigon;
He wes Vðeres, þas æðelen kinges,
He wes ihaten Goswhit, ælchen oðere vnilic.[1]

This calls to mind, not Wace's matter-of-fact descriptions, nor any
of those in French and English romances, but rather the arming of
Beowulf ('the war-corslet linked by hand, . . . the gleaming helmet
encircled by lordly chains, as a weapon-smith had made it in
olden times'). It calls to mind, too, other allusions to weapons in
Old English poetry; in particular, the fairy smith Wite3e recalls
Weland, the cunning smith of heroic legend, and justly so, if Wite3e
is the Old English Widia, son of Weland.

Some echoes of Old English poetry appear in unlikely places, as
when Loch Lomond is set in the fen-land (like Grendel's mere)
and has nickers bathing in it![2] In descriptions of sea-journeys and
battles, as might be expected, these echoes are constant and all-
pervasive. But it is La3amon's battle-descriptions that show most
clearly the hold the older poetry had over him. He does not
attempt to individualize a battle by describing the disposition and
movement of armies. Instead, he gives himself over to the memories
of battles he knows in poetry, and, by means of the old methods
and phrases, he creates an impression of battle—its noise, con-
fusion, and excitement—as in the lines from Arthur's last fight.[3]
He has, it is true, a nearer precedent for his cumulative method of
description in Wace, for he too piles up numbers of parallel phrases,
but the almost completely different details which the two poets
select for mention (for instance, in their accounts of the battle of
Julius Caesar against Cassibelaunus[4]) make it clear that it is not
Wace that La3amon is thinking of. La3amon's descriptions are not
to be despised. They are more stirring than many carefully worked
out accounts, and though the objection that all his battles are alike

---

[1] 'Then he put on his mail-coat of linked steel, which a fairy smith had made
with excellent skill; it was called Wygar, and Wite3e made it. He hung by his
side his sword Excalibur; it was made in Avalon by magical arts. A high helmet
of steel he placed on his head, on which was many a precious stone, all en-
compassed with gold. It had been Uther's, the noble king's. It was called
Goosewhite, and was unlike any other' (ii, pp. 463–4).
[2] *Brut*, ii, p. 489.   [3] See p. 29.
[4] Wace, *Brut*, 4021 ff.; La3amon, *Brut*, i, p. 319.

is unanswerable, it is rather the number of them that gives rise to it than his method.

These memories of 'far-off things, And battles long ago' are inextricably bound up with the verse and the old words and phrases through which he learnt of them. But it should not be thought that the words meant to him just what they did in Old English heroic poetry. In *Beowulf* such words as *hæleþ*[1] and *duguþ* have reference to a particular kind of society; but *duguþ*, which in certain passages in *Beowulf* meant 'a body of tried retainers', 'comitatus', is mostly used by Laȝamon in the vaguer sense of 'body of men, host of warriors'. And so it is with many other of the old words; something of their meaning has gone and they have become less pregnant, more generalized. It cannot be assumed, either, that Laȝamon made the same connexions as we do, if we know heroic poetry. When, for instance, he applies the term 'Godes wiðersaka'[2] to the giant Geomagog, he need not intend to connect him with Grendel, descendant of the evil brood of Cain, of whom the same term is used. For, however much he may remind us of Old English heroic poetry, it is most unlikely that he knew what we know. Nowhere are the similarities between Old English poetry and his poem like those between a model and something directly imitated from it. The relationship is always much less clear-cut. Even when he is most reminiscent, Laȝamon gives an impression of only half-recalling what he reminds us of—an impression similar to that made by the dimmed meaning of the old words he uses, and explicable in both cases if the old conceptions and words reached him not as the result of reading, but of continued oral transmission. Since, as has been shown, Laȝamon's verse-form is related not to 'classical' Old English verse, but to the 'popular' type, it is reasonable to suppose that it was from 'popular' verse, orally handed down, that he got his reminiscences of early heroic poetry. Presumably Laȝamon acquired his loose, repetitive, easy-flowing style from the same source; but all that can be said is that it seems to have some relation to that of the 'popular' verses in the *Anglo-Saxon Chronicle* and to that of Middle English writings in the verse-form related to the 'popular' type, especially the *Departing*

---

[1] 'Warrior'.   [2] 'Adversary of God' (i, p. 77).

Soul's Address and the *Proverbs of Alfred*. On the one hand devices characteristic of 'classical' Old English verse (litotes and 'kennings', for instance) are lacking or rare in all these writings, and their style is altogether less close-packed, owing in part to a more sparing use of compound words. On the other hand, the Middle English writings have in common certain forms of repetition, in particular the repetition of formulas, and some of the same expressions appear in two or more of them. The early, non-alliterative romance *King Horn* also has these characteristics. Some of the resemblances have been thought to point to direct borrowing, by the *Brut* from the *Proverbs*, for instance, and by *King Horn* from the *Brut*; but this would not be inconsistent with the view that these early Middle English writings had behind them a common style deriving from oral poetry.

This assumption would explain what may be called La3amon's basic style; but some of his best effects depend either on similes which have no parallel in any surviving Old or early Middle English verse, or on what appear to be original uses of the repeated formula.

La3amon's repeated formulas (often referred to as 'epic formulas') are the most conspicuous feature of the style of his poem. La3amon must have known this device in the verse with which he was familiar, for he often used it as others did, but he also developed it for his own purposes. Of the many simple formulas which recur, some frequently, throughout the whole poem, a number can be paralleled in late Old English or early Middle English. Such are the many 'fill-ups', used to complete a line ('widen and siden', 'nu and æver mare'), statements making a transition in the narrative ('þe king hine biþohte wat he don mahte'); descriptive phrases like 'æðelest alre kingen', 'Bruttene deorling'. Also to be included here are phrases which seem to be attached to certain circumstances or events, like 'feollen þæ fæie',[1] so common in battle-descriptions, or 'wind stod at wille'[2] often included in an account of a voyage; and also formulas which have the effect of summarizing an action, like 'balu wes on folke'[3] frequently used as a comment on defeat in battle. Parallels to some

---

[1] 'The doomed men fell.'   [2] 'The wind blew as they desired.'
[3] 'Woe came upon the people.'

of these can be found in *King Horn* where the couplet (or slight variations of it) 'þe se began to flowe¹ And Horn Child to rowe' occurs several times in describing a voyage; and in the Worcester *Departing Soul's Address* where there is a refrain-like repetition of the summarizing line, 'Al is reowliche þin siþ efter þin wrecche lif.'² Here, however, it has a more important function than Laȝamon's summarizing formulas, since it emphasizes a main idea of the poem.

So far Laȝamon's repetition of formulas seems to be merely a conventional trick, and it is often a tiresome one to modern readers. But when some one formula is confined to a particular story or episode, for which it has been specially selected, it can be effective: and it is in these instances that Laȝamon seems to be most original.

The stories of Vortiger and of Leir and his daughters provide examples of the effective use of formulas. In the long account of Vortiger's treachery and ultimate downfall, recurring descriptive phrases act like a ground-bass, drumming home the craftiness and guile of the man. At the first mention of his name, before we know anything about him, Laȝamon remarks 'ȝæp mon and swiðe war',³ and he repeats this, with variations, several times while he tells how Vortiger succeeded in getting the monk Constans made king. Once Constans has been crowned, Vortiger plots against him and contrives that he shall be slain by a company of Pictish knights, whom he then openly accuses of murder so that the Britons are roused and kill them. Throughout these doings the recurrent phrase is 'þe swike wes ful derne'.⁴ But already, before this, Laȝamon has slipped in the phrase 'of ufele he wes wel iwar'⁵ which, with variations, is to be used of Vortiger almost to the end of his story. Its use even when Vortiger is himself being deceived by Hengest may seem careless and meaningless, but it could be intended as an ironical reminder, as if Laȝamon repeatedly said 'remember, thus is the Vortiger who betrayed Constans'. At any

---

¹ 'The tide began to flow in.'
² 'All pitiful is thy departure after thy wretched life.'
³ 'A crafty man and most wary' (ii, p. 118).
⁴ 'Who was a most secret traitor' (ii, pp. 144 ff.).
⁵ 'He was well practised in evil' (ii, p. 129).

rate, La3amon was well aware what he was doing at the end of this
episode, for, just as Hengest's treachery is about to be fully
revealed, he suddenly changes the formula, while keeping an echo
of its earlier form and exclaims, 'Her he wes to unwar!'[1]

In the story of Leir and his daughters, formulas serve a slightly
different purpose—that of linking various parts of the narrative.
It is one which lends itself naturally to this kind of treatment and
there are several verbal echoes between the different parts of it,
both of phrases and of key-words. In the first part La3amon drives
home the falseness of Gornoille and Regan, and Leir's folly in
trusting them, by reiterating the word lesinge, 'lie'. Leir 'believed
his daughter's [Gornoille's] lie'; 'all her [Regan's] lie her father
believed': 'Cordoille heard the lies which her sisters spoke to the
king' and she swore that she would speak 'soþ' to her father.[2] This
last statement is caught up again towards the end of the tale when
Leir laments, 'Soþ seide Cordoille, for cuð hit is me nouþe',[3] and
again, 'truth the young woman spoke', 'but my daughter spoke the
truth . . . and both her two sisters told me lies'.[4] There is a hint
for these later repetitions in Wace,[5] though Wace does not, like
La3amon, use repetition to link the earlier and later scenes. The
formula which provides the most effective link in La3amon's story
has no parallel in Wace. It is first used when the husbands of
Gornoille and Regan decide that they will take over the rule
of the country and that Leir, while he lives, shall be supported
by them

> Dæies and nihtes, mid feowerti hired cnihtes;
> And heo him wolden finden haukes and hundes
> Þat he mihte riden 3eond alle þanne þeoden.[6]

Just after this we are told that he went to Scotland and was received
by Gornoille and her husband 'mid feowerti hired cnihtes, mid

[1] 'Here he was too unwary' (ii, p. 213).
[2] Brut, i, pp. 126–8.
[3] 'Cordoille spoke truth; now I know it' (i, p. 147).
[4] Brut, i, pp. 147–8.
[5] Wace's Brut, 1937, 1949.
[6] 'By day and by night, with forty men of his household, and they would
provide for him hawks and hounds so that he could ride all over the country'
(i, p. 138; cf. pp. 139, 140, 151).

horsen and mid hundes'. Gornoille's complaint to her husband soon follows:

> He halt here fauwerti cnihtes, daies and nihtes;
> He haveþ her þas þeines and alle heore swaines,
> Hundes and havekes.[1]

Much later in the story comes the last echo. Cordoille, having been told of Leir's plight by his servant, bids him go back to her father and provide for him richly. He is to buy for him fine clothes and 'hundes and havekes and durewurðe[2] horses' and is to maintain in his house 'feowerti hired cnihtes'.[3]

In the stories of Vortiger and of Leir Laȝamon uses his repeated phrases organically, in the one instance to ensure some continuity of impression throughout a very long narrative, in the other to bring out similarities and contrasts between various parts of the story and so to make the reader conscious of its essential movements. This would seem to indicate some sort of artistic awareness; and there are similar indications in Laȝamon's use of his most striking similes. While brief simple similes occur throughout the poem, the longer and more impressive ones are all concentrated in one part of it—the account of Arthur's wars against Colgrim, Baldulf, and Childrich. The earlier part of this account contains the long exultant speech in which Arthur compares Childrich to the fox who climbs seeking the rocks in the wild places, making holes for himself, carefree, because he believes himself the boldest of all animals. 'But then men below the hills come towards him with horns and hounds, with loud cries. . . . They drive the fox over hill and dale. He flees to the cliff and seeks his hole. . . . Men on every side dig towards him. There the proudest of all animals is then most wretched. So was it with Childrich, the strong and mighty.'[4] In the later stage of the war, when Childrich and his men are forced to flee across the river Avon with Arthur in pursuit, we are told that so many Saxons lie dead in the river that 'al wes Auene stram mid stele ibrugged'.[5] Childrich, Colgrim, and Baldulf climb

---

[1] 'He maintains here forty knights, day and night; he has these thegns here, and all their serving-men, hounds and hawks' (i, p. 140).
[2] 'valuable'.   [3] *Brut*, ii, p. 151.
[4] *Brut*, ii, pp. 451–2.
[5] 'The whole river Avon was bridged with steel' (ii, p. 469).

to the hill above Bath and Arthur again exults: 'Yesterday was Colgrim the bravest of all men; now is he like the goat' who 'high on the hill fights with his horns when the fierce wolf approaches him.' He then taunts Baldulf and Childrich in similar fashion, each speech echoing the beginning of the first: 'Yesterday was Baldulf . . .', 'Yesterday was Childrich . . .', and each elaborated by a comparison. The one addressed to Baldulf is the most remarkable:

> ȝursterdæi wes Baldulf cnihten alre baldest;
> Nu he stant on hulle, and Auene bihaldeð,
> Hu ligeð i þan stræme stelene fisces
> Mid sweorde bigeorede. Heore sund is awemmed,
> Heore scalen wleoteð swulc gold-faȝe sceldes;
> Þer fleoteð heore spiten, swulc hit spæren weoren.[1]

The effectiveness of this image depends on the reversal of the normal order of its terms which has the effect of slowing down the comprehension of it. We see with Baldulf the river filled with gleaming fish, and only gradually comes the recognition that these fish are dead warriors.

Laȝamon's account of the wars against Childrich and his allies, in which these speeches occur, is one of the most original passages in his poem. It has a wealth of incident and detail much of which is not even hinted at in Wace's much shorter and more sober version. In Laȝamon's imagination the whole action evidently became momentous and exciting, and the concentration in this story of elaborate similes, together with the use of such formal devices as the parallelism of Arthur's taunting speeches, are signs that he felt a heightened style to be appropriate to it.

To judge from this account, and from his best uses of the repeated formula, Laȝamon had some notion of suiting his style to his matter and of using stylistic devices for his own ends: that is to say, he possessed some degree of artistic consciousness, and, perhaps, even some knowledge of the art of poetry as it was understood in his own time and set out in manuals of instruction. This second suggestion runs counter to the usual view of Laȝamon, and

---

[1] 'Yesterday was Baldulf the boldest of all knights. Now he stands on the hill and looks upon Avon—how steel fishes lie in the river, girt with swords. Their swimming is impaired. Their scales gleam like gold-decked shields. There float their fins as if they were spears' (ii, pp. 471-2).

it cannot be held to be proven by these examples alone. It is possible that more light might be thrown on his knowledge by a thorough study of his various kinds of repetition, both of formulas and of important words; but it would be necessary to take into account not only what he may have found in native poetry, but also how far he was influenced by Wace, with whom repetition of some kinds is a favourite device, and from whose practice he certainly learnt more than has been recognized.

Yet, whatever La3amon may have known of the art of poetry, and whatever skill he may display in some parts of his work, artistry is not pre-eminent among his qualities. He is too lacking in restraint and discretion. The very devices which he can use well, he will at times use carelessly, even to the point of spoiling his own good effects, as when he says of Hengest, 'Hengest was of ufele war',[1] which, though true, is disturbing when the reader has come to feel that this kind of phrase belongs particularly to Vortiger.

His great gift is for imagining scenes of action. Arthur's wars against Childrich provide plenty of examples of his power of imagining warlike scenes, but he can also create others quite different from these, and by different means. At the climax of Arthur's story, when he has defeated the Emperor of Rome, La3amon prepares for the coming change in Arthur's fortunes by narrating some events which are not in Wace. He describes the arrival of a knight from Brittany with news of Modred. Arthur talks to him for a long time but the young knight will not tell the truth about Modred. Next morning Arthur relates a dream which he takes to be a warning of evil, and he ends the recital with the lament 'I know surely that all my joy has gone, and for as long as I live I must endure sorrow. Alas, that I have not here Wenhaver, my queen.'[2] At last the knight tells Arthur of Modred's treachery and then La3amon brings the scene before us, conveying in a few simple statements, more or less parallel in form, the effect of the news on Arthur's court:

> Þa sæt hit al stille in Arðures halle.
> Þa wes þer særinæsse mid sele þan kinge.

---

[1] *Brut*, ii, p. 208.   [2] *Brut*, iii, p. 121.

Þa weoren Bruttisce men swiðe vnbalde vor þæn.
Þa umbe stunde stefne þer sturede;
Wide me mihte iheren Brutten iberen;
And gunnen to tellen a feole cunne spellen
Hu heo wolden fordeme Modred and þa quene.[1]

Laȝamon's sensitiveness to the emotional quality of a scene appears particularly in moments of tension or suspense. There is an example in his version of the legend of St. Ursula. At first he follows Wace, describing the departure from the Thames of Ursula and the great company of virgins, and the terrible storm that came upon their ships and wrecked many of them; but at this point he introduces a scene that is not in Wace, though he mentions the persons concerned in it—Wanis and Melga.[2] Laȝamon tells us that these men, who were outlaws, had come out from Norway and, knowing the signs of the weather, had laid up in an island:

And swa heo leien i þan æit-londe, and iseȝen þat weder stronge.
Iseȝen scipen an and an, while ma, while nan,
Þeonne feowere, þenne fiue; sellic heom þuhten a þissen liue
Whæt weoren þa ȝemere scipen þa ȝeond þa sæ weolken.[3]

There is a feeling of suspense here, even if one does not know that Ursula is to fall into the hands of these ruthless men. What is more notable, however, is that by a simple scene, apparently of his own invention, Laȝamon brings home the utter helplessness and abandonment of the women, which is to him the essence of their pitiful story. It is this instinct for the essential quality or significance of a story, or of an episode or description, and the power to make the reader feel it, that gives Laȝamon a claim to be regarded as a poet, in spite of the obvious defects of his work. These are not limited to its rough metre and a style that is often slack and careless. The work suffers, too, from the disadvantages of the chronicle

[1] 'Then all was still in Arthur's hall. Then there was sorrow for the good king. Then were the Britons exceedingly downcast thereby. Then after a while voices stirred there; on all sides could be heard the cries of the Britons and in many different speeches they told how they would destroy Modred and the queen' (iii, pp. 124–5).
[2] In Geoffrey, Wanius king of the Huns and Melga king of the Picts.
[3] 'And so they lay up in that island and watched the fierce storm. They saw ships one by one, at times more, at times none, then four, then five; it seemed to them a marvel what the wretched ships might be that tossed on the sea' (ii, p. 77).

form which Laȝamon received from his predecessors. These might have been less apparent if Laȝamon had been able to make Arthur, the most important figure in his history, more human and credible. But he cannot present a complete personality, nor even a complete epic hero. He can, on separate occasions, show Arthur being fearless, impetuous, self-willed, often savagely ferocious, once or twice merciful to women in distress; but these traits appear singly, each in connexion with some one action, and they remain the materials for a character, rather than part of one.

This incapacity of Laȝamon's is to some extent obscured by his ability to make the reader feel the emotions of his people, as he does with Cordoille, in the story of Leir. He does this largely, though not entirely, by describing their physical manifestations. Cordoille sits very still after she has made her reply to her father, and when he has given his judgement she goes to her room and is 'shamefast' ('mortified'); she is silent and turns red when, at the end of the story, Leir's man comes to ask for her help. But her emotions arise naturally from her situation; they are not peculiar to her as an individual. Laȝamon's awareness of them is part of his power of rising to a situation, particularly to a moment of tension.

Since his history contains many kinds of stories and situations, this power of his means that his poem does not lack variety of interest. As occasion offers he can present the mystery of the supernatural; in the story of Arthur's birth, for example, and of his passing and in some passages about Merlin. In his accounts of war he shows heroic and violent action and bloodthirsty sentiments; his theme is suffering and pity in such stories as those of St. Ursula and of Leir. Like most of the Old English poets, however, he is not interested in romantic love; here he even tones down what little Wace has to offer.

Laȝamon's *Brut*, the most considerable and by far the best of the early Middle English alliterative poems, was written in the west of England, in Worcestershire, and this is precisely where the native alliterative verse might be expected to flourish most vigorously and to survive longest.

III

THE ALLITERATIVE REVIVAL

1. The Alliterative *Morte Arthure* and other poems

NOTHING that has survived from the early Middle English period prepares us for that later outpouring of alliterative poetry which has conveniently, though probably inaccurately, been termed the 'alliterative revival'. Suddenly (so it appears to us), in the middle of the fourteenth century, a number of poets began to use alliterative verse in the kinds of poetry then most popular—romances, chronicles, political satire, religious and moral allegory—and, continuing throughout this century and the next, they produced, among a good deal that is second-rate or worse, some of the most spirited of Middle English poems, and a few that can stand comparison with good poems of any age. The fact that so much in this poetry is obviously traditional suggests that the suddenness of its beginning must be illusory; for, if it be supposed that the traditional features were the result of a deliberate revival, this demands answers to the questions—what were the models, and, how were they known? Laʒamon's *Brut* does not provide a satisfactory answer, if only because its uncertain rhythms could not have inspired the far more confident rhythms of the later poems. To answer that other earlier works, now lost, might have been preserved in written or oral form till the second half of the fourteenth century is tantamount to admitting a continuous interest in alliterative verse; and such an interest is at least as likely to have resulted in new compositions as in the constant repetition of old. Moreover, as will appear, the nature of one of the earliest poems of the group seems to indicate that it was not the first of its kind. It is likely then, that alliterative poetry continued to be composed on a considerable scale from generation to generation without a break, and that the features in fourteenth-century verse that appear to be new to the alliterative tradition were adopted gradually, to meet the demands of new subjects and new tastes.

These new features are of various kinds. The traditional vocabulary is often enlarged by a wealth of technical terms, usually French, to do with hunting, architecture, armour, and so forth. The influence of stanzaic verse is seen in the occasional grouping of the alliterative long lines, sometimes in quatrains, sometimes in stanzas using rhyme. Fashionable formal devices such as the dream or the debate are employed, and alliterative poets become as addicted as any others to describing spring mornings, hunting scenes, and elaborate feasts. Yet their poetry remains distinctive in manner and feeling, as well as in metre. Some of the most striking differences between Middle English alliterative poetry and poetry written in other metres are in manner, a liking for specific detail resulting in solid, realistic description; in feeling, a seriousness of outlook which gives unusual strength and purpose, at least to the best of the poems.

There are many and puzzling resemblances in phraseology, style, and theme between the various alliterative poems. Some of these can undoubtedly be explained as the result of deliberate imitation, though ignorance of the exact date of most of the poems often makes it impossible to decide which way the borrowing went. Common authorship has been held to account for some others; but the game of hunting for similar phrases and assigning all works that contain them to a single author was carried much too far by some early critics. It has been shown that many of the poems which were at one time attributed on this evidence to the poet Huchoun, whose name we chance to know from Andrew Wyntoun's *Orygynale Cronykil*, differ in dialect and in important points of style and metrical technique. Nowadays theories of common authorship are viewed with caution, and scholars prefer to leave the authors of most of the alliterative poems unnamed.

Something is known, however, about where the authors lived. From the remark of Chaucer's Parson:

> But trusteth wel, I am a Southren man,
> I kan nat geeste 'rum, ram, ruf,' by lettre,
> Ne, God woot, rym holde I but litel bettre
> *(Canterbury Tales*, I. 42–44)

we may judge, not, as is often suggested, that Chaucer despised alliterative verse (there are good reasons for not believing this), but that he did not think such verse was composed in his own southern district. The investigations of modern scholars show him, on the whole, to have been right. The original dialects of the alliterative poems, so far as they can be ascertained, have, with very few exceptions, been localized in the western counties from Gloucestershire to Cumberland; the majority of them in the northern half of this district.

If, as we may also infer, Chaucer thought these poems 'provincial', he was right in this too; for most of them came from districts which, as the southerner Trevisa tells us, 'þe kynges of Englelond woneþ fer fram'—districts, that is, far removed from the recognized centres of culture. Yet the odd thing is that some of these poems are not at all what we should expect a provincial poem to be. They have a self-assured air, as if their writers, who were evidently familiar with polite literature, knew what they wanted to achieve and how to set about it. In the no doubt extreme case of *Sir Gawain and the Green Knight*, there is a knowledge of aristocratic society as complete as in Chaucer's poetry. Such a poem must have been written for a cultured society of some kind, and it is possible that some great families of the west who were in opposition to the king—the Mortimers, Bohuns, and Beauchamps, for instance—may deliberately have fostered verse of native origin as a rival to that poetry, more closely dependent on French, which was written for the court by Chaucer and others. We know that one alliterative poem at least, *William of Palerne*, was written at the request of Humphrey de Bohun, Earl of Hereford.

Not all alliterative poetry can have been intended for aristocratic society, however. The greatness of *Piers Plowman* does not obscure its comparative lack of art, and, however successful modern critics may have been in showing that it is not the shapeless mass that it once seemed to be, it still remains evident that its writer (or writers) felt no compulsion to polish his work. This does not prove that *Piers Plowman* was written for the common people, though John Ball's letter to the peasants of Essex (1381) shows that they knew of it; but it does suggest that it was intended for a public less literary and less critical than that for which *Sir Gawain* was written.

We must not draw too sharp distinctions between the poems, dividing them into 'aristocratic' and 'popular', for some of the interconnexions that have been mentioned cut across any groupings that might be made. But we may suppose that, in the later fourteenth century, in the districts where it flourished, alliterative poetry was popular in more than one stratum of society. Perhaps there had been, in the preceding period, separate streams of tradition, kept alive in different classes of society, which for some reason or other, and to some extent, intermingled in the fourteenth century.

Of the fourteenth-century poems in unrhymed alliterative long lines, *Winner and Waster* and *The Parliament of the Three Ages*, which are preserved in the same fifteenth-century manuscript, have been thought to be among the earliest. Certainly *Winner* can with good reason be assigned to the years 1352–3; but there is no real evidence for the date of *The Parliament*.

Winner and Waster is a topical satire cast in the form of a dream. The poet, having fallen asleep, sees two armies arrayed to do battle against one another. Their leaders, Winner and Waster, state their cases before a 'comely king', whose appearance and dress, with the blue garter embroidered upon it, proclaim him to be Edward III, and the king gives judgement. Winner, whose army displays the banners of the Pope, of men of law, of the four orders of friars, and of all sorts of merchants, is to go 'by Paris to þe Pope of Rome' (that is, to the Pope at Avignon) where the cardinals will make much of him. Waster is to betake himself 'into þe chepe'[1] and entice the unwary traveller to a tavern to drink all night, or to Bread Street to stuff himself with fat sheep and poultry.

The author is precise about the classes of men who follow Winner, that is, who amass wealth, often caring little for the means they employ. The 'wasters' appear to be chiefly military men and landed gentry, who, so Winner complains, leave their lands untilled and spend what money they have on rich clothes, food, and drink. Since the king claims that both Winner and Waster are 'servants of our house', the poem is clearly, in spite of its respectful references

[1] 'the market', possibly here Cheapside.

to the king, a sharp, twofold attack upon Edward III for the extravagance of his living, and of his wars, and for the means by which he obtained the money for both.

The poet has his material well in hand. Apart from a pointless opening reference to Brutus the Trojan and his founding of the kingdom of Britain,[1] he introduces nothing irrelevant, and he is sometimes ingenious in his handling of conventions. The accusations which Winner and Waster bring against one another are enlivened by many details from real life, as when Waster describes the roof-beams bending in Winner's house because of the bacon that hangs there, or Winner names the London streets that are Waster's haunts and tells how he sits in a tavern crying out 'fille in' and 'feche forth'. On the other hand, the writer sometimes descends to mere cataloguing, and he is too ready with hackneyed alliterative phrases—'ledis[2] of the land', 'fostrede[3] and fedde', 'dynttis[4] to dele', and so forth.

The many features of this poem which are seen to be conventions and even commonplaces, when the whole body of later alliterative verse is considered, raise the question of its relation to these later poems. If *Winner and Waster* is one of the earliest of the group, must it be supposed that later poems derive from it those things they have in common with it? Though this may be so in some instances (*Piers Plowman*, for example, may be directly indebted to it for some things), it can hardly be so in all. *Winner and Waster* does not seem sufficiently outstanding to have had such far-reaching influence, and, to judge by its survival in a single manuscript, its circulation was not wide. Many of its similarities with other poems can be more satisfactorily explained by the assumption already suggested, that behind the earliest poems we know in the fourteenth century there was much alliterative verse that has been lost.

If *The Parliament[5] of the Three Ages* does date from much the same time as *Winner*, it affords an even stronger argument for this assumption, for it would appear to be a mosaic of conventions. Gollancz wrote of it: 'One's first impression is that *The Parliament*

---

[1] Found elsewhere in alliterative poems.   [2] 'men'.
[3] 'fostered'.   [4] 'blows'.   [5] 'Debate'.

is a sort of summary of longer poems—an epitome reminiscent of lines and passages in the chief alliterative poems of the second half of the fourteenth century.' Its opening lines

> In the monethe of Maye when mirthes bene fele,[1]
> And the sesone of somere when softe bene the wedres,
> Als I went to the wodde . . .

remind one, primarily perhaps, of *Piers Plowman*, but also of many other poems, not all alliterative. The description that follows, of the stalking of the deer, the kill and the breaking-up has something in common with the hunting scenes in *Sir Gawain and the Green Knight*. This forms the prologue to a dream in which Youth, Medill-Elde,[2] and Elde[3] appear, and debate with one another, Middle Age attacking Youth, who defends himself, and Old Age reproving both. Familiar themes are introduced into the debate; Youth discourses at length on the sport of hawking, and Old Age gives an account of the Nine Worthies and other famous personages who have 'passed the pase[4] þat I schall passe sone'.

There is some good description in the poem, particularly in the passages on deer-stalking and hawking, where the poet writes circumstantially and, it would seem, from first-hand observation. We can share the excitement of the deer-stalker as he watched to see 'by waggynge of leues'[5] where the wind was, and then, taking up his stand behind a crab-apple tree, remained long motionless, in spite of the gnats that 'gretely me greuede and gnewen myn eghne',[6] while the hart 'stotayde and stelkett and starede full brode'.[7] The writer knows and sometimes makes good use of the tricks of his trade. He employs a number of rhetorical devices, taking pains, for instance, to link the sections of his narrative, either by repeating a phrase from the end of one at the beginning of the next, or by beginning successive sections with similar phrases. But he has little sense of fitness or proportion. The far too lengthy digression on the Nine Worthies is characteristic as a whole and in detail; the account of Alexander is a long and

---

[1] 'pleasures are many'.   [2] 'Middle Age'.
[3] 'Old Age'.   [4] 'path'.   [5] 'moving of the leaves'.
[6] 'sorely vexed me and bit [gnawed] my eyes'.
[7] 'paused, and moved on softly, and stared around'.

breathless recapitulation of facts from every source known to the poet, while Judas Maccabeus and Godfrey of Boulogne, of whom he knows little, are dismissed in a few lines.

Gollancz was convinced that *The Parliament* was by the author of *Winner*, and written about the same date.[1] But this remains to be proved, and in the meanwhile the poem can be taken as what it appears to be—an imitation of *Piers Plowman*, *Sir Gawain and the Green Knight*, and others.

It is with *Piers Plowman* and the late *Death and Liffe* that both *Winner* and *The Parliament* have especially close links. These four poems, all of them, broadly speaking, didactic or satiric in purpose, use the same framework of the dream and the allegorical debate, and there are marked resemblances in phraseology between them. *Death and Liffe* (? *c.* 1450) is directly indebted to the shorter poems for some things; in tone and feeling it comes nearest to *Piers Plowman*. Its solemn theme is treated with deep seriousness, and a powerful imagination makes itself felt in the contrasting descriptions of Life and Death and in their debate. This culminates in a moving exposition of the meaning of the Crucifixion. Death boasts that she conquered all men who ever lived and has even 'jousted' with 'Jesu of heauen' (a clear reminiscence of *Piers Plowman*); but Life replies that Death was put to shame in that joust:

> But, Death, how didst thou then, with all thy derffe[2] words,
> When thou prickedst att his pappe with the poynt of a speare,
> And touched the tabernackle of his trew hart,
> Where my bower was bigged[3] to abyde for euer?
> When the glory of his godhead glented[4] in thy face,
> Then was thou feard of this fare[5] in thy false hart,
> Then thou hyed into hell-hole to hyde thee beliue[6] . . .
>
> (380–6)

She recalls Christ's resurrection, and His victory over the powers of hell, and concludes, addressing mankind,

> Haue no doubt[7] of yonder Death, my deare children;
> For yonder Death is damned with devills to dwell,

---

[1] *Winner and Waster* (O.U.P., 1920), preface.
[2] 'bold'. [3] 'built'. [4] 'shone'.
[5] 'action'. [6] 'quickly'. [7] 'fear'.

Where is wondred[1] and woe and wayling for sorrow.
Death was damned that day, daring[2] full still;
Shee hath no might ne no maine to meddle with yonder ost[3]
Against Euerlasting Liffe, þat Lady soe true.   (439-44)

About the same time as *Winner* there appear the first attempts to render in alliterative verse some of the famous 'matters' of romance. The poets seem, in general, to have avoided love-romances and to have preferred historical, or pseudo-historical, subjects such as the Trojan war, the life of Alexander, the conquests and death of Arthur. One of the few exceptions, *William of Palerne*, shows how right this instinct was. This is a rendering of a twelfth-century French romance made for Humphrey de Bohun, Earl of Hereford, who died in 1361; it must therefore be one of the earliest alliterative romances. The French poet says that he wrote at the instance of Yoland, daughter of Baldwin IV, Count of Hainault, and it is obvious that his work was designed to please a courtly circle. Love is the motive force of the story. William, the unknown foundling, and Melior, daughter of the Emperor of Rome, suffer the pains expected of a pair of courtly lovers, and the French poet analyses their thoughts and emotions at length. Whenever possible he dwells, too, upon the sentiments of other characters; even his animals display the sensibility and behave with the courtesy in which courtly society delighted.

The story which conveys these proper sentiments is fantastic even for a romance. As a young child, William is carried off successively by a kindly werewolf (who swoons with grief when he loses him), an equally kindly cowherd, and the Emperor of Rome, whose daughter Melior eventually falls in love with him. To avoid an uncongenial marriage, Melior runs away from her father's court, and she and William wander through Italy and Sicily disguised first as white bears, and later as a hart and hind. Throughout their journeyings they are provided with food and other necessities by the 'witty'[4] werewolf (as the English version calls him). After many adventures, including some fighting in which William, of course,

[1] 'misery'.   [2] 'crouching with fear'.
[3] 'host' (i.e. the multitude that Death has slain).
[4] 'wise, sagacious'.

distinguishes himself, everything comes out right for the lovers, and for everybody else. The werewolf, being disenchanted, proves to be the son of the King of Spain. The unravelling of the threads of the story gives occasion for affecting recognition scenes which are followed by piteous separations as the various characters finally return to their own countries.

This unreal story, which is related with much circumstantial and even matter-of-fact detail, has something of the lure of a fairy-tale; and the 'niceness' of the characters is attractive. These virtues the English poem retains, for the translator follows the French tale closely. He does his best, too, to convey the sentiment, but he is defeated by the essential unsuitability of his medium. Passages meant to be moving, as when William, dreaming of Melior, clasps to himself a pillow and wakes calling to it and kissing it, are made ludicrous by the heavy insistence of the alliterative lines. Possibly a more flexible and imaginative writer might have done better, but this man is not even skilled in his chosen style. He has little feeling for words and repeats certain favourite ones in and out of season, whenever they are useful for the alliteration.

Among the earliest 'historical' romances in the alliterative metre are two fragments on the life of Alexander, usually known as *Alexander A* and *Alexander B* or *Alexander and Dindimus*. These seem to have been written at much the same time, in the same west Midland dialect, and they are both derived from one version of the famous *Historia de Preliis*.[1] Though their latest editor does not believe that they are by one author, he considers that *B* may be part of a continuation of a complete translation of the *Historia* of which *A* is the beginning. A third fragment, *Alexander C* or *The Wars of Alexander*, was written farther north, and later, and is derived from a different version of the *Historia*.

Alexander A combines with the legendary matter of the *Historia de Preliis* extracts from the reputedly historical *Historia adversus Paganos* of Orosius telling of Philip of Macedon's ancestry, marriage, and wars. The *De Preliis* provides the story of how Nectana-

[1] See pp. 55 ff.

bus, magician-king of Egypt, left his own country and came to Macedon where, in Philip's absence, he seduced Philip's wife, Olympias, by his magic arts and begat Alexander upon her. From it, too, come the accounts of the marvels preceding Alexander's birth, of Alexander's slaying of Nectanabus and his taming of Bucephalus. The story of the birth and childhood of Alexander is absent owing to a lacuna in the manuscript.

Alexander B, from a much later portion of the *Historia de Preliis*, tells of some of Alexander's adventures in India. It begins with his visit to the people known as the Gymnosophists ('is that name to mene the Nakede Wise') and then describes how, on arriving at the river Ganges, he sees on the other side men said to be Brahmins. Letters are exchanged between him and their king Dindimus, in which the Brahmins' simple way of life is contrasted with Alexander's life of luxury and conquest. The underlying intention in this correspondence was to elaborate the familiar contrast between the Contemplative and the Active Life, and, at the same time, to contrast the Christian life with the pagan. The Middle English text breaks off in the middle of a sentence and, since it has no set opening either, it was presumably part of a longer work. In the manuscript, Bodley 264, it is preceded by the French *Roman d'Alixandre*, and, to judge by a note in English appearing in the course of that work, the English fragment was added by a scribe who thought, though wrongly, that a passage was missing from the *Roman*.

The far longer *Alexander C* (*Wars of Alexander*) covers, in one or other of the two extant manuscripts, the whole of the life of Alexander as told in one version of the *Historia de Preliis* (that known as J^{3a}), except for a small portion at the end; in addition, it includes in an abridged form the episode known as the *Fuerres de Gadres* ('Foraging in Gadres': *Alexander C*, 1193–336).

Of the three, *C* keeps closest to its original; this seems certain, even though in the exact version of the *Historia de Preliis* on which it is based is not extant for comparison. The writer of *A* expands considerably, particularly when he is following Orosius's bald narrative. The statement 'Olympiadem Arubae regis Molossorum sororem duxit uxorem' moves him to a neatly ordered catalogue of

Olympias's physical beauties, from the expected rose-red complexion and hair like gold wire, down to her feet:

> Þe fairest feete þat euer freke kende,
> With ton tidily wrought and tender of hur skynne.[1]

He also supplies details about battles merely mentioned by Orosius, helping himself along by means of familiar tags, sometimes quite meaningless as he uses them. The *Historia de Preliis* provides him with more detail, and he rarely adds passages of any length when he is following it; but, because he cannot resist introducing commonplaces, his version is much longer than the Latin, and more tedious. It has been suggested that *Alexander A* was composed for oral delivery, and the style, with its painfully obvious transitions, suggests the 'patter' of the minstrel, never at a loss, but never inspired.

The pedestrian writer of *Alexander B* does not, perhaps, use so many meaningless tags, but he draws out the narrative by lengthy paraphrase and repetitive lines and phrases. Such slight contributions as he makes to the matter seem designed to point a moral or to stress the Christian point of view. Where the renderings of *B* and *C* can be compared, *C* is in general shorter, more direct, and more lively. When the Gymnosophists, to whom Alexander has offered to give whatever they wish, ask for immortality, Alexander replies 'Mortalis cum sim, immortalitatem nullatenus dare possum', and they 'Et si mortalis es, quare vadis discurrendo et faciendo tanta et talia mala?' *B* renders this exchange in eight lines, but *C*, keeping something of the terseness of the Latin, is more effective:

> 'Be driȝtin, sirs, I am a duke dedelike myselfe,
> Forþi vndedlynes to dele I dowe be na ways.'
> 'Now sen it worthis' quod þa wees 'wriche, for to die,
> Quarto hiȝis þou fra half to halfe and all þis harme werkis?'[2]

The greater fidelity of the *Wars of Alexander* to the Latin, often brought as a reproach against it, is, on the contrary, almost always

---

[1] 'The fairest feet that ever men knew, with toes neatly made and delicate of skin' (193–4).
[2] ' "By God, sirs, I am myself a mortal lord, therefore I can by no means give immortality." "Now since it will happen, wretch", said those men, "that you will die, to what end do you hasten from realm to realm and work all this mischief?" ' (4057–60).

a cause of gain. But this is not by itself the reason for its superiority; its writer is more intelligent, and a better poet than the writer of *B*, and he grasps the point of the Latin where *B* sometimes misses it, and has some feeling for its quality. Such expansions of his original as he makes are usually in descriptions of the kind most congenial to poets of the alliterative tradition. He writes of fighting in energetic lines conveying swift action and the noise of battle,[1] and he is responsible for the colour and vividness of the scene when the people of Jerusalem deck their streets for Alexander's visit (1513–72). In such passages, he has an easy command of word and rhythm, and his poetry, though not of the highest order, can hold the attention. Sometimes he conveys impressions of a different kind, as in the pleasant passage describing the Brahmins' enjoyment of nature, where he speaks of the things

> Þat ilk sensitife saule mast souorly delyte,
> As in þe woddis for to walke vndire wale schawis
> Quen all is lokin ouire with leuys, as It ware littill heuen.
> Þan haue we liking to lithe þe late of þe foules,
> Þe swoȝing of þe swift wynde and of þe swete wellis.[2]

The passages just mentioned do not show great originality, but the poet's ear and imagination are still sufficiently alive to the possibilities of the poetic tradition he inherited to enable him at times to write real poetry and in general to be adequate to his task. Some striking similarities in phraseology make it fairly certain that there is some connexion between the *Alexander C* and the work of the *Gawain* poet, and *C* is not entirely unworthy to be either the inspirer or the imitator of the greater poem.

Another famous Latin work, the *Historia Destructionis Trojae* of Guido delle Colonne, is the source of the alliterative *Destruction of Troy*. In the index to the only surviving manuscript we are told that some knight caused the rendering to be made, and we are promised his name and that of the man who 'translated it out of latyn into englysshe'; but the manuscript is defective where the

---

[1] 777–806, 1385–420, 2221–30.
[2] '. . . which please most fully [literally, "savourily"] each sensitive man, as to walk in the woods under pleasant groves, when all is vaulted over with leaves, as it were a little heaven. Then we take delight in listening to the song of the birds, the soughing of the swift wind and the sweet streams' (4381–5).

names should have appeared. This reference suggests that the translation was undertaken as hackwork, and that, on the whole, is the impression it gives. It faithfully follows the course of Guido's book, including his digressions, whether moral, like the diatribes against false gods,[1] or descriptive, such as the series of portraits of the Greek and Trojan leaders.[2] The style is careless; the longer sentences are often clumsy and ill-co-ordinated, and there is much repetition of phrases and epithets. On the other hand, the verse is unusually regular in rhythm and alliteration; but, in a work of 14,044 lines, this regularity becomes monotonous.

Yet the poem is not unreadable. Guido's story was alive to the English writer, and he worked with a mind alert and open to suggestion. The thoughts and emotions of the characters, their long speeches, their appearance and actions were all of interest to him, and he reproduced them, not slavishly, but with added details and occasional cuts of irrelevant matter. Like other poets of the tradition, he is most impressive when describing violent action—battles and storms at sea in particular. The energy which is his most marked characteristic finds natural and effective outlet in such lines as:

> With a ropand rayne rugh was the se;
> The wyndes full wodely wackont anon,
> Rut vp the rughe se on rokkes aboute;
> As hilles hit hepit in a hond while.
> So þe bre and the brethe burbelit togedur,
> Þat hit spirit vp spitously fyue speire lenght
> With walterand wawes, þat þe wynd dryues
> All fore as a fyre þe firmament ouer.[3]

But the striking phrase 'ropand rayne' becomes less impressive when it is met with in a second storm, and a third.

The weakness of these 'historical' romances is their formlessness. The writers do not attempt to arrange their matter in accordance with any idea of their own but simply follow the course of the narrative as they find it. The author of *The Siege of Jerusalem*,

---

[1] *Destruction*, 4295 ff.   [2] 3741 ff.

[3] 'The sea was rough with a beating rain; soon the winds wakened madly, dashed the rough sea up about the rocks; it was heaped up like hills in a short time. The sea and the wind so bubbled together that it [the sea] spurted up furiously five spears length with weltering waves which the wind drives before [it] like a fire over the firmament' (3693–700).

however, seems to have tried to give his story some shape by selecting and combining material from several sources, and by dividing it into four sections, each marked by a brief concluding invocation, such as 'and god ȝyue us joye'. His attempt is not very successful, for not all his divisions are natural ones, and he includes a good deal of unnecessary historical matter. His other formal device, the grouping of the long lines in quatrains may have acted as some check on the exuberance of his descriptions, yet he still lavishes descriptive detail on things that are only incidental to the story— Vespasian's fleet (281 ff.), the elaborate 'standard' built like a belfry (385 ff.) which he erected as his headquarters, the elephant with a castle on its back in which Caiaphas sits (461 ff.). Descriptions of battle are proper to the story, and here, among much that is familiar elsewhere in alliterative poetry, there are flashes of imagination, as when we are told that the battlefield grew bright as the beams of the sun from the golden and jewelled armour that lay there (544–5), or later, that it was strewn so thick with dead bodies that a horse could not put down its foot but on steel armour (600–1). But such exaggeration is effective only in small doses, and this writer does not know when to stop. He spares the reader few of the horrors of the siege of Jerusalem; indeed, his ghoulish relish for the horrible is so marked that one feels it may account for his having chosen the siege as his subject.

To turn from the *Siege* to *Joseph of Arimathie* is to become aware of the variety of style of which alliterative poetry is capable. This poem, probably one of the earliest of the group under consideration (? *c.* 1350), is certainly the earliest to deal with any Arthurian matter. Its story is part of the early history of the Holy Grail, a condensed version of the first part of the French prose *Lestoire del Saint Graal (Grand Saint Graal)*. The opening is missing in the only extant manuscript, but it evidently told of the imprisonment of Joseph of Arimathie by the Jews, during which he received from Christ a dish containing His blood shed on the cross. The text begins when Joseph is being released by Vespasian. He is bidden by the voice of Christ to make a box for the blood, and to go to Sarras (whence the Saracens come) to preach His word. Arrived there, he tells Evalak, the king, of Christ's death, of the Incarnation, and of the Trinity. Evalak doubts the possibility of what he says, and that night two visions appear to him to show him the truth. His land is invaded by Tholomer, King of Babylon, and Joseph, after revealing a miraculous knowledge of his early life, sends him forth to battle with a cross of red cloth upon his shield. Evalak is at first successful, but is presently taken prisoner. He then looks upon the shield and prays, and at once a white knight appears who rescues him and his brother-in-law, Seraphe, and slays Tholomer. When Tholomer's army retreats, the white knight vanishes. Evalak's queen is discovered to be a Christian, and Evalak himself and more than 5,000 others are baptized. The poem ends abruptly with a brief reference to the events which immediately follow in *Lestoire del Saint Graal*.

If, as Skeat thinks, little of the poem has been lost, the poet must have intended to confine himself to the single episode of Joseph's conversion of Evalak. On the whole his cuts in the French material and rearrangements of it are consonant with this view. If he retains some matter not strictly relevant to this episode as, for instance, the vision granted to Josaphe, Joseph's son, on looking into the box containing the blood, and Christ's consecration of Josaphe as bishop, this is explained by his underlying purpose, which is to manifest the power of Christ and of His sacrifice. It is this that engrosses his attention and, with simple earnestness, he relates his tale as an illustration of it. His language is for the most part plain, at times even bald; he has few stock alliterative phrases or exclusively poetic words, and such rhetorical devices as he uses are of the simplest. To judge from his clumsy transitions and occasional inappropriate phrases he was an inexperienced writer, and the irregularity of his metre also suggests this. The subtler parts of the French work are beyond him, and he fails to convey the full significance of Evalak's visions or of Joseph's exposition of the Trinity. Yet on the whole his plain style suits his subject, and it can be effective, as in the reply which Josaphe gives when his father asks him why he is looking into the box:

> 'A Fader, touche me not in þis ilke tyme,[1]
> For much gostliche grace me is here i-graunted.'   (279–80)

[1] 'at this time'.

or in the description by Evalak's queen of Christ's appearance to her and her mother:

> Þenne com Iesu Crist so cler in him-seluen,
> aftur þe furste blusch we ne miȝte him bi-holden,
> And a wynt and a sauor whappede us vmbe,
> we weore so wel of vr-self we nuste what we duden.[1]

In his account of the battle he comes nearer the traditional manner of alliterative poetry, but, compared with most of the other poets, he is still brief and sparing of detail; and he gains not a little in force thereby.

The central story of the Arthurian cycle—the conquests of Arthur, his recall to Britain by the news of Modred's treachery, his unequal last fight and death—was the inspiration for one of the most impressive of alliterative poems, the *Morte Arthure*. This work, which survives in a unique copy in the Thornton MS., has recently achieved a sort of fame, even among those who have not read it, by the discovery that Malory based upon it the 'Noble Tale of King Arthur and the Emperor Lucius', as Professor Vinaver calls it.[2] Here, however, it will be considered in its own right as, in spite of some obvious defects, it well deserves.

The *Morte Arthure* is, in subject and treatment, a thoroughly masculine work. Its heroic theme resembles those beloved by the Old English poets. Arthur is the mighty conqueror, haughty to his enemies, generous to his knights, and undaunted in defeat; his sole occupation, and that of his men is fighting; courage and loyalty are the virtues they prize. The temper which they (and the poet) admire is well illustrated in the speech of Sir Idrus when, in the last battle, Arthur bids him rescue his father, who is hard pressed:

> He es my fadire in faithe, forsake sall I neuer,
> He has me fosterde and fedde and my faire bretheren . . .
> He commande me kyndly with knyghtly wordes,
> That I schulde lelely one þe lenge and one noo lede elles;
> I sall hys commandement holde, ȝif Crist wil me thole.
> He es eldare than I, and ende sall we bothen,

---

[1] 'Then came Jesus Christ so bright in Himself that after the first glance we could not behold Him; and a wind and a scent lapped us round, we were so full of joy we knew not what we did' (656–9).

[2] Book v in Caxton's version of the *Morte Darthur*.

He sall ferkke before, and I sall come aftyre.
3iffe him be destaynede to dy todaye one þis erthe,
Criste comly with crown take kepe to hys saule.[1]

In all that concerns the relations between Arthur and his knights resemblances to Old English heroic poetry are striking. The knights, some of them Arthur's kinsmen and all of them ready to boast of their high lineage, are councillors as well as warriors, like the picked band of tried men, the *duguþ*, who in *Beowulf* support Hroþgar. Like them, they make their vaunts about the great deeds they will do in battle, and receive from their lord rewards for their valour. The speech of Sir Cader, encouraging his men to brave a great army of the Romans, reads like a fourteenth-century version of one from *The Battle of Maldon*. 'Think', he cries, 'on the valiant prince who has ever enriched us with lands and honour . . . given us treasure and gold and many rewards, greyhounds and fine horses . . .' (1726 ff.). How much of this is due to the Middle English poet we do not know, but if, as the latest opinion holds, he got his story from a French romance, or combined material from several romances, it seems likely that he developed it on lines that were traditional in English heroic poetry, as La3amon had done before him.

But the monsters encountered in *Morte Arthure* are not those of *Beowulf*, even though the same or similar phrases are sometimes used of them. In place of the indefinite but immensely suggestive description of Grendel, that misshapen haunter of the waste lands, that 'helle gast'[2] of the brood of Cain, who is evil and terrifying even today, the *Morte Arthure* has the giant of Mont St. Michel, presented with a wealth of definite details which, horrible as they are, yet fail to terrify. The giant's kirtle, 'spun in Spain' and 'garnished in Greece' and bordered with beards of slain kings, is a fancy befitting the story of Jack the Giant-killer rather than a

---

[1] 'He is in truth my father, whom I shall never forsake. He has fostered and fed me and my good brothers. . . . Fittingly he bade me in knightly speech that I should stay loyally by you and by no other man. I shall keep his command, if Christ will allow. He is older than I, and we both must come to our end; he will go before and I shall come after. If he is destined to die on this field today, may the gloriously crowned Christ have care of his soul' (4142 ff.).
[2] 'spirit of hell'.

thing to be believed in. More impressive is the description of the giant as Arthur first sees him:

> He lay lenand on lange, lugande vnfaire,
> Þe thee of a manns lymme lyfte vp by þe haunche;
> His bakke and his bewschers and his brode lendez
> He bekez by þe bale-fyr and breklesse hym semede;
> Þare ware rostez full ruyde and rewfull bredez,
> Beerynes and bestaile brochede togeders,
> Cowle full cramede of crysmede childyre;
> Sum as brede brochede, and bierdez þam tournede.[1]

Other marvels in the story—the prophetic dreams, the balm that heals Sir Priamus and Sir Gawayne—belong wholly to the world of romance, and are treated in a matter-of-fact way, as necessary 'properties' of the story. Nor are these the only features traceable to the romances. The poem opens according to pattern, with a prayer and a call for attention; there are the expected descriptions of feasts, of clothing, of the arming of knights. The stigmatization of Arthur's enemies, even in Britain, as Saracens reflects the familiar romance conflicts between Christian and Saracen, and, though in the earlier part of the story Arthur fights merely for personal glory, he enters upon his last campaign displaying a banner on which is 'a chalke-whitte mayden And a childe in hir armc þat chefe es of hevyne' (3648-9), and his end is marked by Christian devotion. Of the gentler virtues comprised under the term 'courtesy', he and his knights show little trace, however, in spite of the opening description of them as 'Kynde men and courtays and couthe of courte thewes' (21).[2] More characteristic of them are the grim jests they make in battle, as when Arthur cuts through the knees of the giant Golapas, crying, 'Come down and speak to your companions. You are too high by half, I promise you truly. You shall be more convenient in height, with my Lord's help' (2126 ff.). This recalls similar jests in the Icelandic sagas, and

---

[1] 'He lay, leaning at his length, disposed uglily, holding up by the haunch the thigh from a man's leg. His back and his buttocks and his broad loins he warms by the bonfire—and breechless he seemed. There were horrible roasts and pitiful meats, men and animals on the spit together, a tub crammed full of anointed children, some spitted as meat, and women turned them' (1045-52).

[2] 'versed in courtly behaviour'.

demonstrates how superficial the relation between this poem and the romances of chivalry really is.

For this is a tragic tale, 'þat trewe es and nobyll' (16). Fittingly, it is given a firm foundation in time and place. So, Arthur justifies his rage at the summons to appear before the Roman Emperor Lucius by an 'historical' account of his ancestors' lordship over Rome; and the stages of his own journey thither are so clearly indicated that it would be possible to trace them on a map. Descriptions are solid, for the most part realizable in terms of the known. In recounting the siege of Metz, the poet specifies the siege instruments that were brought up and suggests the resulting destruction by details that come home to present-day readers perhaps even more than they did to the fourteenth century:

> Stone-stepells full styffe in þe strete ligges,
> Chawmbyrs with chymnés and many cheefe innes
> Paysede and pelid down playsterede walles.[1]

Constantly a scene is brought to life by some realistic detail, as when the sheriffs 'sharply shift' the commons to make room for the great lords who are to embark for the expedition against Lucius (725), or, as when Arthur, having climbed to the top of Mont St. Michel, lifted his visor and 'caughte of þe colde wynde to comforthe hym seluen' (a touch that did not escape Malory). There are details like this in the accounts of battles, but they are mingled with others, more conventional and less real, for the tradition of such descriptions in alliterative poetry is too strong to be ignored. Here is a characteristic passage:

> Than the Romaynes and the rennkkez of þe rounde table . . .
> Foynes ful felly with flyschande speris,
> Freten of orfrayes feste appon scheldez.
> So fele fay es in fyghte appon þe felde leuyde,
> That iche a furthe in the firthe of rede blode rynnys,
> By that swyftely one swarthe þe swett es byleuede,
> Swerdez swangen in two, sweltand knyghtez
> Lyes wyde-opyn welterande on walopande stedez.[2]

---

[1] 'Stone steeples full strong lie in the streets; they battered down chimneyed rooms and many of the chief buildings and pounded plastered walls' (3040-2).
[2] 'Then the Romans and the warriors of the Round Table . . . thrust full

In all descriptions there is much use of the cumulative method, detail being piled on detail, often in phrases of similar construction, as in Old English poetry. But the poet of *Morte Arthure* is less restrained than the best of the Old English poets, and his long, overloaded descriptions slow down the narrative considerably. It is noticeable how often Malory improves upon him by selecting only the most significant of the details he offers. A sense of over-elaboration is increased by some of the poet's tricks of style and metre. Often he uses the same alliterating sound for several lines on end, for as many as ten on one occasion; or he will begin consecutive lines with the same phrase or rhythm. Phrases and even whole lines from one passage are repeated in another, not usually for the purpose of linking sections of the narrative, as in some alliterative poems, but merely to produce a sort of echo. In one instance only is this repetition justified by its effect. When Arthur tells his council of Modred's treachery, which he has just learnt from Sir Cradok, his repetition of several of Sir Cradok's phrases helps to convey his stunned horror at the news. In general the effect of these various kinds of repetition is like that of a battering-ram. The mind wearies of what it feels to be a continual striving to impress. Excess is, indeed, the great defect of the poem, and not only in matters of style. There are too many giants, almost all 'engendrede of fendez' ('begotten of devils'); there are too many speeches at the opening council, and here, and elsewhere, they are too long; there is far too much fighting.

But a distinction must be made between the earlier and later parts of the poem, for in the later, though from line to line the method of narration is not essentially different, the tale is made far more engrossing. It may be that the poet turned to a fresh source for the last part of his tale (the fact that Malory makes no use of the poem after about l. 3218 needs some explanation); or it may be that the incidents are in themselves so stirring that they called forth in the poet powers which do not appear in the earlier

fiercely with slashing spears, tore away gold fringes fastened upon shields. So many doomed men were left on the field in the fight that each ford in the forest runs with red blood. Soon the life-blood is left on the green grass, swords beaten in two, dying knights with gaping wounds lie lolling on galloping steeds' (2135 ff.).

part. Whatever the reason, the story moves more purposefully from the point where Arthur, nearing the end of his victorious progress through Europe, stands at the top of the St. Gotthard pass looking down upon Lombardy, and cries, 'In yon pleasant land I think to be lord' (3109). Descending into Italy, he receives at Viterbo the Pope's message that he will crown him sovereign in Rome. That very night he has a dream in which he sees eight kings clinging to Fortune's wheel and striving in vain to reach a silver chair. Fortune sets Arthur in the chair, but at midday she turns against him. A philosopher tells him that the kings are eight of the Nine Worthies, all renowned conquerors in their day. Arthur himself will be the ninth; he is now 'at the highest', and will achieve no more. Arthur rises and goes out alone 'with anger in his heart', and almost at once he sees a man, dressed as a pilgrim and hastening on the road to Rome, who proclaims himself Sir Cradok, a knight of Arthur's chamber, come from Britain to tell him that Modred has had himself crowned king and has taken Guinevere for his wife. Arthur quickly calls a council and, then, leaving a few knights to guard his conquests, he hurries back through Italy, Germany, and Flanders to take ship for Britain.

In this climax of the story the events are so ordered as to bring out the drama inherent in them, and they are related without digression, indeed, with a certain urgency, which is not lost even in the long account of the dream. After this, even though the excitement of the unexpected is lacking, the poet remains to the end in control of his story. He achieves a fine contrast between the maddened fighting and violent end of Gawain and the slow griefstricken tributes of his slayer, Modred, and of Arthur. In Arthur's lament, the most widely quoted passage in the poem, the repetitive, cumulative style is at its most effective:

> Þan the corownde kyng cryes full lowde:
> 'Dere kosyn o kynde, in kare am I leuede,
> For nowe my wirchipe es wente and my were endide.
> Here es þe hope of my hele, my happynge of armes,
> My herte and my hardynes hale one hym lengede,
> My concell, my comforthe, þat kepide myn herte!
> Of all knyghtes þe kynge þat vndir Criste lifede,

Þou was worthy to be kynge, þofe I þe corown bare;
My wele and my wirchipe of all þis werlde riche
Was wonnen thourghe sir Wawayne and thourghe his witt one!'[1]

Vowing to avenge Gawain, Arthur pursues Modred to Cornwall,
and, after fierce fighting, slays him, but receives his own death-
wound. The rest of the poem is on a quieter note. Arthur laments
his fallen knights, and asks to be carried to Glastonbury to the
Isle of Avalon, where, after calling for a confessor, he dies, saying
'In manus'. The poet concludes: 'So ends King Arthur, as writers
tell, who was of the kin of Hector, the son of the king of Troy.'
Characteristically, this 'true' tale knows nothing of a mystic boat
with wailing women, nor of the prophecy that Arthur shall return
to the Britons.

The poem, as a whole, is animated by an energetic and powerful
imagination, not always sufficiently kept in check. Though the
poet lacks subtlety, he has a sure sense of the dramatic, and never
fails to recognize the significant moments in his story. He has,
particularly at such times, a clear mental picture of action (though
he is not capable of subtle or consistent characterization), and he
understands the emotions that prompt it or arise from it. He knows,
too, the value of contrast in bringing out the emotional quality of
a scene or an action. Even in the earlier, less stirring parts of the
poem perception is quickened by such contrasts as the Roman mes-
sengers bowing in knightly fashion before delivering the Emperor's
summons and then, suddenly terrified at Arthur's anger, 'crouching like dogs' before him, or Arthur, when he is discovered
wounded after his terrific fight with the monstrous giant of Mont
St. Michael, telling his knights that his sword and shield lie on the
top of the crag together with the giant's club, and asking simply
that they should go and fetch them.

[1] Then the crowned king cries aloud, 'Dear cousin of my race, in grief am
I left; for now my fame is passed and my fighting days ended. Here is the hope
of my success, my good fortune in arms. My confidence and my valour depended
wholly on him, my counsel and my comfort which my heart held fast. The king
of all knights that lived under God, thou wert worthy to be king, though I wore
the crown. My prosperity and my honour from all this mighty earth were won
through Sir Gawain and through his genius alone' (3955–64).

11. *Patience, Purity,* and *Sir Gawain and the Green Knight*

The only alliterative poem which has caught the spirit of
Arthurian romance as the French understood it is *Sir Gawain and
the Green Knight.* This, the finest of the alliterative romances and,
indeed, of all Middle English romances except perhaps Chaucer's
Knight's Tale, has such close connexions with the poems *Pearl,
Patience,* and *Purity (Cleanness)* that they must be considered as a
group.

Unlike the works of Chaucer or Langland, which have been
continuously read ever since their composition, these poems
remained almost unknown till Sir F. Madden edited *Sir Gawain*
in 1839, and described the manuscript, Cotton Nero A x, in
which all four have been preserved. They appear there in the same
late fourteenth- or early fifteenth-century hand, and they are
provided with crude illustrations, probably contemporary with the
texts. It is natural that the poems should have been ascribed to the
same author, and, on the whole, modern scholarship supports this
view. The Nero texts, which are not originals, are all substantially
in the same dialect, one not very different, it would seem, from that
of the originals, and certainly of the north-west Midlands, though
whether of Derbyshire, Cheshire, or south Lancashire is a matter
of dispute. Such evidence as there is points to the last quarter of
the fourteenth century as the period of composition. Striking
similarities of vocabulary, of phrasing, and (in *Sir Gawain, Purity,*
and *Patience*) of metre provide obvious links between the poems.
Similar stylistic devices are used in all four, and there is a recurrence of certain conceptions, of the doctrine of the Beatific Vision,
for instance, and of the pearl as a symbol of perfection. Since, in
addition, all four, in various manners and degrees, display not
merely a liking for symmetrical arrangement, but a marked sense
of form, it seems easier to assume a common author than to suppose
that two or more men writing in the same locality and the same
period, and certainly closely associated with one another, possessed this rare and, one would think, inimitable quality.

No attempt to identify this author has so far been successful,
and curiosity has to be satisfied with what can be learned from the

poems themselves. Though these reveal a good deal about the poet's opinions and outlook, they provide little evidence for any life-history. What is certain is that the poet had the opportunity for considerable reading, both secular and religious. In French, he had read the *Roman de la Rose* and some Arthurian romances; in English, he was familiar with much alliterative poetry and probably with a number of non-alliterative writings. More unusual reading for an Englishman of his time is suggested by the possible indebtedness of *Pearl* to Dante's *Divina Commedia* and to Boccaccio's *Olympia*. The poet's intimate knowledge of the Bible and his evident familiarity with Biblical commentary and interpretation suggests that he may have had an ecclesiastical education. If so, his independence of mind is the more remarkable. Professor Menner has remarked that, in *Purity*, he is 'less fettered than most homilists by theological doctrine and conventional interpretations', and in *Pearl* he employs both in a manner still more individual. From *Sir Gawain and the Green Knight* it is obvious that he was sufficiently at home in courtly, or at least aristocratic, society to be able to depict with fidelity its manners, pastimes, and setting. Verifiable details of dress and armour, of architecture, of sport, are accurate for the period in which the poem was written. This suggests the kind of public for which *Sir Gawain* was intended; and *Pearl*, too, can hardly have been written for other than cultured readers.

This is all that can be said with certainty of the poet's circumstances, and it leaves many questions unanswered, including one legitimately of interest to those who would understand the poems —the question of the order in which they were written. It can be plausibly argued that *Patience* and *Purity* preceded the other two, and that, of these, *Patience* is the earlier; but grounds for deciding whether *Sir Gawain* or *Pearl* came next are insufficient.

Patience and *Purity* (*Cleanness*) are alike in aim and in general structure. Each is a homily commending one of the virtues in the Beatitudes, and illustrating its value, and to some extent its nature, from Biblical story. By a twist which is perhaps characteristic of the poet, the illustration goes, as it were, by contraries. In *Patience* it is the story of the impatient Jonah that is chosen; in *Purity* the stories of the Flood, of the Fall of Sodom, and of Belshazzar's Feast illustrate God's anger against the impure (or 'unclean', as the poet calls them). The structural similarity of the two poems extends to some details. Each opens by naming the virtue to be extolled ('Patience is a poynt, þaȝ hit displese ofte', 'Clannesse who so kyndly cowþe comende') and, early in each, a paraphrase of the relevant Beatitude provides the text for the whole homily. Each ends with a restatement of the theme, though the last line in *Purity* does not, as in the other, echo the first. *Patience* is simpler in conception than *Purity* and therefore neater and more unified in construction. The poet concentrates on the story of Jonah, confining exposition and exhortation almost entirely to the introduction and brief conclusion. In *Purity* the homiletic element is more important, for the poet attempts to use the argument as a framework to link together a number of Biblical stories, including the three main ones. The opening sections provide an example of his method. After paraphrasing his text (Beati mundo corde, quoniam ipsi Deum videbunt), he elaborates upon it. He first states the converse, that no one who has any 'uncleanness' shall come to the sight of God, and this he illustrates by the parable of the man without a wedding garment; second, he emphasizes the point that no sin angers God like uncleanness. He was not angry when He cast out Lucifer or drove Adam from Paradise, but for the third crime, 'fylþe of þe flesch', He called forth the Flood which destroyed almost all living things. The story of the Flood is then related, and is followed by a short passage of exposition which also serves to introduce the next story, that of the Fall of Sodom. This more ambitious scheme is not entirely successful, for, in order to include the story of Belshazzar's Feast, the poet has to juggle with his interpretation of 'uncleanness' and make it cover the defiling of what belongs to God as well as unchastity. Moreover, since he is still mainly interested in narrative, he tends to tell his stories at disproportionate length. But, in this attempt to provide the poem with a comprehensive argument, he anticipates in part the design of *Pearl*.

Both in *Patience* and in *Purity* it is the narratives that impress. The poet has seen and felt the Biblical stories afresh and he re-creates them for his readers, fusing into them points from other books or of his own invention. Alike in comparatively homely scenes and in scenes far removed from normal experience, his imagination is quick to seize upon, or to conjure up, details that will make them realizable. Abraham, preparing to serve his three angelic visitors,[1] runs to fetch a tender calf and gives it to the servant to cook (as in the Vulgate), and then 'catches up a clean cloth and spreads it on the green grass' (not in the Vulgate). Jonah enters into the whale's mouth

> As mote in at a munster dor, so mukel wern his chawle3[2]

and, as he is carried along in its belly, which the poet has not hesitated to describe, he hears the great seas beating on its back and sides.[3]

Like other alliterative poets, the writer is especially kindled by scenes of violence and tumult, and in his descriptions of the storm and shipwreck in *Patience*, and of the Flood and the destruction of Sodom and Gomorrah in *Purity*, he reveals his considerable resources of style and language. The following lines correspond to Genesis xix. 24–25, 'Igitur Dominus pluit super Sodomam et Gomorrham sulphur et ignem a Domino de caelo et subvertit civitates has':

> Þe grete God in his greme bygynne3 on lofte;
> To wakan wedere3 so wylde þe wynde3 he calle3,
> And þay wroþely upwafte and wrastled togeder,
> Fro fawre half of þe folde flytande loude.
> Clowde3 clustered bytwene, kesten up torres,
> Þat þe þik þunder-þrast þirled hem ofte.
> Þe rayn rueled adoun, ridlande þikke,
> Of felle flaunkes of fyr and flakes of soufre,
> Al in smolderande smoke smachande ful ille,
> Swe aboute Sodamas and hit syde3 alle,
> Gorde to Gomorra, þat þe grounde laused . . .[4]

---

[1] *Purity*, 629 ff.
[2] 'Like a speck of dust in through a church door, so vast were his (the whale's) jaws'. *Patience*, 268.   [3] *Patience*, 302.
[4] 'In His anger the great God on high begins; He summons the winds to waken storms so wild, and they angrily arose from the four quarters of the earth and wrestled together, contending noisily. Clouds massed themselves in the

Effective though this is, it might become monotonous if it were not that the writer soon turns our attention from the upheaval in nature to its victims; and this is characteristic of him. He is always interested in human beings, or rather, for his sympathy extends to animals too, in what is living. In his description of the Flood, there is a moving passage on the plight of men and beasts. The animals, driven by the waters to seek the heights, 'stared to þe heven, Rwly wyth a loud rurd rored for drede'[1] and, when the floods had risen so high that every man saw that he must drown:

> Frende3 fellen in fere and faþmed togeder,
> To dry3 her delful destyné and dy3en alle samen;
> Luf loke3 to luf and his leve take3,
> For to end alle at one3 and for ever twynne.[2]

For the characterization of individuals *Purity* affords little scope, though the poet knows more of the character of Lot's wife than the Bible told him; but Jonah's character is his main concern in *Patience*, and he rises to the occasion. Incredible as Jonah's adventures are (and the poet himself remarks that what happened to him would be a wonder, if it were not for the witness of Holy Writ) he himself is always credible. This is partly because we are told so much that is relatable to common experience, how he snores as he lies asleep in the boat and is roused by a kick from a sailor, how in his relief at the shade of the gourd he lies lolling under it all day not bothering to eat; but it is mainly because he is depicted as a consistent character whose speeches and musings explain the motives for his actions. When God commands him to go to Nineveh to announce its impending destruction, Jonah (in the Bible) 'surrexit ut fugeret in Tharsis a facie Domini'; but the poet tells us how he thinks and feels. God tells me, he says to himself, that those men are wicked fellows. If I go with that news, they will put me in prison and thrust out my eyes. This is a strange

---

midst, throwing up towers, which the frequent thunder-bolt pierced again and again. The rain of cruel sparks of fire and flakes of sulphur came down, falling thick, all in suffocating smoke, evil smelling; it drove round Sodom and all its neighbourhood, rushed upon Gomorrah so that the ground gave way. . . .' *Purity*, 947 ff.   [1] 'Pitifully, with a loud voice, roared for dread'. *Purity*, 389–90.
   [2] 'Friends sank together and clung to each other, to suffer their grievous fate and die in company. Lover gazes on lover and takes leave, to end in the same instant and part for ever.' *Purity*, 399 ff.

message for a man to preach among so many and such accursed
enemies. And he decides to go some other way, where God is not
looking, 'and perhaps when I am lost, He will leave me alone.'
In this speech of self-justification Jonah shows himself petulantly
and stupidly rebellious, and later, when God has taken pity on the
Ninevites and forgiven them, the poet rearranges and amplifies the
Biblical version of Jonah's protest so that his words have the same
ring of testy self-justification. Here, and elsewhere in this poem,
the poet shows a mastery of colloquial speech—a feature which
also distinguishes *Sir Gawain*. When God asks Jonah why he is so
disturbed at the withering of the gourd, 'Why art þou so waymot,[1]
wyȝe,[2] for so lyttle?', Jonah's 'Hit is not lyttel'[3] is exactly right.

The passages that have been quoted prove that the poet can
vary his style with the occasion. He is no untutored versifier
writing as he must. Though the homilies have not the accomplished
artistry of *Sir Gawain* and *Pearl*, the same resources and many
of the same qualities are discernible in them. The vocabulary of
Purity is as wide and as varied in kind as in either of the greater
poems and it is handled with the same boldness; words are used
figuratively or with an eye to their associations, old phrases are
remodelled or applied in fresh contexts. It was apparently from
the common medieval phrase 'hound of hell' that the writer
evolved the striking first line of his description of hell opening to
receive the doomed cities of Sodom and Gomorrah:

> For when þat þe helle herde þe houndeȝ of heven
> He watȝ ferlyly fayn, unfolded bylyue.[4]

His handling of words indicates a training in the art of rhetoric and,
in fact, the homilies, like the other poems, bear many signs of this.
Sometimes his fondness for rhetorical 'colours' results in effects
too obviously sought after for present taste, as in the lines:

> Þat he fylsened þe faythful in þe falce lawe
> To forfare þe falce in þe faythe trwe.[5]

---

[1] 'sad'.   [2] 'man'.   [3] *Patience*, 492–3.
[4] 'For when Hell heard the hounds of Heaven, it was wonderfully glad and
opened up quickly.' *Purity*, 961–2.
[5] 'So that He helped those who were faithful to the false religion to destroy
those who were false to the true faith.' *Purity*, 1167–8.

But the careful introductions to both poems, and the neat transitions show what he had learnt from that branch of the art which has to do with arrangement (*dispositio*), and in *Purity* he makes a very effective use of the device of repetition. The ideas contained in the Beatitude which is its text are kept constantly in the mind by the recurrence of the words 'clannesse', 'clene' and their opposites, and by the frequent use, generally at the end of a section or a story, of varied phrases representing the words 'Deum videbunt'; and at the end of the poem these are combined, as they were in the text at the beginning. The effect is not unlike that of a leading *motif* in music, and has something in common with the use of the refrain in *Pearl*.

The treatment of the metre in *Patience* and *Purity* has marked affinities with that of *Sir Gawain*, though there are some differences in detail. In all of them the lines tend to be of even length, unstressed syllables being used with moderation. The verse is thus more regular, and at the same time weightier, than, for instance, that of *Piers Plowman*; and at times, notably in some descriptive passages, its weightiness is increased by the poet's use of more than the necessary amount of alliteration. The tendency in *Patience* and *Purity* for the long lines to be grouped in fours seems to indicate a hankering after some sort of stanza form; in *Sir Gawain and the Green Knight* a stanza has been achieved by other means.

The Gawain stanza consists of a varying number of alliterative long lines terminated by five short rhyming lines (the 'bob and the wheel'). So far as is known, it is unique though related to other stanza forms which employ the alliterative long line; but, if the poet did not invent it himself, he was fully alive to its potentialities. For the most part he develops his story in the leisurely long lines, using the crisp, rapid lines of the 'bob and wheel' for special purposes, to sum up or conclude a part of the action,[1] for gnomic comments upon it, not unlike some in *Beowulf* (562 ff.), and for remarks that need to be given special force or point (2280). It is noticeable that it is in the last, specially emphatic, line of the 'wheel' that we are told the most surprising fact about the mysterious

[1] 487 ff., 991 ff.

visitor to Arthur's hall—that he was 'oueral enkergrene'.[1] The poet adapts his long lines to a wide variety of effects; his management of subtle and witty conversation in this seemingly unsuitable medium shows exceptional metrical skill. There is a danger, with a stanza that ends so emphatically, that the narrative might seem to move in a series of jerks, but this effect is minimized by varying the length of the stanzas so that their ends can often be made to coincide with natural pauses, and further counteracted by the device, common in alliterative poetry, of linking the stanzas by repetition. Here this device is unobtrusively used, and in varied forms; an idea, a word, or the alliteration is caught up by the first line of a stanza from some line in the preceding 'wheel'. The repeats are not carried mechanically right through the poem, but there are enough of them to impart a sense of continuity.

The subtle variations of common practices seen in the metre of *Sir Gawain* are characteristic of the poem in every aspect. It is, of course, immediately recognizable as a romance. Its strange and thrilling story, its setting, the preoccupations of the characters, are all of a kind to satisfy the taste of a reader of romances. It even displays such minor features of the romances as the call for attention, the list of famous knights, the references to the 'book' whence the story came. But the differences between *Sir Gawain* and most Middle English romances are striking. It is no simple tale of adventure and love, but the story of a test of character for which adventure and love-making provide the means. This in itself would give the poem a unity uncommon in romances, but, in addition, the poet concentrates on one adventure of his hero, avoiding the temptation to dwell on others, though he mentions them.

On the other hand, the plot of his chosen episode is complex, combining two stories, known as the Beheading Game and the Temptation, which are found only separately in earlier works. The poem opens with the first of these. On New Year's Day a terrifying visitor to Arthur's court, the Green Knight, makes a challenge, offering to let any man strike him a blow on condition that he may give one in return a year hence. The challenge is accepted by Gawain, and he cuts off the Green Knight's head. The Green

[1] 'bright green all over'.

Knight picks it up, and, as he departs, the head speaks to Gawain, bidding him come to the Green Chapel for the return blow. In due time Gawain sets out, and on Christmas Eve he arrives at the castle of a lord called Bertilak. Here the second story (the Temptation) is introduced. Bertilak persuades Gawain to stay till New Year's morning, and proposes that for three days he shall go out hunting while Gawain rests in the castle; at the end of each day, they shall exchange their winnings. Each day Gawain is visited by Bertilak's wife, who offers him her love. He evades her offers as courteously as he can, but accepts the kisses she gives him. On the third day she persuades him to accept a green girdle which will preserve his life in the forthcoming ordeal. The kisses, and the game which Bertilak has captured in his hunting, are duly exchanged each evening; but Gawain says nothing about the green girdle.

The first story is taken up again when Gawain leaves the castle for the Green Chapel. There the Green Knight appears, makes two feints at Gawain with his axe, and the third time wounds him slightly. Gawain protests that he has had all that was in the bargain and more, but the Green Knight rebukes him, explaining that he is Bertilak, the lord of the castle and knows all about the happenings there. The two feints were for the first two days when Gawain resisted all temptation, but the light blow was for the day when he accepted the girdle. Gawain curses himself for his cowardice and covetousness, but the Green Knight says that his full acknowledgement of his fault has absolved him, and explains that the whole was an enchantment devised by Morgan le Fay to try the honour of the Round Table and to make Guinevere tremble. Gawain returns to Arthur's court wearing the green girdle as a baldric in memory of his transgression, but the court decides that henceforth it shall be worn by all in honour of him.

Both stories, it will be observed, present a test—the first of courage and fidelity to the plighted word, the second primarily of chastity, though loyalty to the host and fidelity are involved, and Gawain's courtesy, the quality for which he was famous, is also tested. The combination of the two results, therefore, in a comprehensive test of knightly virtue. There is, in this poem, no mere lip-service to the ideals of chivalry; its purpose is to expound them by illustration, and as it proceeds we become aware that to live up to them requires constant vigilance and self-discipline, and, in the last resort, divine protection. The first concern of the poem is thus with conduct; that is, it is moral in the true sense of the word.

The attitude in the poem towards the art of love is interesting. The lady of the castle thinks (or pretends to think) that Gawain's reluctance to make love to her is unexpected and even unnatural[1] and, in spite of his disclaimers, he does know how to speak the language of love and is not, therefore, quite as ignorant of the art as he tries to make out. But he regards the love which the lady offers and demands as a sin, a temptation to be guarded against.[2] At no point in the poem is there any trace of the idea, stressed for example in Chaucer's *Troilus and Criseyde* and common among apologists for Courtly Love, that love is an ennobling force, the source of knightly virtues. It is significant of Gawain's attitude, and perhaps of the poet's, that when the lady says she would choose him above all others for her lord, he replies '3e haf waled wel better';[3] for to recommend a husband as more desirable than a lover is hardly in accordance with the usual canons of Courtly Love. It is also significant that, while there is much talk of love at Bertilak's castle, which is a place of temptation, there is none in Arthur's court, which is not. Clearly, the poet has made his own choice among the qualities customarily held to be proper to a knight, and his choice accords with Christian morality.

Yet, moral as the poem is, the poet rarely moralizes. His conception of the Christian gentleman is conveyed through the actions and speeches of the characters and, in particular, of Gawain. At the same time none of the characters is a mere peg on which to hang a moral, like Chaucer's Griselde. From the first swift sketch of Arthur:

> He wat3 so joly of his joyfnes, and sumquat childgered:
> His lif liked him ly3t, he louied þe lasse

---

[1] 1509 ff.
[2] 1549–51, 1774–5.
[3] 'You have chosen much better' (1276).

> Auþer to longe lye or to longe sitte,
> So bisied him his ȝonge blod and his brayn wylde[1]—

we feel ourselves in the presence of living flesh and blood. The preposterous visitor, green (the fairy colour) from top to toe and riding a green horse, huge and 'aghlich',[2] is mysterious enough at first, but he gradually takes shape as the poet minutely describes his appearance, his clothes, his horse and its trappings; and his speech and his movements completely establish him as a living being. It is impossible to doubt his reality when, his challenge uttered, he stands awaiting the blow and:

> Wyth sturne schere þer he stod he stroked his berde,
> And wyth a countenaunce dryȝe he droȝ doun his cote.[3]

But his reality does not make his behaviour any the less alarming, and, as he rushes out of the hall, carrying his head in his hand, there is such a sudden relaxation of tension that we are not surprised when Arthur and Gawain find relief in laughter: 'At þat grene[4] þay laȝe and grenne.'

Gawain is, naturally, more fully drawn than any other character. Not only do we observe him ourselves, we are told how he impressed other people in the story and how he himself thought and felt. We see him behaving, as all expect him to do, with exquisite courtesy; but we also see what is not apparent to the other characters, that such behaviour does not always come easily to him. All the time that he is parrying the lady's advances, we are aware that he feels himself to be on a knife-edge between discourtesy and compliance:

> For þat pryncece of pris depresed hym so þikke,
> Nurned hym so neȝe þe þred, þat nede hym bihoued
> Oþer lach þer hir luf, oþer lodly refuse.
> He cared for his cortaysye, lest craþayn he were,
> And more for his meschef, ȝif he schulde make synne.[5]

---

[1] 'He was so gay in his youthfulness and somewhat boyish: he liked a merry life and cared the less either to lie long or sit long; so his young blood and wild brain stirred him' (86–89).   [2] 'terrible'.

[3] 'With grim countenance, as he stood there, he stroked his beard, and, with unmoved face, he drew down his coat' (334–5).

[4] 'green one', i.e. the Green Knight (464).

[5] 'For that noble lady (princess) pressed him so hard, urged him so near the

So, too, we see, behind the actions that proclaim his courage, his inward fears and anxieties. Throughout his stay in Bertilak's castle his mind is continually occupied with the perilous meeting at the Green Chapel. He is worried lest he may not arrive in time, and, very naturally, he is fearful about what will happen to him there. He has bad dreams and sleeps little on the night before he is to set out. When he agrees to accept the lady's gift of the green girdle that will preserve his life, and promises to keep it secret, we understand how he came to do so because we have shared the anxiety that brought him to it. But justice would not be done if, at the end, when the Green Knight reveals his knowledge of Gawain's fault, we were still to feel with Gawain and were to concur in the bitter condemnation which he heaps upon himself. So here we are given another and less biased point of view when the Green Knight proclaims him: 'On þe fautlest freke þat euer on fote 3ede';[1] and this judgement is confirmed for us when Arthur's court decrees that the green girdle shall be worn ever after as a sign of honour.

Thus, by the double process of revealing his hero's mind and letting other persons in the story comment upon him, the poet makes us judge his hero's character and conduct as he would have us do. But this alone would not make Gawain the intensely vital figure that we feel him to be. It is what he says and does that gives this impression. The poet has an unusually sharp eye for movements that are natural, or specially significant, at the moment when they are made. 'Now take your grim weapon, and let's see how you deal a blow', cries the Green Knight to Gawain. 'Gladly, sir', he replies, and 'his ax he strokes'. On the occasion of the lady's first visit, it is by a series of slight movements that the poet brings the whole scene to life. Gawain is lying in bed:

And as he slipped in and out of sleep, he heard a little noise, warily, at his door and heard it quickly open. And he lifted up his head out of the bed-clothes and pulled up a corner of the curtain a little and warily looked out to see what it might be. It was the lady, very fair to see, who drew the door after her softly and secretly, and moved towards the bed.

limit (thread), that he must needs either accept her love there or rudely refuse. He was anxious for his courtesy, lest he should behave like a villain, and more for his own harm if he were to commit sin . . .' (1770–4).
[1] 'The most faultless man that ever walked' (2363).

And the man was embarrassed and stealthily lay down and behaved as if he were asleep (1182–90).

When he speaks, Gawain's tone varies with the occasion. Naturally courteous in speech, he is exaggeratedly so in his request to Arthur to be allowed to accept the Green Knight's challenge (343), for Arthur's prestige has suffered from the insulting behaviour of the Green Knight. In his polite answers to the lady there is something laboured, though he can make some neat counterstrokes. There are, too, some subtle indications that with each of her visits, he is a little less on his guard; he addresses her rather more intimately, and once, during the third visit, he slips from the formal plural (ye, you) into the familiar singular:

> I wolde I hade here
> Þe leuest þing for þy luf þat I in londe welde.[1]

As he exchanges jests with Bertilak in the castle he affects a hearty tone; but when he meets him as the Green Knight at the Green Chapel he speaks without ceremony and very much to the point.

The background against which the characters play their parts is always concretely presented; and this writer, like other alliterative poets, is lavish with his details. The three hunts, Gawain's armour, the clothes he was given at the castle, and even the cushions placed on his chair—all these, and much more, are minutely described. For the most part, the things the poet chooses to describe are those elaborated by other romance writers; but he had a mind stored with unusually vivid memories of sight and sound; and he knew how to select the telling details and phrases that would convey them. The cold weather is made sensible by the reference to 'mony bryddeȝ vnblyþe[2] . . . þat pitosly þer piped for pyne of þe colde' (746–7). A brief simile sets before us the whole elaborate structure of Bertilak's castle standing out against the sky: 'pared out of papure[3] purely hit semed' (802). In many of the descriptions there is movement. In the hunting scenes, the ceaseless activity of the hunted animals, of the men and

---

[1] 'I wish I had here the most precious thing I possess on earth, for love of thee' (1801–2).

[2] 'unhappy'.   [3] 'cut out of paper'.

the hounds, conveys all the excitement of the chase. Like Chaucer, the poet can give the impression of a number of people doing different things at the same time, and both in Arthur's hall and in Bertilak's castle, though our chief attention is on the main characters, we are conscious of the bustling life that goes on around them.

In description, as in most else, the poet varies his method of presentation. Sometimes he uses comparison, as in the description of the two ladies in the castle:

> Bot vnlyke on to loke þo ladyes were,
> For if þe ȝonge watȝ ȝep, ȝolȝe watȝ þat oþer;
> Riche red on þat on rayled ayquere,
> Rugh ronkled chekeȝ þat oþer on rolled.[1]

Sometimes, instead of an objective account, he describes things as they appeared to the hero, as in the long account of Bertilak's castle, first seen in the distance, shining and shimmering through the great oaks that surround it. Coming up to it, Gawain finds the drawbridge up and the gates fast shut. He stops and notices first the deep double moat, the stone walls going down into the water and rising thence a huge height up to the cornices. Then, his eyes having travelled to the top, he sees the watch-towers, and, farther in, the hall and a mass of towers, pinnacles, chimneys, and roofs. The details are presented in the order in which they would appear to a man arriving at the castle.

Most of the descriptions of nature are related to Gawain in some way or other. Gawain is lying sleepless in bed, thinking of the coming day's meeting with the Green Knight, while

> Þe snawe snitered ful snart, þat snayped þe wylde;
> Þe werbelande wynde wapped fro þe hyȝe,
> And drof vche dale ful of dryftes ful grete';[2]

and the foul weather sharpens his fears, and ours for him. The

---

[1] 'But unlike in appearance were those ladies; for if the younger was fresh, the other was yellow; a brilliant complexion adorned the one; rough wrinkled cheeks hung in folds on the other' (950–3).

[2] 'The snow whipped down very sharply, and nipped the wild creatures cruelly, the whistling wind blew from the heights and drove each valley full of great drifts' (2003–5).

description of the seasons at the beginning of Part II, conventional enough in some of its details, serves a double purpose. It introduces a fresh section of the story, as similar passages do in the romance of *Kyng Alysaunder* and elsewhere; and, prefaced by the warning,

> A ȝere ȝernes full ȝerne, and ȝeldeȝ neuer lyke,
> Þe forme to þe fynisment foldeȝ ful selden,[1]

it suggests the rapid passing of the year's respite granted to Gawain. It is thus another example of the poet's power of turning to fresh account something that is familiar, as a result of which the familiar does not stale his work, but enriches it by the associations it brings.

To play upon associations of all kinds is natural to this poet, and his magic in large part depends on it, especially in *Pearl*. In *Sir Gawain* it is perhaps chiefly by the words he chooses that he calls up the associations he wants. In the central part of the story, for instance, he alternates between the technical terms of hunting, which would claim the serious attention of those skilled in the sport, and the equally technical terms of love-making. But it is the words belonging to the alliterative tradition that are most effectively used in this poem. When the poet wishes to curdle the blood by indefinable terrors, he chooses ancient words belonging to the vocabulary of alliterative poetry. The Green Knight, he thinks, might be 'half etayn'.[2] The dread creatures which Gawain encountered on his journey (and which the poet does not want to delay over) are swiftly conveyed by words like 'wormeȝ'[3] 'wodwos',[4] and, again, 'etayneȝ':

> Sumwhyle wyth wormeȝ he werreȝ, and with wolues als,
> Sumwhyle wyth wodwos, þat woned in þe knarreȝ;
> Boþe wyth bulleȝ and bereȝ, and boreȝ oþerquyle,
> And etayneȝ, þat hym anelede of þe heȝe felle.[5]

---

[1] 'A year runs full swiftly and never brings back the same thing; the beginning seldom accords with the end' (498–9).

[2] 'giant', with a strong suggestion of the supernatural; OE. *eoten*. In Beowulf *eotenas* are among the evil brood descended from Cain.

[3] 'dragons', the *wyrmas* of OE. poetry.

[4] 'wood-trolls', OE. *wudu-wasa*.

[5] 'Sometimes he fights with dragons, and with wolves too, sometimes with trolls that dwelt in the crags; both with bulls and bears and at other times with boars, and with giants that snorted after him from the high fell' (720–3).

With all the wealth of detail that is to be found in every part of the poem, there is never any lack of control. On the contrary, the poet has succeeded in fashioning a narrative not merely unified but cunningly and satisfyingly shaped. The fourfold division suggested by the larger capitals and the flourishes in the manuscript, brings into relief the essential features of the story: the challenge and Gawain's acceptance of it, his journey and arrival at Bertilak's castle, the temptation, the second meeting with the Green Knight; but, where the breaks might be too disrupting, the parts are linked by passages giving warning of what is to come.

These passages are one of the means by which the poet creates and maintains a feeling of tension which he heightens and brings to its climax in Part III. The theme of the Beheading Game is kept in the reader's consciousness throughout, even when the second theme of the Temptation occupies the foreground. The skill with which, in the last two parts, the two are kept running concurrently, each being brought to the fore at the right moment, can justly be placed to the credit of the *Gawain* poet, even if, as many believe, he knew a French poem which combined them. For, unless the English is a mere literal translation (and it can hardly be this) there are many possibilities of going astray in so delicate a matter.

Yet there is a good deal more to the ordering of the poem than this. The poet has produced, as it were, an internal and an external order at the same time. While the character and actions of the hero give coherence and meaning to the events of the story, making of them a unified narrative, the events are also so ordered as to produce something of the effect of a pattern. This 'patterning' is made by the parallelism of incident or description; it is most obvious, of course, in the scenes at Bertilak's castle, where it is also most complex. The parallelism between the three hunts and the three visits of the lady, and also that between Gawain's blow on New Year's Day and the Green Knight's on the same day a year later, may have been provided by the poet's source, though nothing exactly like them is known elsewhere. But, even so, there are others, less likely to be in any source. The action of the poem ends as it began, with a scene in Arthur's court, preceded in the one case and followed in the other by a similarly worded reference to Brutus and the siege of Troy. Gawain's ordeal is preceded and followed by an adventurous journey, though because the climax of the story is over, his journey home is much more lightly sketched. There is some parallel between Gawain's arrival at Bertilak's court, and the festivities that follow, and the festivities at Arthur's court and the arrival of the Green Knight. But this is an extreme instance of the combination of similarity of theme and dissimilarity of detail which marks all the parallels; indeed, in some ways these two descriptions are rather the antithesis of one another, since, for the defiance and insolence of the Green Knight we have the courtesy of Sir Gawain, and for the terrified hostility of Arthur's court, the genial friendliness of Bertilak and his household. This sort of effect has its nearest analogy in music and can give the same kind of pleasure as variations on a musical theme. It is undoubtedly an outcome of rhetorical teaching, but it is rare to find among Middle English poets one who knows how to make organic use of this teaching.

It is easy to relate most things in this poem to various sources and influences, it may be that the combination in it of some of the best things in the alliterative tradition with some of the best in French romance makes for its richness of texture as compared with most other Middle English romances. But there is a limit to what can reasonably be attributed to any outside influence. It was not from literature that the poet learned the delicacy of touch with which he handles the scenes between Gawain and the lady, or the understanding of human feeling shown in the blustering words of Gawain as he hears the Green Knight whetting his axe behind the rock. Gawain has not yet seen him and is not sure precisely what the noise is, and he speaks half fearfully, half ironically:

> 'Bi Godde', quoþ Gawayn, 'þat gere, as I trowe,
> Is ryched at þe reuerence me, renk, to mete
> bi rote.'[1]

Such things are not to be explained, they can only be remarked and

---

[1] 'By God', said Gawain, 'that contraption, I believe, is meant for a salutation, to meet me, by the way' (2205–7).

enjoyed; and this poem is fuller of them than any contemporary work save that of Chaucer.

A comparison with Chaucer is not, indeed, wholly to the disadvantage of the lesser-known poet, for he surpasses Chaucer in some things—in architectonics, for instance, and perhaps in natural description—and, though his range is narrow, within it he shows himself a subtle delineator of character. In outlook he is as civilized as Chaucer, but sterner, much more of a moralist, a great deal less of a humorist. But there is humour of a sort in his presentation of the Green Knight's play-acting in Arthur's hall, and in some of Gawain's rueful remarks; and the poet has some of Chaucer's capacity for seeing his story and his characters from both inside and out, so that his readers can sympathize with the hero and at the same time see him and his doings in perspective.

III. *Pearl*

Pearl stands much farther apart from other Middle English writings than *Sir Gawain*. Though its form is influenced by the familiar dream convention, and though it is thoroughly medieval in spirit and workmanship, yet as a whole it is unlike any other Middle English poem. In some respects it is nearer to *Lycidas* than to anything else in English, for—without prejudice to the controversial question of whether or not *Pearl* is an elegy—it begins, like *Lycidas*, by lamenting a loss; from this the poet is led on to consider certain spiritual and moral problems, and he finally reaches understanding and acceptance of God's will. Like *Lycidas*, *Pearl* is cast in a conventional literary form, is built with scrupulous artistry and expressed in highly charged language—language, that is, selected and ordered for particular ends. Though the differences between the two poems are, of course, many and important, they are essentially of the same order.

So far as *Pearl* is concerned, there is much in this statement that needs justification, and it would be well to begin by outlining the poem as impartially as possible. It opens with praise of the pearl which the poet has lost in an 'erbere',[1] and he tells how, on going back to the spot, he finds it covered with so many sweet flowering

---

[1] 'herb garden'.

plants that he is overpowered by their fragrance and falls asleep. He passes in spirit into a marvellous country and, on the other side of a river, he perceives a maiden clad in gleaming white garments set with pearls. He recognizes her: 'I knew hyr wel, I hade sen hyr ere',[1] 'Ho watȝ me nerre þen aunte or nece';[2] and he begins to question her: 'What fate has carried away my jewel and plunged me in such grief?' (249–50). The maiden rebukes him, saying that he has no cause for grief, for, though she was but young when she departed, her Lord the Lamb took her in marriage and crowned her queen.

The dreamer cannot believe this, for surely Mary is the Queen of Heaven. But the maiden explains that in heaven no one dispossesses any other, and all are kings and queens; and then, as he protests that she is too young to be a queen, she relates the parable of the workers in the vineyard to show that the first shall be last, and the last first. The dreamer still protests, for this means that he who works less receives more. The maiden replies that there is no question of more or less in God's kingdom; His grace is enough for all. The sinner who repents finds grace, why not the innocent who never sinned? 'When such knock there upon the dwelling, quickly shall the gate be unlatched for them' (727–8). In the kingdom of heaven is endless bliss, the pearl of great price, which the merchant sold all that he had to purchase. In answer to the dreamer's further questions, he is permitted to see the New Jerusalem and, in the streets of it, a procession headed by the Lamb. In the throng that follows Him he sees his 'lyttel quene'.

Longing to be with her, he is about to start into the stream, but he suddenly awakes, to find himself back in the 'erbere'. Though full of grief at his banishment from the fair country of his vision, he cries:

> If hit be ueray and soth sermoun,
> Þat þou so strykeȝ in garlande gay,
> So wel is me in þys doel-doungoun,
> Þat þou art to þat Prynseȝ paye.[3]

---

[1] 'I knew her well, I had seen her before' (164).
[2] 'She was nearer to me than aunt or niece' (233).
[3] 'If it is indeed sober truth that thou movest thus in a gay garland, then I am content, in this prison of grief, that thou art to the Prince's pleasure' (1185–8).

He reflects that, had he been more submissive to God's will, he might have come to know more of His mysteries, and he ends by offering up his vision to God, praying that God may 'grant us to be the servants of His household and precious pearls for His pleasure'.

This summary is perhaps sufficient to suggest the nature of the appeal made by *Pearl*, but it cannot convey the qualities which make it an outstanding example of poetic art.

In this poem, as in all great poems, form and content are not separable; and both are evident alike in the smallest detail and in the conception and shaping of the whole.

As in *Sir Gawain and the Green Knight*, the matter of *Pearl* is ordered so as to form a pattern. Naturally the means by which this is done here differ from those employed in the narrative poem, and the pattern is all-embracing, as it is not in *Sir Gawain*. Of the twenty equal sections of the poem[1] the first four are mainly devoted to presenting the dreamer's state of mind and to description of the dream-country and of Pearl herself; argument and exposition occupy the central twelve sections, and the last four again contain description, this time of the New Jerusalem, and end with the poet's reflections. This pattern is emphasized by the echoing of the first line of the poem, 'Perle, plesaunte to prynces paye',[2] in the last, 'Ande precious perleȝ vnto his pay'. The metrical scheme, which subdivides the poem into smaller sections and at the same time links all its parts into a continuous sequence, forms a second pattern, subsidiary to the main one but concurrent with it. There are 101 stanzas of twelve four-stressed lines, rhyming a b a b a b a b b c b c. Two or more of the stresses are usually marked by alliteration. The stanzas fall into groups of five, the same refrain being used in the last line of each of the five, and it is thus that the poem is divided into the twenty equal sections, though section XV, exceptionally, contains six stanzas. A key-word or phrase in the refrain is always echoed in the first line of the following stanza; this means that the sections are linked to one another, since a significant word is repeated, in the first line of each new section, from the refrain of the preceding one. The echo

---

[1] Indicated by initial capitals in the manuscript.
[2] 'Pearl, a precious thing for the Prince's pleasure'.

between the first and last lines of the poem gives the effect of a completed circle, intended perhaps to suggest the idea of the pearl, which in l. 738 is called 'endele3 rounde'.[1]

The same stanza form, and the linking, are found elsewhere in Middle English, in some lyrics in the Vernon MS. for instance; but nowhere else is there anything like this complex scheme, nor is the stanza handled with such mastery. This poet makes good use of the natural break after the eighth line, and, within the line, he allows himself freedom in the use of alliteration and varies the rhythm and the number of syllables. Thus, within the rigid metrical scheme of the whole, the line, its smallest unit, is flexible. The following stanzas, one descriptive, one argumentative, illustrate some of these characteristics. They also illustrate what appears to be a general practice, the greater use of alliteration in description:

> The dubbemente of þo derworth depe
> Wern bonke3 bene of beryl bry3t;
> Swangeande swete þe water con swepe,
> Wyth a rownande rourde raykande ary3t;
> In þe founce þer stonden stone3 stepe,
> As glente þur3 glas þat glowed and gly3t;
> As stremande sterne3, quen stroþe men slepe,
> Staren in welkyn in wynter ny3t;
> For vche a pobbel in pole þer py3t
> Watz emerad, saffer, oþer gemme gente,
> Þat alle þe lo3e lemed of ly3t,
> So dere wat3 hit adubbement.[2]

> Grace innogh þe mon may haue
> Þat synne3 þenne new, 3if him repente,
> Bot wyth sor3 and syt he mot hit craue,
> And byde þe payne þerto is bent.
> Bot resoun of ry3t þat con not raue
> Saue3 euermore þe innossent;
> Hit is a dom þat neuer God gaue,

[1] 'endlessly round'.
[2] 'The beauties of those precious deeps [i.e. deep waters] were pleasant banks of bright beryl; swinging softly, the water swept with a whispering voice, flowing straight on. In the depth there lay bright stones that glowed and glittered like lights through glass; shimmering like stars, which, while men on earth are sleeping, gleam in the heavens on a winter night. For every pebble set there in the pool was an emerald, sapphire or precious gem, so that all the water shimmered with light, so splendid was its adornment' (109–20).

Þat euer þe gyltleȝ schulde be schente.
Þe gyltyf may contryssyoun hente,
And be þurȝ mercy to grace þryȝt;
Bot he to gyle þat neuer glente,
As innoscente is saf by ryȝte.[1]

The refrains are the most difficult part of this scheme to manage, but on the whole the poet is amazingly successful with them. Often they appear to fit naturally into his train of thought, but when necessary he will vary them slightly. The emphasis which certain words receive from so much repetition is rarely misplaced; indeed, most of the reiterated words and phrases are so essential to the poem as a whole that, taken in order, they almost form a key to its contents. There are some sections, certainly, in which the repetition seems mechanical, and others in which the meaning of the repeated word or phrase has to be ingeniously stretched to fit every context in which it is used. Yet the poet can make a poetic virtue even of this kind of ingenuity, or of something very closely akin to it. In Section VIII the refrain word 'cortasye', is used to mean, not only 'courtesy', 'courtliness', but 'generosity', 'benevolence', and, as critics have pointed out, it is sometimes almost a synonym for 'grace' (divine favour or condescension). No one of these meanings fits every context in this section, but the poet uses now one, now another, while keeping all the time some reflection of the basic meanings 'courtliness', 'courtesy', and its implications. This is achieved by the use of many words such as 'queen', 'king', 'emperor', 'empress', 'court' which are naturally associated with 'courtliness' and 'courtesy'. So the lesson of Section VII—that though Mary is Queen of Heaven, she is also Queen of Courtesy, and none who comes there is, or feels himself to be, dispossessed, but each is 'king and queen by courtesy'—is doubly conveyed by clear statement which can be intellectually apprehended and by all the associations of the word 'courtesy'.

[1] 'Grace enough may that man have who sins afresh, if he will repent; but with sorrow and lamentation he must crave it and endure the pain that is bound with it. But Reason, Who cannot swerve from justice, evermore saves the innocent. It is a judgment that God never gave that ever the innocent should be discomfited. The guilty man may cling to contrition and by mercy be drawn back to grace—but he who never turned aside to sin, being innocent is saved by right' (661–72, emending MS. *at* to *as*, and MS. *&* to *by* in the last line.)

Such exploitation of the association of words is a marked feature
of the whole poem and takes many forms, from mere word-play,
dependent on similarity of sound, as in the line 'So is hys mote
wythouten moote',[1] to the vividly metaphorical language of the
following lines:

> I loked among his meyny schene
> How þay wyth lyf wern laste and lade[2]

or of these:

> For þo3 þou daunce as any do,
> Braundysch and bray þy braþe3 breme,
> When þou no fyrre may, to ne fro,
> Þou moste abyde þat he schal deme.[3]

Some words already have poetic or literary associations which are
of value to the context in which they are used. So, 'douth', having
dignified associations from its use in old heroic poetry, but having
lost the precise significance of the Old English 'duguþ',[4] is at once
impressive and mysterious enough to be used of the hosts of hell,
earth, and heaven that gaze upon the Lamb (839–10). In writing of
his longing for the Pearl the poet evokes, by the word 'luf-
daungere',[5] memories of the separation of lovers, and of the love-
longing so often described by poets of the *Roman de la Rose*
tradition. Especially in descriptive passages, his phrasing is full of
echoes; and it is here that they have most value, for in all his
descriptions the poet is attempting to present something trans-
cending ordinary human experience. In the description of the
maiden, he calls to his aid conceptions of feminine beauty by using
terms from the romances, and throughout the opening descriptions
there are reminiscences, verbal and otherwise, of the Garden of
Love in the *Roman de la Rose*. The flowers on the spot where Pearl
was lost are, like those in the Garden of Love, fragrant spices

---

[1] 'So is His dwelling without spot' (948).
[2] 'I gazed among His radiant following [and saw] how they were loaded and
weighed down with life' (1145–6).
[3] 'For, though you skip about like any doe, rush to and fro, and bray out
your fierce wrath, when you can go no further, forwards or backwards, you must
put up with what He decrees' (345–8).
[4] 'a band of noble retainers'.
[5] 'separation in love' (11). 'Danger', in the *Roman de la Rose*, comes between
the lover and the beloved.

known for their healing properties; and the trees, the birds, the
river of the country of the poet's vision could not fail to remind his
readers of that beautiful garden. Yet the details—the 'flaumbande
hwe3'[1] of the birds, the tree-trunks 'blwe as ble of ynde',[2] the
emeralds, sapphires, and other gems that lie at the bottom of the
stream—are peculiar to this description and less realistic than those
in the *Roman*; for this land is more remote from normal experience
than the Garden of Love and surpasses it in beauty. At one point
the poet compares the banks of the river to 'fyldor fyn',[3] normally
associated with jewellery or, in simile, with golden hair, and the
effect of this fantastic comparison is to convey the splendour of
the banks and at the same time their unreality. To the modern
mind, however, the associations with nature evoked by some of the
poet's similes are probably more effective—the comparison, for
instance, of the precious stones glinting through the water to stars
that shine on a winter night,[4] or of the sudden appearance of the
procession of Virgins to the rising of the moon:

> Ry3t as þe maynful monc con ry3
> Er þenne þe day-glem dryue al doun,
> So sodanly on a wonder wyse
> I wat3 war of a prosessyoun.[5]

More than any secular book it is the Bible that fills the poet's
mind and imagination. When he describes his distress, 'My herte
wat3 al wyth mysse remorde, As wallande water got3 out of welle',[6]
he is recalling the Psalmist's 'Sicut aqua effusus sum'; at the words
of the Lamb, 'Cum hyder to me, my lemman swete, For mote ne
spot is non in þe' (763–4), the maiden is invested with the associations of the Song of Songs ('et macula non est in te. Veni de Libano
sponsa mea . . .'). In the central portion of the poem the poet
makes constant appeal to the authority of the Bible, buttressing his
argument by passages drawn from it. The ease with which he
passes from one part of it to another is an indication both of his

---

[1] 'flaming colours'.   [2] 'blue as indigo'.
[3] 'fine gold thread'.   [4] See p. 88.
[5] 'Even as the mighty moon rises before the gleam of day has quite descended
thence, so suddenly, in a miraculous way, I was aware of a procession' (1093–6).
[6] 'My heart was all stricken with grief [so that I was] like rushing water
pouring from a stream' (364–5).

familiarity with it and of the alert independence of his mind. In Section XIV and the beginning of XV, where the maiden is replying to the dreamer's question 'Quat kyn þyng may be þat Lambe?',[1] her answer is a tissue of reminiscences of Isaiah liii, of the Gospels, of the Book of Revelation and of other passages, all co-ordinated into a coherent and moving statement.

However closely dependent on the Bible the poet may be, he always follows his own line of thought. The parable of the workers in the vineyard, which is a close paraphrase of Matthew xx. 1–16, is interpreted in a way that is relevant to the argument and, so far as is known, unique; and, in the description of the New Jerusalem, the poet makes his own choice of details from the Book of Revelation and presents them in his own order.

With the parable of the pearl of great price (Matthew xiii. 45–46), from which the symbolism of the poem largely derives, it is not the Bible alone that the poet has in mind, but, in addition, various interpretations of it. The parable is alluded to and partly paraphrased in ll. 729–32, just after the reference to Jesus calling the little children to Him, and the implication would seem to be that the precious pearl (the 'spotless pearl' in the words of the poem) means innocence. But at the same time it means the kingdom of heaven, the reward of innocence, for ll. 729 ff. state explicitly that the pearl which the merchant sought is 'the joy that cannot cease' which is found in the kingdom of heaven, and in the next stanza (lxii) the maiden shows in what respects the pearl resembles that kingdom. She finally identifies it with the pearl she wears upon her breast which, she says, her Lord the Lamb placed there in token of peace. Of the many interpretations of the pearl of great price which might have been familiar to the poet, Gregory's statement that 'margarita vero mystice significat . . . dulcitudinem coelestis vitae', or that of Petrus Chrysologus that the pearl is 'vita aeterna', may lie behind his thought here; and there may even be a hint at the interpretation, used in Usk's *Testament of Love*, that the pearl of great price means grace. The poet shifts to yet another interpretation in the first line of stanza lxiii, when the maiden herself is addressed as the 'spotless pearl'. Here he is

---

[1] 'What kind of thing may that Lamb be?'

probably thinking of St. Bonaventura's 'Bonae margaritae sunt omnes sancti'. It is evident that in this passage the poet is playing upon various ideas connected with the pearl of great price in much the same way as he plays upon the meanings of the word 'cortasye', and he sums up the complex symbolism of the passage in the lines which the dreamer addresses to the maiden:

'O maskele3 Perle in perle3 pure,
Þat bere3', quod I, 'þe perle of prys . . .'[1]

It is likely that, to a medieval lover of poetry, many of the passages that have been quoted in the preceding pages would have conveyed a rather different impression from that which they make on a modern critic. While not less alive to their effects, he would at the same time have recognized them as examples of the rhetorical 'figures' and colours which Chaucer's Host begs the Clerk to keep till he composes in the 'high style'; and he would have noticed many others, for rhetorical devices of all kinds abound in the poem. In *Pearl*, as in *Sir Gawain and the Green Knight*, the whole method of composition, including the planning of the poem, is determined by the precepts of the rhetoricians. But, again as in *Sir Gawain*, it is not rhetorical doctrine but the poet's artistic sense that is the ultimate court of appeal. In some of his descriptive passages, where he needs to create an impression of gorgeous beauty, he writes in the 'high style' enriching his expression by every means he knows; but when he wishes, he can write simply, with few devices, comparatively little alliteration, and few words that were not in common use. The paraphrase of the parable of the workers in the vineyard is for the most part in this simple style, and a comparison of this passage with the description of the dream-country makes it possible to answer the criticism that the poet's vocabulary is 'faulty in too great copiousness'. It is obvious that there is 'copiousness' where it is in place, but not everywhere.

Another objection might perhaps more legitimately be brought against *Pearl*. It might be argued that a work so meticulously wrought must be lacking in vital force, that such close attention to form and expression cannot be compatible with the creation of

[1] ' "Oh spotless Pearl, in pure pearls, that wears", said I, "the pearl of price" ' (745–6).

poetry that is 'the breath and finer spirit of all knowledge'. To this the only answer is a personal one. To many readers, the present writer among them, the human emotion manifested in the poem appears to be its driving force and its motive. Whether the poet is describing his grief, or wrestling in argument, or realizing the joy of those who follow the Lamb, there is an urgency and a passionate sincerity in his writing which forbids one to regard it as a mere exercise in the poetic art. This has been widely felt, even though there has been no general agreement about the nature of the poet's loss or the meaning of his poem.

These are problems still in dispute, and possibly incapable of final solution, since it will not do to argue that, because the poet makes us feel a sense of loss, Pearl must represent a real child and cannot be the allegorical representation of some virtue or, as has even been suggested, of the poet's own soul in a state of perfection. For men have grieved for such losses as much as for the loss of a child. Yet, on the whole, it seems most satisfactory to assume that the poem was inspired by the death of a loved child, not necessarily a daughter or a sister, for the line 'Ho[1] watȝ me nerre[2] þen aunte or nece' need not imply blood-relationship. The poet's grief is intensified by his uncertainty about her fate, for she died too young to please God by works or even to pray (484). In the vision that is granted him, he is convinced, both by argument and by the sight of his 'lyttel quene' in the New Jerusalem, that she is saved and that she is among those who follow the Lamb; and with this reassurance he is able to resign himself to God's will.

R. Wellek has shown that the child's fate could have presented a real problem at the time when Pearl was written.[3] Though belief in the salvation of the baptized child through free grace was widely held from the time of Augustine, yet the matter was still under discussion in the fourteenth century. The reaffirmation by Thomas Bradwardine (d. 1340), in De Causa Dei contra Pelagium, of the doctrine of salvation by grace, against those who held the Pelagian heresy of salvation by merit, points to an interest in fourteenth-

---

[1] 'She'.   [2] 'nearer'.
[3] 'The Pearl: an interpretation of the Middle English Poem', Studies in English by Members of the English Seminar at the Charles University, iv (Prague, 1933).

century England in matters fundamentally connected with this. Hence the poet's anxiety to know what had happened to the child, and his concern with the nature of grace, are understandable. Clearly the maiden's answer, that the innocent who have been baptized (626–7) are saved, 'For þe grace of God is gret innoghe',[1] is not, as one critic has suggested, unorthodox; and it would appear that R. Wellek was right in maintaining that there is nothing unorthodox, either, in the high position in heaven which is assigned to the child. The intellectual and spiritual struggle presented in the poem is not waged against orthodox beliefs; rather, it is a struggle to accept the teaching of the Church by one who wishes to do so, but is beset by doubts.

The battle, must, of course, have been won before the poem was written, since it is the poet who, in the person of Pearl, provides the answers to his own difficulties. But it is not the least of his powers as a poet that he conveys the agony of the struggle as if it were still to win. There is a close parallel to the *Divina Commedia* here. Small as the scale of *Pearl* is compared with Dante's poem, the method is essentially the same. In both, the process of enlightenment is presented by means of a dialogue between a mortal seeking it and a celestial being, once a loved mortal, who now possesses knowledge, by virtue of her position in heaven. In both, the poet has, as it were, split himself into two, so that he can present at once his ignorance and uncertainty and his knowledge and confidence; and, since his serene confidence, and even his power to understand, was not achieved unaided, but was the result of divine revelation both direct and through the teaching of the Church, the person of the instructor is rightly represented as insusceptible of human emotion, remote and incomprehensible, while the person of the instructed remains human and prone to emotion, and for that reason able to arouse emotion. Though the dialogue form is often used in medieval literature to convey instruction, the similarity here is unusually close; and it is between something so fundamental to each poem that it affords far better grounds for thinking that the poet of *Pearl* knew the *Divina Commedia* than some of the lesser parallels that have been cited.

[1] 'enough'.

If this be the right way of looking at the poem, there is little point in the old argument as to whether *Pearl* is an elegy or an allegory. Though it has, of course, elegiac and allegorical elements in it, it is not to be comprehended by either term, and it could with as much justice be called a homily, a debate (*disputatio*), or a vision of the other world. None of these labels, by itself, is any more illuminating than the bare terms 'elegy' or 'pastoral' would be, if applied to *Lycidas*.

This brings us back to the starting-point and by now it should have become clearer in what respects *Lycidas* and *Pearl* are alike and in what they differ. Perhaps the most surprising thing is the marked similarity of their conclusions. The vision of the Catholic poet of *Pearl* ends where the Protestant Milton's does:

> For Lycidas your sorrow is not dead,
> . . . but mounted high
> Through the dear might of him that walked the waves . . .
> And hears the unexpressive nuptial Song,
> In the blest Kingdoms meek of joy and love,
> There entertain him all the Saints above,
> In solemn troops and sweet Societies.

IV

CHAUCER'S LOVE VISIONS, WITH PARTICULAR REFERENCE TO THE *PARLEMENT OF FOULES*

CHAUCER, perhaps almost more than any other great English poet, has suffered from being considered, as it were, in compartments. Those whom it is now the fashion to call 'academic critics' have, particularly during this century, been busy accumulating great stores of erudition relating to his works, while, on the other hand, those who like to call themselves 'literary critics' have rarely been deterred by ignorance from 'evaluating' the work of one who is recognizably a poet of the first rank. At one extreme we have books like Burke Severs's lengthy study of the sources of the *Clerkes Tale*[1] or Carleton Brown's book on the many versions of the tale told by the Prioress,[2] studies which seem to have very little to do with Chaucer's poetry. At the other extreme, we find excessive praise of whatever appeals to the individual critic or seems likely to appeal to his twentieth-century reader, often regardless of its importance or function in the work in which it is found. An example is the praise which is so frequently lavished on the description of the little dog in the *Book of the Duchess*. Alternatively, a critic will attempt to interpret a poem in terms quite foreign to it, as when Mr. Speirs[3] sees in the *Nun's Priest's Tale* of the Cock and the Fox, an allegory of the Fall of Man.

Both these ways of approaching Chaucer are, in their extreme forms, unprofitable, and there is little to be gained by abandoning one for the other. If we are frequently revolted by what seems to be

---

[1] *The Literary Relationships of Chaucer's Clerkes Tale*, New York, 1942.
[2] *A Study of the Miracle of Our Lady told by Chaucer's Prioress*, Chaucer Society, 1910.
[3] J. Speirs, *Chaucer the Maker* (London, 1950), p. 189.

pointless learning, we must remember that however 'modern' Chaucer may often seem to be, he *is* separated from us by more than five centuries, and, if we are honest, we shall have to admit that there are many things in his writings that make little sense to us. What then are we to do with these things? We must either study them historically and try to see what they meant to their own age, and therefore probably to their author; or ignore them, and thereby run the risk of ignoring something vital to the work in which they are found.

Mr. Raymond Preston in the Preface to his book on Chaucer remarks that 'a twentieth century reader cannot, except in fantasy, become a fourteenth century reader; but he may read a fourteenth century book, and it is the task of the critic who would encourage him to see that the twentieth century reading is a development, not a contradiction, of the fourteenth century reading'.[1] This is good sense, but it is almost too modest an aim. I would go a little farther, and suggest that it is the critic's task to apply the knowledge which has been accumulated, so that Chaucer's poetry may be better understood, and so that as much as possible of its subtleties, its ironies, and its varieties may become clear to us. In fact, a critic should be at once 'academic' and 'literary' for, as a reviewer in *The Times Literary Supplement* put it, 'learning without sensibility is futile, and so is sensibility without learning'. I shall do my best here to carry out, in relation to Chaucer's Love Visions, what I believe to be the critic's task when he is faced with medieval poetry.

In any consideration of Chaucer's Love Visions it is necessary to remember that he was a court poet. When, probably in 1368, he became an esquire of the royal household, it would be one of his duties to entertain the court by singing and composing poetry. The young Squire described in the Prologue to the *Canterbury Tales* knew how to compose and write songs—'he koude songes make and wel endite'—and it seems likely that in this description Chaucer is not merely giving an account of the pattern Squire, but is remembering his own early life. Alceste, in the *Legend of Good*

[1] *Chaucer* (London and New York, n.d.), p. xv.

Women, refers to the 'balades, roundels, virelays' which Chaucer had written in his youth; and Gower, too, in the *Confessio Amantis* makes Venus send greetings to Chaucer who 'in the floures of his youthe' made 'Ditees' and 'songes glade' for her sake. That he was still composing for the Court a good many years later is evidenced by the famous picture in one of the manuscripts of *Troilus and Criseyde* which shows him reading the poem to the Court, and by those lines in the first Prologue to the *Legend of Good Women* which indicate that the *Legend* was to be given to the Queen.

To say that most of Chaucer's early poetry, that is, almost everything before the *Canterbury Tales*, and probably a good deal of them, was written for the Court, is to imply certain very definite things about that poetry. Its subjects, methods, and style would have to appeal to a small, exclusive, and sophisticated audience. In general, the kind of poetry which would be acceptable to an English courtly audience in Chaucer's day would have to be modelled on the poetry written for French courtly and aristocratic circles. The most popular subject would be love—love of the kind first celebrated by the Troubadours of Provence, later, with certain modifications, by the poets of northern France, and ultimately by those of most European countries.

Something was known in England about what we now term 'Courtly Love' as early as the beginning of the thirteenth century, for the writer of the *Owl and the Nightingale* understood it; but a court poet like Chaucer would not have been likely to gain his knowledge of it from English sources. And, indeed, the form of his love poetry makes it quite certain that he did not.

Though the earliest poems celebrating Courtly Love, those of the Troubadours, had been lyrics, as early as the twelfth century French poets became interested in a more abstract and intellectual treatment of Courtly Love than was possible in lyric. Chrétien de Troyes used Arthurian stories in his *Lancelot* and *Yvain* as a means of illustrating some of the ideals of Courtly Love, and his poems contain long digressions devoted simply to exposition and reflection upon it. In the next century the impulse towards exposition seems to have become stronger still, and some poets abandoned narrative for allegory. The outstanding example of this tendency, and the most important for the understanding of Chaucer, is the *Roman de la Rose*, in particular the first part of it, which was composed by Guillaume de Lorris.[1] The fame and influence of this poem in medieval Europe during the next 200 years can hardly be overestimated. In Chaucer's lifetime, more than a hundred years after its first appearance, French poets such as Machaut, Deschamps, and Froissart were still exploiting its possibilities; and, though they developed these possibilities in different ways, their subject was still the same, and its form still recognizably that used by Guillaume de Lorris—the Love Vision. Some at least of contemporary French poetry was certainly known at the English court; some of Froissart's verse was actually written for it. So, when Chaucer began to write longer poems to please his royal patrons, it was natural that this kind of French poetry should be his model.

It is in the nature of courtly poetry, at least in the Middle Ages, that it should tend to follow fixed forms and conventions. W. P. Ker has spoken of the abstract patterns of poetry that fascinated the seventeenth-century poets.[2] He was thinking of the conception of the 'heroic poem' and the classical tragedy, but his words apply almost equally to Chaucer's age, to Court poets like Chaucer and Gower.

Chaucer's four Love Visions, the *Book of the Duchess*, the *House of Fame*, the *Parlement of Foules*, and the *Legend of Good Women*, prove that there must have existed in his mind an abstract idea or pattern of the Love Vision, which he could use again and again for different purposes. This pattern of his is not the same as that of the *Roman de la Rose* itself, though it is ultimately derived from it. The original pattern of the Love Vision, the pattern of the *Roman de la Rose*, was unique and inimitable, for, as Mr. Lewis has shown,[3] in the first part of the *Roman de la Rose* Guillaume de Lorris's conception and the form in which he conveys it, are indivisible. When later poets used the details of his allegory to convey other conceptions, however closely related to the original they might be, this bond was broken, and the details tended to lose their original significance. This had already happened in the work

[1] For a useful analysis of this work see C. S. Lewis, *The Allegory of Love*, pp. 112 ff.   [2] See *The Art of Poetry* (Oxford, 1923), p. 53.
[3] *The Allegory of Love*, pp. 112 ff.

of the later French writers. Poet after poet followed de Lorris, and depicted himself as dreaming of a beautiful garden; but, though the flowers, birds, and streams of the garden were suggested by those of the garden of the *Roman*, they no longer needed to have any symbolic significance. Yet the garden itself does stand for something, for wherever we meet it, it calls up associations with the whole complex of ideas, or ideals, which we call Courtly Love—and it is meant to do so.

It was this modified form of the Love Vision which was current in Chaucer's day, and which was his chief model, though of course he knew the *Roman de la Rose* itself. Just what the 'pattern' of the Love Vision meant to him is clear enough from his own poems. Whatever the precise subject of the poem, it must begin in a particular way, with the poet falling asleep and dreaming. Following the example of contemporary French poets, Chaucer could elaborate (as Guillaume de Lorris had not troubled to do) on the reasons for his sleeping, or his dream. Froissart, in *L'Espinette amoureuse*, had depicted himself falling asleep as he read a book. Chaucer adapts this device in the *Parlement* and the *Book of the Duchess*, and in each case takes occasion to describe his reading at some length. In his dream he finds himself in a spring landscape, the Garden of Love (*Parlement*), or some variation of it, the woods (*Book of the Duchess*) or the meadows (*Legend of Good Women*). Here, in the *Book of the Duchess* and the *Legend*, the main action takes place. This is not so in the *House of Fame*, nor, as I think, in the *Parlement*. The vision over, the poem is concluded by the poet's wakening from his dream.

I want especially to speak of the *Parlement of Foules*, for in it Chaucer seems to me to have made a particularly successful and brilliant use of his pattern of the Love Vision. The *Book of the Duchess* perhaps impresses some modern readers as more charming and delicate, but it has more loose ends. The *House of Fame* has things that seem more obviously Chaucerian (the treatment of the Eagle, for instance), but as a whole it is not a success, and was perhaps left unfinished for that reason. The Prologue to the *Legend of Good Women* can hardly be considered by itself. It needs to be related to *Troilus and Criseyde* on the one hand, since it is in a sense a light-hearted comment on that poem, and on the other to the Legends themselves. The *Parlement of Foules* is recognizable, even today, as the most perfect of Chaucer's Love Visions, and it would certainly have seemed so to Chaucer's contemporaries. Its interest lies in the fact that, although it is highly conventional, it is also, as a whole, highly original.

It is not merely in its basic pattern that it conforms to French models. Most of the ways in which Chaucer fills out the pattern had already been exploited. I shall take some of the major ones.

Chaucer's poem is clearly conceived as a Valentine poem. In his Retractations he calls it 'the book of St. Valentine's day, of the Parlement of Briddes'. He tells us that the assembly of birds took place on St. Valentine's day, and at the end of the poem the birds praise St. Valentine in their roundel. One of the French poets who developed the convention of writing poems to celebrate St. Valentine's day was Sir Oton de Graunson, whom Chaucer certainly knew, for he names him as 'floure of hem that make in France' at the end of the *Complaint of Venus*. In Graunson's *Songe sainct Valentin*, the poet, like Chaucer in the *Parlement*, dreams that he sees a great assembly of birds of every kind met to choose their mates. It is possible that Chaucer knew this poem,[1] but even if he did not he must have known some of the many medieval writings in which a council or parliament of the birds is described.[2]

In the later portion of Chaucer's poem, the part that depicts the parliament of birds, and the part that is often remarked on as most original, there are other features that would be familiar to a contemporary audience. One of these is the debate of the birds. To give an early English example of this device, the *Owl and the Nightingale* is a debate between birds. But it is not only the *form* of the debate that would be familiar: its subject would be equally so. When each of the three tercel eagles in turn claims that he has most right to the lady (the formel), he is debating one of the 'questions of love' that were popular as subjects of discussion in love poetry, and possibly also in real life in courtly circles. This

---

[1] See Haldeen Braddy, *Chaucer and the Poet Graunson*, Lousiana, 1947.
[2] Cf. Robinson, *The Complete Works of Geoffrey Chaucer* (Cambridge, Mass., 1933), p. 361, for full references.

particular question is debated in another work of Chaucer's, when, in the *Knight's Tale*, Palamon and Arcite quarrel about Emily.

There are many other familiar features in the earlier parts of the poem. Chaucer in his introduction, like Guillaume de Lorris at the beginning of the *Roman de la Rose*, thinks of the dream of Scipio and of Macrobius, its famous commentator. I quote from the English translation of the *Roman*:

> This may I drawe to warraunt
> An authour that hight Macrobes,
> That halt nat dremes false ne lees,
> But undoth us the avysioun
> That whilom mette kyng Cipioun. (A, 6–10)

In the vision itself Chaucer introduces the most common of the mythological or allegorical figures which were customary in love visions: Cupid, Venus, and Nature; and in his description of the Garden of Love there are the familiar personifications—Beauty, Youth, Flattery, Desire, &c.—and the familiar decorative details, such as the lists of trees.

But it is not only in its main formal elements and its contents that the *Parlement* conforms to established literary convention. It does so also in the manner of its expression. The French poets to whom Chaucer was, perhaps, most directly indebted in his Love Visions, Machaut and Froissart, wrote in a style whose principles had been laid down in the early-thirteenth-century treatises on the Art of Poetry, such as Geoffrey de Vinsauf's *Nova Poetria*, or Matthieu de Vendôme's *Ars Versificatoria*.

Chaucer evidently learnt both from the French poets and also directly from the treatises. This can be seen from his description of Blanche in the *Book of the Duchess*. In method this description follows the recipe for a description given by Geoffrey de Vinsauf; but Machaut had followed the same recipe in his *Jugement dou Roy de Behaigne*, and Chaucer combines details from both. He uses other devices of the rhetoricians in the *Parlement*. *Contentio*, for example, is used as a figure of words; that is, an idea is expressed by contrasting words:

> For out of *olde* feldes, as men seyth,
> Cometh al this *newe* corn from yer to yere. (22–23)

As a figure of thought, *contentio* contrasts ideas, often using contrasted words as well, as in:

> For bothe I hadde thyng which that I nolde,
> And ek I nadde that thyng that I wolde. (90–91)

The Prologue to the *Parlement* opens with several instances of this device, all used to describe love:

> The lyf so short, the craft so long to lerne,
> Th'assay so hard, so sharp the conquerynge,
> The dredful joy, alwey that slit so yerne:
> Al this mene I by Love. (1–4)

This kind of device, and many others, Chaucer's French predecessors and Chaucer himself undoubtedly used deliberately, with a consciousness of their nature and of where they had learnt them and had met them in other writers.

But in the *Parlement* and in Chaucer's other Love Visions (and also, I believe, in *Troilus*, and in some, though not all, of the *Canterbury Tales*) such devices are not casually introduced. On the contrary, the whole manner and arrangement of the expression depends on the teaching of the so-called 'rhetorical manuals', or, as I prefer to call them, the 'Arts of Poetry'. This I have tried to show elsewhere,[1] and I will not repeat what I have said there. But a further illustration of Chaucer's methods from the *Parlement*, will show how he 'knits' (to use his own word) or co-ordinates his various thoughts. In the first stanza he introduces the subject of love in the indirect way I have just indicated: 'al this mene I by love'; and he goes on to dwell on the miraculous power and the cruelty of love, of which, though he himself has not experienced it, he has read in books:

> For al be that I knowe nat Love in dede,
> Ne wot how that he quiteth folk here hyre,
> Yit happeth me ful ofte in bokes reede
> Of his myrakles and his crewel yre.
> There rede I wel he wol be lord and syre;
> I dar nat seyn, his strokes been so sore,
> But 'God save swich a lord!'—I can na moore. (8–14)

[1] See pp. 149 ff., 'Some Reflections on Chaucer's "Art Poetical"'.

This statement leads, by way of a general remark on his habit of reading, to a reference to a particular old book which he had been reading in order, he says, 'a certeyn thing to lerne':

> Of usage—what for lust and what for lore—
> On bokes rede I ofte, as I yow tolde.
> But wherfore that I speke al this? Nat yoore
> Agon, it happede me for to beholde
> Upon a bok was write with lettres olde,
> And therupon, a certeyn thing to lerne,
> The longe day ful faste I redde and yerne. (15–21)

The suggestion in the words 'a certeyn thing to lerne' is here left unexplained; but it is, I think, taken up again later.

The account of the book which follows is, in rhetorical parlance, a descriptive *digressio*, but Chaucer does not proceed to it at once. Instead he makes an elaborate transition, introducing for the purpose a *sententia*, or proverbial saying, which, like others in this poem, takes the form of a *contentio*. The use of a *sententia* was one of the recognized ways of making a transition. Picking up the suggestion in the phrase he used about the book—it 'was write with lettres olde'—he continues with the lines I have already quoted:

> For out of olde feldes, as men seyth,
> Cometh al this newe corn, from yer to yere,

and then uses this *sententia* as a *comparatio* (comparison):

> And out of olde bokes, in good feyth,
> Cometh all this newe science that men lere. (22–25)

The *digressio* which describes the contents of the book proceeds more or less straightforwardly, but the device of *repetitio* is used in it a good deal to introduce the various stages of the story: 'Thanne shewede he hym the lytel erthe that here is' (57); 'And after shewede he hym the nyne speres' (59); and, later, 'Than tolde he hym' (67). This kind of repetition is advocated by the rhetorical manuals, and Chaucer makes considerable use of it in all his works. In his later writings, however, its effect is often very different.[1]

Repetition of a different kind also appears in this account of the

---

[1] For an instance from the Wife of Bath's Prologue, see below, pp. 145 ff.

Dream of Scipio. Certain important words are emphasized by its means. In Scipio's dream his ancestor Africanus takes him to a 'sterry place' whence he shows him first Carthage, then the whole earth which is so small 'At regard of the hevenes quantité' (58); and he tells Scipio that since the earth is so little and so full of torment, he should not take delight in it. But such men as here on earth loved common profit shall 'into a blysful place wende, Ther as joye is, that last withouten ende' (48–49). The phrase, 'blysful place' is repeated at the end of Scipio's dream and kept in mind during the account of it by the lines 'that place deere That ful of blysse is' (76–77), and by the phrase 'hevene blisse' (72), all occurring in the course of the dream. It can hardly be accidental that, in the next section of the poem, when Chaucer himself is brought by Africanus to the gate of the park, the first inscription he reads over the gate is 'Thorgh me men gon into that *blysful place*' (127).

I need not continue this minute analysis of the style and manner of the *Parlement*, but I want to lay stress on one point: that in the composition of such a poem nothing is likely to be unconsidered. On the contrary, one would expect everything to be planned and carefully co-ordinated. So, however apparently haphazard or even incongruous some things may appear to be, it would be dangerous to assume that Chaucer introduced them without good reason.

It has been the fashion with this poem to dismiss most of the early part as literary convention, prettily and even elegantly treated but merely introductory to the debate of the birds, which has been universally, and perhaps extravagantly, praised for its freshness and originality. This, I am sure, is the wrong way to look at the poem. The debate begins at l. 416, and so far as the lesser birds are concerned—and it is in them that the twentieth century delights, not in the tercels, with their formal speeches—it begins a good deal later, at l. 491. The whole poem is only 699 lines long. Are we to suppose that Chaucer, who, in smaller matters wrote with such conscious art, allowed himself to patter on to no purpose —or to little purpose—for about three-quarters of the poem before he, as we arrogantly suppose, 'found himself', and said what he wanted to say? Or, to put the question another way, are we to ignore what *we* think is conventional, and to find meaning and pleasure only in what *we* think is fresh and original?

This surely is not merely to misunderstand the *Parlement* but, what is worse, to misunderstand the whole aim and trend of medieval poetry. Nor do we get much further by spying into the so-called conventional parts and comparing them carefully with other examples of the same thing. We can, of course, remark that in describing the Garden of Love in the *Parlement* Chaucer has turned from the usual French sources to the Italian, and so produced something clearer in detail and more decorative than similar descriptions in the French poets; or we can note that the personified virtues 'Dame Pees . . . with a curtyn in hire hond' (240), 'Dame Pacience . . . With face pale, upon an hil of sond' (242–3), and the goddess Venus herself, have a particularity reminiscent of contemporary Italian paintings. Such observations may make us more appreciative of the details of Chaucer's work, but they do not help us to an understanding of the poem as a whole; and, again, I think that they tend to run contrary to the spirit, not merely of Chaucer, but of medieval poetry as a whole. For, to the medieval poet, the art of poetry was not the creation of something new, but the much humbler one of the selection, arrangement, and representation of what was known and familiar. At its best this resulted in new combinations and revealed new relations, but it meant that even the good poem was likely to be familiar in all its parts, and that it would be valued for this and would appeal as much by its likeness to what was known as by its difference from it.

The notes to Skeat's or Robinson's text of the *Parlement* make it abundantly clear that Chaucer selected the material from many different sources. In addition to the French poets he uses Boccaccio's *Teseida* for the description of the garden and of Venus; he takes the dream of Scipio from the fourth book of Cicero's *Republic*, as preserved to medieval times by Macrobius its commentator; the description of Nature and some suggestions for the birds come from the Latin work *De Planctu Naturae* by Alanus de Insulis. These are his major debts, but there are many others: to Boethius, to Dante, to Ovid.

Was this selection merely haphazard? I think not. On the

contrary, I believe that each has its purpose in the whole and that the poem as a whole is as closely co-ordinated as is the expression. But before I attempt to show how each part fits into the whole, I should perhaps say a little about the attempts that have been made to explain the poem as a topical allegory.

The German scholar, Koch, was the first to see in it an allegory of the wooing of Anne of Bohemia by Richard II, who actually married her in 1382. Since this theory was first published much scholarly energy has been expended on supporting or attacking it, and much time has been wasted in endeavouring to identify the other two personages who, together with Richard, are presumed to have been portrayed as the three tercel eagles who lay suit to the formel, Anne.

Chaucer may well have been alluding to some particular event, and to some contemporary personages in this poem, for such topical allusions are common in medieval poetry, and particularly in this kind of courtly poetry. In the Valentine poems of Chaucer's contemporary, Sir Oton de Graunson, there are similar allusions; Chaucer's own *Book of the Duchess* certainly, and his *Legend of Good Women* probably, also contain them. I do not think, however, that at this distance of time we are in a position to say what precise event, or which persons, are referred to.

But let us suppose, for the sake of argument, that the *Parlement* does contain topical allegory. Even so we are left with no real explanation of the earlier part of the poem; for, on this assumption, everything up to the point at which Chaucer introduces Nature and the birds must, once again, be regarded merely as introduction. If, instead, we begin at the beginning, it is possible to make sense of the whole.

The poem, as I have already noted, opens with a description of love—a fact which at least suggests that love is its subject. Moreover, the artificial phrases of the description indicate that Chaucer is thinking of Courtly Love; 'the craft so long to lerne . . .' (1), 'the dredful joye' (3). Further, he makes it clear that it is not his own love with which he is concerned: 'For al be that I knowe nat Love in dede' (9); but, as he says, he had often read of loves 'myrakles and his crewel yre' (11). When, therefore, he tells us that he read all day in an old book 'a certeyn thing to lerne', it is reasonable to suppose that this thing was love.

But the dream of Scipio and his vision of the 'blysful place' to which come only those who work for the common good, seems little to his purpose. He suggests this himself when he says that, when he had to stop reading for lack of light, he went to bed

> Fulfyld of thought and busy hevynesse;
> For bothe I hadde thyng which that I nolde,
> And ek I nadde that thyng that I wolde (89–91)

—that is, he had had a vision of true felicity but had learnt nothing about love. The lesson of the book had been 'That he ne shulde hym in the world delyte' (66), which was not what he then wanted.

To the modern reader it is not immediately clear why Chaucer should have chosen to relate this dream at this point, and at such length. But there are several indications of its real significance. The first comes from *Troilus and Criseyde* where, almost at the end of the poem, there are lines remarkably like some in this passage of the *Parlement*:

> And whan that he was slayn in this manere,
> His lighte goost ful blisfully is went
> Up to the holughnesse of the eighthe spere,
> In convers letyng everich element;
> And ther he saugh, with ful avysement,
> The erratik sterres, herkenyng armonye
> With sownes ful of hevenyssh melodie.

> And down from thennes faste he gan avyse
> This litel spot of erthe, that with the se
> Embraced is, and fully gan despise
> This wrecched world, and held al vanité
> To respect of the pleyn felicité
> That is in hevene above. (*Troilus*, v. 1807–19)

> Thanne axede he if folk that here been dede
> Han lyf and dwellynge in another place.
> And Affrican seyde, 'Ye, withouten drede',
> And that oure present worldes lyves space
> Nis but a maner deth, what wey we trace,
> And rightful folk shul gon, after they dye,
> To hevene; and shewede hym the Galaxye.

Thanne shewede he hym the lytel erthe that here is,
At regard of the hevenes quantité;
And after shewede he hym the nyne speres,
And after that the melodye herde he
That cometh of thilke speres thryes thre,
That welle is of musik and melodye
In this world here, and cause of armonye.

Than bad he hym, syn erthe was so lyte,
And ful of torment and of harde grace,
That he ne shulde hym in the world delyte.

(*Parlement*, 50–66)

In both poems Chaucer is contrasting, or rather making his speaker contrast, the transitory things of earth with the 'pleyn felicité that is in hevene above'. In *Troilus*, a few stanzas later, there is further an explicit contrast between heavenly and earthly love. In the *Parlement* this contrast is never explicitly made, probably because it is on so much smaller a scale and is so much lighter in tone and intention than *Troilus*; but this does not mean that it was not here too in Chaucer's mind.

That we are on the right track seems more certain when we look again at the lines in which Chaucer commented on his reading:

For bothe I hadde thyng which that I nolde,
And ek I nadde that thyng that I wolde. (90–91)

These lines echo some words spoken by Philosophy in Boethius's *Consolation of Philosophy*.[1] Philosophy is discoursing on the difference between true and false felicity. She has just explained to Boethius that riches and honour do not bring true happiness. 'When you had riches,' she asks Boethius, 'were you never anxious or sorry?' Boethius replies that he does not remember that he was ever free from anxiety. '"And was nat that" quod sche "for that the lakkide somwhat that thow woldest nat han lakkid, or elles thou haddest that thow noldest nat han had?"' Once again, it is clear that Chaucer is thinking of the contrast between true and false felicity. With this idea at the back of his mind he proceeds to relate his dream, and it is with this idea in mind that we should read it.

---

[1] iii, pr. 3; Robinson, p. 401.

There is more than one indication that Chaucer's dream of the Garden of Love is to be related to Scipio's dream of true felicity, and one result of the juxtaposition of the two visions is that the reader is made to view the Garden of Love in a special way—ironically, and with a kind of detachment. Both irony and sense of detachment are in fact interconnected, and both, to some extent, pervade the whole poem. The detachment is partly indicated and sustained by Chaucer's manner of presenting himself. He is, as often in other poems, the slightly bewildered spectator, sympathetic and well-intentioned, but never quite understanding what is going on. He tells us at the beginning of the poem that he worships Love, but he is so astounded by Love's works that when he thinks of him he does not know whether he is swimming or sinking. He is so 'astoned', again (142), at the inscriptions over the gate that he has not sufficient sense either to run away or to go in, and is then told by Africanus that 'this writyng nys nothyng ment bi the' (158), but only concerns the initiates, Love's Servants. And at the end of the whole poem Chaucer makes no comment at all on what he has seen, but simply turns again to his books, hoping, in terms vague enough to suggest that he is still at sea, that some day his reading will result in a dream that will enable him to fare better.

This portrayal of himself is in itself ironical, but irony is also suggested by several other things early in the poem: by the fact that it is the same Africanus who gave such solemn advice to Scipio, who leads Chaucer into the Garden of Love; by the *two* inscriptions over its gate which are, as Chaucer says, 'of ful gret difference', the one describing the joys, the other the pains of love, a contrast bringing some reminder of the earlier one drawn by Africanus between the bliss of heaven and the miseries of earth. And for those who know the *Divina Commedia* there is deeper irony in the reminiscences of it which Chaucer introduces when he describes his entry into the Garden. Scipio acts and speaks in a manner which recalls Virgil's actions and words to Dante at the entry to the Inferno. The wording of Chaucer's inscriptions over the gate echoes Dante's inscription over the gate to the Inferno.[1]

[1] Cf. p. 143 below.

At the end of the *Parlement*, when the lesser birds discuss the dilemma of the aristocratic eagles, the irony is obvious enough, not only in their behaviour, but also in their formal speeches. The common-sense but crude comments by which the lesser birds reveal their attitude to Courtly Love may be said to be treated ironically; Chaucer portrays both parties faithfully, but holds the scales equally between them, giving no sign of sympathizing with either.

But he leads up to this more obvious irony gradually, by way of long descriptions, first of the Garden, and then of the two goddesses, Venus and Nature. The significance of the descriptions of the goddesses becomes apparent when we compare them in detail, bearing in mind their significance in medieval writings.

Chaucer shows us Venus lying in a 'privé corner' of her dark temple, filled with the sound of sighs,

Whiche sikes were engendred with desyr. (248)

She lies on a bed of gold, her golden hair bound with a gold thread, naked from the breast upward and covered otherwise with a thin 'coverchef of Valence'. Then he describes Nature, who surpasses in beauty all other creatures as the bright summer sun surpasses the star. She sits on a green hill surrounded by flowers, leaves, and branches. Venus is petitioned by the two lovers, whose fate we are not told, and the painted walls of her temple depict the stories of unhappy and frustrated lovers, 'al here love, and in what plyt they dyde' (294). Nature, who, following Alanus, is described as the deputy (vicaire) of the Almighty Lord, who knits all the elements into harmony, is petitioned by all the birds of the air, and at the end of the debate she grants them their desire. We know from Alanus and the writers of his school that Nature represents the general order of things[1] and that in Alanus, *De Planctu Naturae*, she upholds natural love, so that, even without the contrasted petitioners, we might guess that in the goddesses we have a contrast between artifical Courtly Love and the natural love of creature for creature, a contrast which the end of the poem reinforces when, after the debate is over, the aristocratic birds are left without

[1] Cf. *The Allegory of Love*, pp. 94 ff.

satisfaction, while the lower birds, who know only Nature's rule, are happily united.

This, then, is how I think the poem as a whole should be interpreted: as delicately ironical fantasy on the theme of love and not merely of Courtly Love presented through a series of contrasts, variously achieved.

It is not mere accident that Chaucer introduces so many examples of the rhetorical device of *contentio*, of contrasted phrases and statements, in this poem. It is, I believe, an indication of how his mind was working when he wrote it. His opening lines suggest that he is going to write about Courtly Love, but he quickly passes on, in the dream of Scipio, to a description of true felicity, and a suggested contrast between it and the delights of the world— a contrast which gains point through the linking of this dream to Chaucer's own dream of the Garden of Love. At the entrance to the Garden the contrast is made between the happy lover who comes to the 'welle of grace, There grene and lusty May shal evere endure' (129–30) and the frustrated lover who is compared to a fish left high and dry in a fish-trap. The Garden itself is beautiful, and its air is so temperate 'That nevere was ther grevaunce of hot ne cold' (205), but there is no happiness in the temple of Venus, and Venus herself seems without pity, unlike Nature who sympathizes with the difficulties of the courtly birds, and is also solicitous for the common birds. If these descriptions are intended to contrast, as I have suggested, Courtly Love and Natural Love, the same contrast is also presented from a rather different viewpoint in the debate of the birds and their fate.

We should not, I am sure, attempt to draw a moral from all this. Above all we should avoid the temptation of saying that Chaucer ridicules Courtly Love in this poem. He presents the aristocratic birds sympathetically, and the irony comes only from seeing how the vulgar birds (who *are* vulgar) react to them. What we *can* say, however, is that the Chaucer who wrote this poem can have been no unthinking devotee of Courtly Love. His courtly audience no doubt wished to hear about Courtly Love, and, perhaps even about some particular courtship, and he gave them what they wanted in a poem that pleased them. But he also showed those who wished to see that there were many ways of looking at love.

If, after reading this poem, we turn to *Troilus and Criseyde*, which we believe to have been written later, we shall not expect to find in that greater poem a simple or straightforward presentation of love, courtly or otherwise, for at least the *Parlement* makes it clear that Chaucer had already thought much, and even deeply, on the subject.

V

TROILUS AND CRISEYDE

> The double sorwe of Troilus to tellen,
> That was the kyng Priamus sone of Troye,
> In lovynge how his aventures fellen
> Fro wo to wele, and after out of joie,
> My purpos is, or that I parte fro ye.[1]

SO in the 'high style' Chaucer begins the story of Troilus's
love, in a manner which recalls Virgil's opening: 'Arms and
the man I sing', and, appropriately to this manner calls upon
Tisiphone to

> help me for t'endite
> Thise woful vers, that wepen as I write.

Before he actually begins the story he restates the theme, and is
a little more explicit about its outcome. It is one

> In which ye may the double sorwes here
> Of Troilus in lovynge of Criseyde,
> And how that she forsook him or she deyde.

At this point he says nothing of his source, but later he is circumstantial, referring frequently to 'the storie' ('the storie telleth
us', v. 1051) or to 'myn auctour' and twice to Lollius: 'myn auctor
called Lollius' (i. 394) and 'as telleth Lollius' (v. 1653). Once he
insists that all he is doing is to translate from the Latin which,
he presumably means to imply, is the work of Lollius. Here he
addresses Clio the muse of History—since History, so he suggests,
is the only art he needs in recording what he elsewhere calls
'storial truth':

> O lady myn, that called art Cleo,
> Thow be my speed fro this forth, and my Muse,
> To ryme wel this book, til I have do;

[1] Quotations are from R. K. Root, *The Book of Troilus and Criseyde*, Prince-
ton, 1945.

> Me nedeth here noon othere art to use.
> Forwhi to every lovere I me excuse,
> That of no sentement I this endite,
> But out of Latyn in my tonge it write. (ii. 8–14)

But the story of Troilus was derived not from a Latin work but from an Italian poem, *Il Filostrato*, written not by Lollius but by Boccaccio. This was known, in part at least, as early as 1430 or thereabouts, for Lydgate, in the *Fall of Princes*, says that Chaucer made a translation 'off a book . . . In Lumbard tunge',[1] i.e. in Italian. But Lydgate adds, to our further mystification, that the Italian book 'callid is Trophé', a title which has never been explained.

That some mystification was intended by Chaucer himself is clear from the fact that the lines I have just quoted are prefixed to Book ii which, of all the books of his poem, is the least indebted to Boccaccio or to anyone else. I doubt, however, whether he invented the name 'Lollius', for he mentions it in the *House of Fame*, among other well-known writers on the story of Troy, and, as Root remarks,[2] there can have been no motive for introducing a fictitious name there. Boccaccio himself implies in *Il Filostrato* that he is following an ancient story,[3] and Chaucer may have believed for some reason (perhaps because he misunderstood some lines of Horace) that this ancient story was the work of a Latin writer called Lollius.[4] If so, he preferred to refer to that rather than to the vernacular work which he must have had before him.

In fact, Boccaccio did much to create the story of Troilus and Criseyde as Chaucer knew it, and as Shakespeare was to know it after him. With the materials out of which Boccaccio built the story I shall not concern myself. His sources have been treated briefly by R. K. Root in his edition of *Troilus*, and much more fully by Griffin and Myrick in their edition of *Il Filostrato*, and they are translated by R. K. Gordon in *The Story of Troilus*. With Boccaccio's poem, however, we must concern ourselves, since it is largely by comparing Chaucer's poem with Boccaccio's that we can arrive at a fuller understanding of Chaucer's meaning.

[1] *Fall of Princes*, Prologue, 283–7.
[2] Op. cit., p. xxxvii.   [3] Cf. Proemio and elsewhere.
[4] For a full discussion of Lollius cf. Root, op. cit., pp. xxxvi ff.

Boccaccio wrote his poem, as he tells us in the long prose Proemio, for the lady whom he loved, Maria d'Aquino, daughter of the Countess d'Aquino and perhaps of Robert, King of Naples and Sicily. The immediate occasion was Maria's absence from Naples for a period of some months. In despair, Boccaccio tells her, he decided to give his grief at her absence 'issue in some suitable lamentation' and to relate his sufferings in the person of someone passionately in love (*passionnato*), as he is. The grief of Troilus at the departure of Criseida from Troy seemed an apt parallel. And, he continues, addressing Maria:

If it chance that you read in them, how often you find Troilus weeping and grieving at the departure of Cressida, so often may you clearly understand and recognize my very cries, tears, sighs and distresses; and as often as you find good looks, good manners, and other thing praise-worthy in a lady written of Cressida, you may understand them to be said of you. As to the other things, which in addition to these are many, no one, as I have already said, relateth to me, nor is set down here on my own account, but because the story of the noble young lover requireth it. And if you are as discerning as I hold you to be, you can from these things understand how great and of what sort are my desires, where they end, and what more than anything else they ask for, or if they deserve any pity. Now I know not whether these things will be of so great efficacy as to touch your chaste mind with some compassion as you read them, but I pray Love to give them this power.[1]

By his flattering reference to Maria's discernment, Boccaccio no doubt hoped to turn her attention away from those features of the tale which were not so appropriate to their situation: par-ticularly from the infidelity of the heroine. He does not, as Chaucer does, mention this at the beginning of the poem.

Boccaccio's aim colours the whole poem. It is reflected in the style—in the passionate intensity of some passages and the lyrical beauty of others. It naturally affects his treatment of the story. It is Troilus and his woes that interest him, and, of the eight parts into which his poem is divided, four are devoted to this. Criseida's departure from Troy takes place about half-way through the poem.

For Chaucer the story had not this personal application. Com-

---

[1] *Il Filostrato*, Proemio, Griffin and Myrick's translation, p. 129 of their edition.

pared with Boccaccio he stands apart from it. He is present only
as the narrator and sympathetic observer of the action. The passionate tone of Boccaccio is absent from Chaucer's work. His pace
is much more leisurely, and he takes time to explain his characters'
thoughts and feelings, and to reflect and comment in his own
person. To him the story is not so much the story of Troilus's
grief as of a great love which ended unhappily. He was at least as
interested in Criseyde as in Troilus, and as interested in Troilus's
wooing of her as in his grief at her loss. The proportions of his
much longer poem reflect this different interest. The departure of
Criseyde takes place at the beginning of the fifth and last book, and
four-fifths of his poem are devoted to Troilus's wooing and the
description of his happy love.

   This difference in the proportions of the two poems is brought
about partly by Chaucer's compression of the end of the story,
but much more by the additions, small and large, which he makes
in his version of the wooing of Criseyde. The largest additions
are two whole episodes, for neither of which more than a hint was
to be found in the *Filostrato*. The first of these, which begins
towards the end of Book ii, at l. 1394, and continues to Book iii,
231, consists of Pandarus's plans for the first meeting of Troilus
and Criseyde and the meeting itself; the second (Book iii, 505–1309)
of the meeting at Pandarus's house which ends in their union.

   But these scenes are not simply thrust into a story which otherwise closely follows Boccaccio's. They come naturally into a narrative in which Chaucer has prepared the way for them. From the
beginning of Book ii he sets about altering Boccaccio's story,
making numerous small additions, rearrangements, omissions,
constant alterations. It would be difficult to summarize their
effect, but the idea behind them becomes apparent through a close
examination of the two poems, and I propose here to compare
certain portions of the earlier books in detail. I do not apologize
for taking some time over this because, besides enabling us to find
out what was in Chaucer's mind, the comparison will serve as an
illustration of his methods of developing a story and of revealing
the mind of his heroine.

   In Chaucer's Book i Pandarus has persuaded Troilus to tell him who it is he loves, and has learnt that it is his niece Criseyde. In Boccaccio the relationship is different: Pandaro is a rather younger man and the cousin of Criseida. He undertakes to prepare the way for Troilus by telling his niece of his love, and at the beginning of Book ii we see him departing for Criseyde's house.

All this Boccaccio also tells us, but in the *Filostrato* Pandaro, having arrived at Criseida's house and been shown into her bed-chamber, comes quite quickly to the point. He begins by praising her beauty, and says at once that he has heard that it has pleased one man so much that he is quite undone by it. Criseida blushes, and admits that there is someone who continually hangs about her door. Pandaro soon perceives that this is not Troilo; he tells her that the man he means is not an insignificant person, but a man known to everybody, and he expatiates a little on his worth. 'Who is it?' Criseida asks, and is told that it is Troilo.

In Chaucer's poem the pace is much slower. When Pandarus arrives he finds Criseyde listening to a maiden reading 'a tale of Thebes', and he greets her in the half-jesting way natural between people who know each other well:

> 'Madame, God yow see,
> With al youre book, and al the compaignie.' (ii. 85–86)

She rises to meet him and, after the conventional greeting, says abruptly that she has recently dreamt of him. Pandarus says jokingly that she will doubtless fare the better for it all that year, and, apologizing for interrupting the reading, asks what the book is, 'Is it of love?' It is his niece's turn for a jest, for Pandarus is well known to languish in hopeless love. 'Uncle', she says, 'youre maistresse is nat here.' With that, Chaucer adds 'they gonnen laugh'. The conversation continues, gay, intimate, and natural. But Pandarus is waiting for an opportunity, and presently he gets it when Criseyde asks about the war, and about Hector. He praises Hector and goes on to speak in praise of Troilus. Then he pretends to take his leave, but is persuaded to stay a little longer to advise his niece about her affairs. Again he rises—'Now is tyme I wende'— but just as he is going he says cryptically that she ought to be merry and cast aside her widow's habit, 'sith yow is tid so glad an aventure'. This, as he intends, fires Criseyde's curiosity. She asks what he means. Pandarus puts her off: it would take too long to tell and might displease her. She promises not to be displeased, and he is apparently just about to tell her what he means. But she is not yet sufficiently prepared, and he continues for a long time to talk darkly about her good fortune, until she is in a fever of impatience:

> 'Now, my good em, for Goddes love I preye',
> Quod she, 'Come of and telle me what it is.' (ii. 309–10)

He is satisfied that now she will not think his news unimportant, and reveals that Troilus loves her. About nine-tenths of this scene was added by Chaucer. In the passages that immediately follow the additions are less extensive, but they are very numerous and, together with constant rearrangements and omissions of Boccaccio's material, they constitute a radical revision of it.

To continue with the comparison. In the *Filostrato* the final speech of Criseida to Pandaro is this:

> I perceive in what direction thy compassionate desire tendeth. I will do what thou askest because I am sure to please thee thereby and he is worth it. Let it suffice thee if I see him. But in order to avoid shame and perhaps worse, pray that he be discreet and act in such a way that it may not be a reproach to me, nor to him either.[1]

When Pandaro has gone she retires to her room to think over all that she has heard. At first she is joyful: 'I am young, fair, lovely, . . . why should I not be in love?'[2] she says to herself. Then she is fearful: and asks herself whether his love will last, and if it does, whether it will remain concealed? Will she not lose her reputation?[3] These doubts lead her to conclude that she should 'leave such loves to those who delight in them'.[4] But immediately after this we are told that Troilo, advised by Pandaro of how she had received the news of his love, went to her house, and

> she was standing at one of her windows and *was perchance expecting what happened*. Not harsh nor forbidding did she show herself toward Troilo . . . but at all times cast towards him modest glances over her shoulder.[5]

---

[1] *Il Fil.* ii. 66.   [2] Ibid. ii. 69.   [3] Ibid. ii. 76–77.
[4] Ibid. ii. 78.   [5] Ibid. ii. 82.

When Pandarus reveals his news to Chaucer's Criseyde she at first accuses him of ill faith, and weeps for her own wretched state, abandoned, so she says, by her best friend. It is only when Pandarus threatens that Troilus will die and he with him, that he extracts from her a promise that she will try to please Troilus provided her honour is safe. But she does not say how, nor does Pandarus dare to press her further.

When Pandarus has gone:

> Criseyde aros, no lenger she ne stente,
> But streght into hire closet went anon,
> And sette hire down as stylle as any ston,
> And every word gan up and down to wynde,
> That he had seyd, as it com hire to mynde.
>
> And was somdel astoned in hire thought,
> Right for the newe cas; but whan that she
> Was ful avysed, tho fond she right nought
> Of peril, why she ought afered be.
> For man may love, of possibilité,
> A womman so his herte may to-breste,
> And she not love ayein, but if hire leste. (ii. 598 ff.)

Boccaccio's Criseida reacted in the same way except that this last idea did not occur to her.

At this moment Criseyde hears a noise in the street and people cry out that Troilus has been putting the Greeks to flight. Her maidens tell her that he is just about to pass her house, and she goes to the window and looks down as he rides by, without his seeing her. She gazes at this knightly figure:

> So lik a man of armes and a knyght
> He was to seen, fulfild of heigh prowesse . . .
> So fressh, so yong, so worthy semed he,
> It was an heven upon hym for to see. (ii. 631–7)

As she sees him pass with his helmet 'to-hewen . . . in twenty places' and his shield bearing the marks of the cruel conflict in which he has just been victorious:

> of hire owen thought she wex al reed,
> Remembryng hire right thus: 'Lo, this is he

Which that myn uncle swerith he moot be deed,
But I on hym have mercy and pitee;'
And with that thought, for pure ashamed she
Gan in hire hed to pulle, and that as faste,
Whil he and al the peple forby paste.
And gan to caste and rollen up and down
Withinne hire thought his excellent prowesse,
And his estat, and also his renown,
His wit, his shap, and ek his gentilesse;
But moost hire favour was for his distresse
Was al for hire, and thought it was a routhe
To sleen swich oon, if that he mente trouthe. (ii. 652–65)

Chaucer then comments:

Now myghte som envious jangle thus:
'This was a sodeyn love; how myghte it be
That she so lightly loved Troilus
Right for the firste syghte, ye pardé?'
Now whoso seith so, mot he nevere ythé;
For every thyng a gynnyng hath it nede
Or al be wrought, withouten any drede.

For I sey nat that she so sodeynly
Yaf hym hire love, but that she gan enclyne
To like hym first, and I have told yow whi;
And after that, his manhod and his pyne
Made love withinne hire for to myne;
For which, by proces and by good servyse,
He gat hire love, and in no sodeyn wyse. (ii. 666–79)

But this time has not yet come. Criseyde's doubts are by no means all resolved, and Chaucer gives us her thoughts at some length. At first she is disposed, not to encourage him, but at least not to discourage him. She thinks of Troilus's 'gentilesse' and of his high estate ('my kynges sone is he'), and that she might regret it if she were to refuse to have anything to do with him, and he were in consequence to dislike her. Suppose she allows his love, and suppose the worst, that it were to become known; surely it has happened before that a man has loved a woman without her leave? It is, after all, not surprising that he should love her:

'For wel wot I myself . . .
I am oon the faireste, out of drede,
And goodliest, whoso taketh hede,
And so men seyn in al the town of Troie.' (ii. 744–8)

These last lines are taken from Boccaccio, but his Criseida speaks
them much earlier. 'Why should I not love?' she continues, 'I am
nat religious'; and, provided she keeps her honour, it can be no
shame to her. But then, suddenly, she is afraid:

'Allas! syn I am free,
Sholde I now love and putte in jupartie
My sikernesse, and thrallen libertee?' (ii. 771–3)

She is, as Chaucer says, 'Now hoot, now cold'. In this state she
goes into the garden. There she hears Antigone sing a Trojan
song in praise of love, and hears her speak of the bliss of lovers.
Later, at night, in bed, 'tho lay she stille, and thoughte Of al this
thing', and as she ponders

A nyghtyngale, upon a cedre grene,
Under the chambre wal ther as she lay,
Ful loude song ayein the moone shene,
Paraunter, in his briddes wise, a lay
Of love, that made hire herte fressh and gay. (ii. 918–22)

And so she falls asleep, to dream that an eagle comes and rends her
heart from her breast and departs, leaving his own in its place.

This is enough detailed comparison to show the kind of continual
change Chaucer wrought in Boccaccio's poem, and now a more
rapid summary will serve. In Boccaccio's poem, as in Chaucer's,
there is an exchange of letters between the lovers, but in the
Italian nothing more happens before Troilo's first visit to Criseida,
and the consummation of their love. In Chaucer's poem, Criseyde's
first meeting with Troilus takes place at the house of Deiphobus,
Troilus's brother, and only comes about through ingenious preparation by Pandarus, in which he shows much adroitness in the
management of men and affairs. This meeting ends with Criseyde
agreeing to receive Troilus 'fully to my servyse', and promising to
do all she can to turn his bitter pains to sweetness. A second meeting in Pandarus's house is needed before the lovers are united.

This meeting, too, has to be elaborately planned by Pandarus; and his efforts are, on this occasion, seconded by Destiny. Criseyde would have gone home after her supper with Pandarus, and might never have known that Troilus was in the house, had not Fortune sent so terrible a storm that she was forced to remain for the night. Chaucer is quite explicit about this:

> But O, Fortune, executrice of wyerdes,
> O influences of thise hevenes hye,
> Soth is that, under god, ye ben oure hierdes,
> Though to us bestes ben the causes wrie.
> This mene I now, for she gan homward hye,
> But execut was al bisyde hire leve
> The goddes wil, for which she moste bleve. (iii. 617–23)

So, with Fortune and Pandarus both working against her, Criseyde is first persuaded to see Troilus, and then to yield to him. Afterwards she herself attempts to throw the responsibility on Pandarus. When in the morning he sees her and asks her 'Nece, how kan ye fare?', Criseyde answers:

> 'Nevere the bet for yow,
> Fox that ye ben, god yeve youre herte care!
> God help me so, ye caused al this fare.' (iii. 1564–6)

But her anger, if it is as much as that, does not last, and Pandarus soon makes his peace with her.

The effect of all these alterations on the character of the heroine is obvious enough. If Boccaccio's Criseida is not exactly forward, she certainly does not hesitate very long when she knows of Troilo's love. But Chaucer's heroine is much more difficult to persuade. Almost every alteration and addition has as its result the portrayal of a woman less approachable, more reluctant, more modest, and more timorous; needing more persuasion from Pandarus before she is willing to accept even the most humble service; yielding finally only when every circumstance points the way, and then yielding for 'pitee' rather than desire.

Mr. Lewis, both in *The Allegory of Love* and in an essay in *Essays and Studies*,[1] has shown that in thus changing the character of Criseyde Chaucer was rewriting the *Filostrato* 'in terms of

---

[1] xvii: 'What Chaucer really did to *Il Filostrato*.'

Courtly Love'. The feelings and behaviour of Chaucer's Criseyde, both her reluctance and her 'pitee', are those expected of a lady according to the canons of Courtly Love. It is safe to be even more precise than this. As he wrote the early part of *Troilus*, Chaucer had at the back of his mind the course of love as it had been allegorically depicted in the *Roman de la Rose*; and the course of Troilus's wooing is made to conform to this. The various difficulties encountered by the Dreamer of the *Roman* in his pursuit of the lady's love—that is, of the Rose—difficulties there represented by the allegorical figures Danger, Chastity, Evil-Tongue, and the rest—are also encountered by Troilus in his wooing of Criseyde. But Chaucer presents them directly, as the thoughts and feeling of Criseyde, her doubts, her fears of what people will say, and so on. So, too, the comfort given to the lover in the *Roman* by such figures as Bel Acueil, Franchise, and Pitee finds expression in Criseyde's graciousness, generosity, and sympathy—the qualities which in both poems give the lover his hope of ultimate success.

I have said that Chaucer rewrote the *Filostrato* in terms of Courtly Love, and the implication might seem to be that Boccaccio's poem had nothing to do with Courtly Love. This, of course, is not true. In the introduction to their edition of the *Filostrato* Griffin and Myrick devote a whole section to a discussion of the ways in which the poem was affected by the doctrine of Courtly Love. They show that it affects only the character and actions of Troilo. He is conceived as the true courtly lover, but Criseida is outside the convention. As they put it: 'Of this highly idealistic conception of love Boccaccio, by diverting attention from Criseida and her perfidy, and concentrating on Troilus and his woes, succeeded in the *Filostrato* in availing himself to the full'.[1]

But this was not good enough for Chaucer. I said earlier that he looked upon the story of Troilus and Criseyde as that of a great love. If it was to be a great love, one fitted to be celebrated in poetry, the lady, too, must be worthy to inspire and receive the humble service of the lover, otherwise his love would be a mockery. Chaucer, therefore, had to re-create Criseida and, as was natural, he did so in conformity with the ideal of the age. It is a sign of his

[1] Op. cit., pp. 88–89.

sympathy with and understanding of that ideal that he could create a woman of such charm and such humanity that, however one may interpret her, it is not necessary to explain or apologize for Troilus's love.

Boccaccio's Troilo Chaucer could accept almost as he was. He does, however, make one characteristic alteration at the beginning; he omits a passage (*Il Fil.* i. 23) in which Troilo refers to a previous love affair, and instead depicts him, when he first appears in the Temple, as one who has 'no devocioun . . . to non' (i. 187–8), and who is so far quite ignorant of love. This is perhaps one reason why his Troilus seems younger than Troilo. He is, too, more given to weeping and swooning—though Troilo does both. For us it is difficult to accept his behaviour as it was meant to be accepted. We tend to see him either as a despicable weakling or as a somewhat comic figure. I am quite sure that neither impression was intended by Chaucer. Troilus and his prototype Troilo are patterns of the true lover in their abandonment to grief and despair, as well as in their complete absorption in their love and their humility—at times almost servility—towards their lady. What seems to us Troilus's weakness, his inability to act, to do anything for himself, is equally in the tradition; though compared with the Dreamer of the *Roman de la Rose* he is an extreme example of the dependent lover. For the Dreamer of the *Roman* does sometimes take action, though not without encouragement from the figure called Frend. Troilus is completely dependent on his Frend Pandarus up to the time when Criseyde has deserted him, when he is beyond Pandarus's help.

How completely Troilus's inability to act and Criseyde's holding back are in the tradition can be seen from a passage in Chrétien de Troyes's romance *Cleges*. There the lover and the lady are in love with one another, but neither makes any attempt to declare their love: they have not yet found a friend to bring them together. They go on a journey, he in the service of his lord and she in that of her lady, and in the course of it they have to cross the sea. Chrétien describes them sitting side by side, both suffering tortures alike from love-sickness and sea-sickness; neither saying a word to the other.

It is customary to speak as if Chaucer were more interested in Criseyde than in Troilus, but I doubt whether this is really true. The reason for this belief is, I suppose, that nowadays we find Troilus so much less credible than Criseyde; and since he is, throughout, the *perfect* lover, Chaucer himself finds less to say about him. But Chaucer never makes fun of him. He always depicts him sympathetically, e.g. in the lines which describe the regeneration love has brought him, as it must do according to the canons of Courtly Love:

> And in the town his manere tho forth ay
> So goodly was, and gat him so in grace,
> That ech hym loved that loked on his face. (i. 1076-8)

In Chaucer's portrayal of the deserted Troilus of the last Book there is deeper feeling than mere sympathy; and, though he is for the most part following Boccaccio, Chaucer intensifies some of his effects. Pandarus's unavailing attempts to distract Troilus by taking him to the house of Sarpedon, and the visit to Criseyde's empty house, where everything reminds Troilus of past happiness, are fully described in both poems, but more fully in Chaucer's. So, too, is the scene of the long watch on the walls of Troy, which Boccaccio places at the gates of the town. Here Chaucer's account seems to gain by the fact that he is an observer and not a participator in Troilus's feelings. By describing more fully than Boccaccio had done the background of normal life, which goes on in complete indifference to Troilus's sufferings, he makes us more aware of the pathos of his situation:

> Tyl it was noon, they stoden for to se
> Who that ther come; and every maner wight
> That com fro fer, they seyden it was she,
> Til that thei koude knowen hym aright.
> Now was his herte dul, now was it light;
> And thus byjaped stonden for to stare
> Aboute naught this Troilus and Pandare. (v. 1114-20)

A last despairing hope is raised by something descried afar off—a detail not in Boccaccio. Troilus cries:

> 'Have here my trouthe, I se hire! yond she is!
> Heve up thyn eyen, man! maistow nat se?'

Pandare answerde: 'Nay, so mote I the!
Al wrong, by god; what seistow man? where arte?
That I see yond nys but a fare-carte.' (v. 1158–62)

Only Chaucer, who sees Troilus in perspective, can risk this anticlimax.

There are two important passages concerned with Troilus which Chaucer added, neither of which, to judge from our manuscripts, was in his first draft. It is Chaucer alone who, when his hero has been slain on the battlefield, translates him to the Eighth Sphere, whence he looks down upon 'this litel spot of erthe' and laughs 'right at the wo Of hem that wepten for his deth so faste' (v. 1815–22). Chaucer took this passage from another poem of Boccaccio, the *Teseida*, where it describes Arcite. I shall leave the consideration of this until later.

The other passage is Troilus's long debate with himself about free will and predestination (iv. 955 ff.), which was lifted bodily from Boethius's *De Consolatione Philosophiae*. This has been condemned, and it is certainly too long and too much a mere translation of Boethius, but I think that what Chaucer meant by it can still be seen. Chaucer's Troilus has the qualities of a true lover, including passivity in suffering. In real life such a man is almost bound to be something of a fatalist, as Troilus is on several occasions shown to be. By giving him this argument Chaucer has attempted to deepen his character, to show him not merely as a fatalist but as one who is a fatalist by reasoned conviction. It is significant that, although he follows Boethius's argument closely, Chaucer omits the conclusion—that man has free will, on certain conditions—which would not suit Troilus or the context.

Chaucer's Pandarus is inevitably more complex than Pandaro. He has so much more to do, and is so much more often on the stage. The mere fact that he is an older man than Pandaro, and is Criseyde's uncle not her cousin, makes his relation to the lovers less simple. Boccaccio's Pandaro is of Troilus's age, a natural companion for a young man. He is like Troilo in many of his tastes and ideas, though he is unlike him in being nothing of an idealist and a good deal of a cynic. The friendship between Pandarus and

Troilus is of a different kind. Pandarus has the affection of an older man for one who depends on him. He is so self-assured and so much on top of his world, and Troilus is so young and so ignorant, that it comes natural to him to encourage and advise Troilus and to aid him in every way. It is, in fact, natural to him to play the part that Frend plays in the *Roman de la Rose*.

Mr. Lewis has stressed this function of Chaucer's Pandarus, and has pointed out that it explains the many occasions on which Pandarus acts as the exponent of Courtly Love, explaining to Troilus the nature of his feelings and what, according to the code, it is fitting for him to do. But Pandarus is also Troilus's friend on a more ordinary level, and as such he does not merely advise, he also rallies, him, and, however sympathetically, laughs at him, calling him 'thou mouses heart' and telling him

> 'thow hast a ful grete care
> Lest that the Cherl may falle out of the moone.' (i. 1023–4)

It is at times like this that we have a sense of being in contact with someone who, while entirely sympathetic to Troilus, yet looks at his affairs from outside.

This, I think, is also what happens in the much discussed passage when, having brought the lovers together and seen them at last in one another's arms, Pandarus remarks:

> 'For aught I kan espien,
> I nor this candel serven here of nought.
> Light is nat good for sike folkes yen;'
>   .   .   .   .   .
> And bar the candel to the chymeneye. (iii. 1135–41)

At this moment when the lovers are absorbed in each other and we in them, we are suddenly brought up against the ordinary world where men are aware of such things as candles. This consciousness of a world outside the world of love is something that Boccaccio does not give us. His poem has no room for such contrast nor, in fact, room for comedy.

Mr. Lewis warns us against seeing this and other actions and speeches of Pandarus as 'broadly comic' inside the magic circle of

Courtly Love.[1] I am sure that he is right in so far as he means that Pandarus believes the love of Troilus and Criseyde to be good in itself (he says so explicitly); and for the most part has no doubts about the part he is playing, a part wholly justified and even moral from the point of view of the code of Courtly Love. Yet, as Mr. Lewis also makes clear, this is by no means the only part he is capable of playing. His dealings with Deiphobus and Helen and other members of Troilus's family show him to be an experienced man of the world, with fingers in other pies than Troilus's. It is impossible that he should be as single-minded as Troilus. His attitude towards his own love affair is significant, for he allows Criseyde to jest about it, and he can laugh at it himself, albeit ruefully. And it is surely not for nothing that Chaucer uses of him the same phrases as he uses of the Wife of Bath: he knows 'the olde daunce of love'.

More significant still are the very occasional misgivings he has about the part he is playing. When he reminds Troilus that

> 'for the am I bicomen,
> Betwixen *game and ernest*, swich a meene
> As maken wommen unto men to comen' (iii. 253–5)

he is surely speaking, for the moment, as one who is outside the circle of Courtly Love.

I see no real inconsistency between this Pandarus and Pandarus the serious exponent of Courtly Love. I think that Chaucer, beginning with the idea of the Frend in the *Roman de la Rose*, imagined a human being of a kind naturally fitted to fulfil that function; but just as he created a Criseyde who is much more complex than the typical courtly lady, so in Pandarus he created something subtler than the traditional Frend, and something human enough to play the game of love with all his energy, and at the same time to be conscious of much outside the game.

So far I have spoken only of Chaucer's characters as compared with Boccaccio's. I want now to consider some other alterations which Chaucer made.

---

[1] 'What Chaucer really did to *Il Filostrato*', *Essays & Studies*, xvii, p. 64.

When one thinks of each poem as a whole, perhaps the chief thing that strikes one is how infinitely more varied Chaucer's is. It reaches out in all directions from Boccaccio's. On the one hand, conversation is more natural, and more colloquially expressed than Boccaccio's. This is one means by which Chaucer brings us closer to real life. Another is the brief depiction of vivid little scenes— Criseyde with her ladies in a paved parlour with a maiden reading aloud to them, or Deiphobus and Helen receiving a letter from Pandarus and descending the stairway to a green arbour where they may read it (ii. 1704). We must be careful here, for Boccaccio has some passages which impress us in the same way. The scene in Book iv. 685 ff. of Chaucer's poem in which Criseyde, having heard that she is to be sent to her father, is visited by a group of ladies who chatter and offer her congratulations and consolation,

> And bisyly they gonnen hire comforten
> Of thyng, God woot, on which she litel thoughte, (iv. 722–3)

is also in Boccaccio. Nevertheless, we do not receive from Boccaccio's poem, as we do from Chaucer's, the continual impression of being within a complete world of people and things—a real world to which the lovers also belong, and in which they play their part.

At the other extreme are the highly rhetorical passages which are found throughout the poem. Chaucer, as I have already said, opens his poem in the 'high style', and each of the books is introduced in a similar style with invocations, rhetorical ornament, and general reflections. Most of these rhetorical introductory passages are designed to prepare us for the action to follow. The third book, which tells of the lovers' union, opens with a hymn to love which Chaucer has removed from the context in which it appears in Boccaccio's poem. The fourth book warns us of Troilus's change of fortune:

> From Troilus she [Fortune] gan hire brighte face
> Awey to wrythe, and took of hym non heede,
> But cast hym clene oute of his lady grace,
> And on hire whiel she sette up Diomede. (iv. 8–11)

It is by these invocations that Chaucer contrives his alteration of the form of Boccaccio's poem, converting its eight parts (divisions which have no vital significance) into his own five books, and thereby, as has been noted, dividing the action in exactly the same way as the five acts divide an Elizabethan Tragedy. This correspondence is, of course, purely fortuitous. Chaucer knew nothing like a five-act Tragedy, and the five movements probably came to his mind as a natural and symmetrical way of indicating the movement of Troilus's fortunes from 'wo to wele, and after out of joie'.

Passages of rhetoric are to be found in other parts of the poem besides the introductions to the five books, for example in the apostrophe to Fortune which occurs at the climax of the wooing of Criseyde:

> 'But O, Fortune, executrice of wyerdes . . .' (iii. 617)

Often they contain what might be called a philosophical comment on the action. For example Troilus, who is scoffing at love, is just about to be smitten by the eyes of Criseyde, and Chaucer writes:

> O blynde world; O blynde entencioun!
> How often falleth al the effect contraire
> Of surquidrie, and foule presumpcioun;
> For kaught is proud, and kaught is debonaire. (i. 211–14)

The effect of these passages, whether we like them or not, and many modern readers do not, is to set the story of the lovers in perspective—to give it a wider background and to bring it into relation with issues and forces that concern all mankind.

Chaucer's many references to planetary influences, to Fortune, and to Destiny had, I believe, the same purpose. Professor Curry has pointed out[1] how much more frequent such references are in Chaucer's poem than in the *Filostrato* (though that poem is not quite without them). Curry shows too that the general conception behind Chaucer's references is that of Boethius. According to Boethius the workings of Fate are manifested to man through the agency of lesser powers, among which were Fortune and the influence of the planets. It is this conception that Chaucer has in mind when he calls Fortune 'executrice of wyerdes'. Curry has a theory that the whole story of the lovers is worked out in close

[1] 'Destiny in Chaucer's *Troilus*', *P.M.L.A.* xlv (1930), pp. 129 ff.

relation to this Boethian conception, and he claims that Chaucer has created a tragedy of Fate 'far in advance of medieval theory and practice'. But in making this claim it seems to me that Curry goes too far. It is true that Chaucer does several times refer to the workings of Destiny at critical points in the story, as, for instance, in the stanza which imputes to Fortune the 'smoky rain' which kept Criseyde in Pandarus's house. But the use of the Boethian conception is not systematic in the poem, nor do we ever get the impression that the lovers' fate is entirely due to Fortune or Destiny. The effect of these allusions is rather to suggest a wider background and wider issues behind the love story.

We find Chaucer doing the same thing on an earthly plane. Several of his additions to Boccaccio are concerned with the approaching doom of Troy, and though Boccaccio also alludes to it, one is more continually aware in Chaucer's poem of the city moving gradually towards its tragic fate. Chaucer stresses it at the beginning when he tells us that Chalchas stole away to the Greeks because he had discovered by consulting the oracle that Troy must be destroyed; and again towards the end of the story we are reminded that

> Fortune, which that permutacioun
> Of thynges hath . . .
> Gan pulle away the fetheres brighte of Troie
> Fro day to day, til they be bare of joye. (v. 1541–7)

In his poem the fate of Troy forms a background and a parallel to the fate of the lovers.

All the passages I have just been considering—rhetorical passages, passages of philosophical reflection, passages on Destiny and on the fate of Troy (all for the most part either added by Chaucer or at least more strongly emphasized)—have been used by Mr. Lewis as examples of what he calls the medievalization of Boccaccio's poem. And from our point of view, at a distance of nearly six centuries, this is how they appear. But this cannot be how Chaucer regarded them. It is inconceivable that, as he sat down to write *Troilus*, he should have deliberately set himself the task of 'medievalizing' this poem of Boccaccio's. It seems more likely that he felt that the story was of a kind that justified, or even demanded,

a treatment as dignified as he could give it. If we remember the
precept of the rhetoricians, that only a great subject was fitted for
the high style, we may conclude that Chaucer felt his subject to be
a great one, and that these passages express his sense of its high
significance. The stanza in which he bids farewell to his book
confirms that he regarded his poem in this way:

> Go, litel book, go, litel myn tragedye,
> Ther god thi makere yit, or that he dye,
> So sende myght to make in som comedye!
> But, litel book, no makyng thow nenvie,
> But subgit be to alle poesie;
> And kis the steppes where as thow seest space
> Virgile, Ovide, Omer, Lucan and Stace. (v. 1786–92)

It is, no doubt, a convention of medieval poetry for a poet to take
leave of his work in some such way as this, But, with Chaucer at
least, to label a certain passage as a convention is not to say that it
is meaningless. In this stanza Chaucer names the greatest poets
he knew: 'Virgile, Ovide, Omer, Lucan and Stace'; and it is worth
noting that we find him, however humbly, mentioning his own
poem in the same breath with them. We may, in this connexion,
remember his opening lines, 'The double sorwe of Troilus to
tellen . . . My purpos is', with their hint of the opening of the
Aeneid.

The deep seriousness of the end of *Troilus*, of what is usually
called the 'Epilogue', certainly fits in with this idea. After Troilus's
translation, Chaucer makes his final comment on the poem, first
in direct relation to Troilus:

> Swich fyn hath, lo, this Troilus for love!
> Swich fyn hath al his grete worthinesse . . .

and then, widening out from this:

> Swych fyn hath false worldes brotelness. (v. 1828–32)

Then follows the famous stanza addressed to 'yonge fresshe
folkes', bidding them turn from worldly vanity to God, and to
love Him, for 'He nyl falsen no wight, dar I seye'. Chaucer then
attacks the 'payens corsed olde rites' and 'thise wrecched worldes

appetites'; dedicates his book to 'moral Gower' and 'philosophical Strode', and concludes with a prayer to the Trinity, adapted from a passage in Dante's *Paradiso*.

This epilogue has long puzzled the critics, and many have been the attempted explanations. Many have dismissed it merely as a palinode. Medieval writers on love were accustomed, it is argued, to add at the end of their works a recantation of what had gone before, and Chaucer is merely following their example. These critics compare with it the Retractation at the end of the *Canterbury Tales*. The implication is that the epilogue to *Troilus* is something apart from the poem, and that the poem can be understood without it. This is true of the Retractation to the *Canterbury Tales*, which are not in any way linked to the *Tales* themselves; but if we examine the epilogue to *Troilus* we shall find that it is closely linked to the final statements Chaucer makes about Troilus himself. One of the most extreme advocates of the theory of the irrelevance of the epilogue is Curry in the article I have referred to. Having made up his mind that Troilus is a 'tragedy, strongly deterministic in tone, the action of which is presided over by a complex and inescapable Destiny'[1] he is obliged to dismiss the epilogue, which does not fit in with this theory at all, as 'dramatically a sorry performance',[2] and he concludes that the 'line of cleavage between the two productions [i.e. the poem and the epilogue] . . . may fairly be said to represent the complete separation of the pure artist from the religious man'.[3]

This seems to me not merely a radically wrong judgement, but even unnecessary from Curry's own point of view. He himself showed that this whole conception of Destiny was derived from Boethius. But to Boethius Destiny, or Fate, is itself the servant of God. For him God is the stable centre of the universe who 'transmits the power of His will through successive stages of action, each of which, as it is discovered to be farther and farther away from the unchangeable source, shows more and more diversity, change and alteration'.[4] Chaucer, according to Curry, showed the lover's fate as the result of the action of an irrational Fortune. What more

---

[1] Op. cit., p. 129.
[2] Ibid., p. 165.
[3] Ibid., p. 168.
[4] Ibid., p. 130.

natural, then, than that, at the end of his story, he should direct
his readers to the stable God in whose mind lies the explanation of
all apparent irrationalities? I do not claim that this is exactly what
Chaucer does, only that this—with much else—may have been at
the back of his mind as he wrote the Epilogue.

At the other extreme is Shanley,[1] who sees the whole poem as
the moral tale of Troilus, illustrating the Christian truth that
nothing but misery comes from trusting in earthly love. The ultimate cause of Troilus's woe, he holds, was not that he trusted in
a woman, but that he placed his hope of happiness in what was by
its very nature temporary and imperfect. Shanley maintains that
Chaucer hints at this moral throughout the poem.

I do not think that either of these interpretations will do.
I believe, unlike Curry, that Chaucer meant the epilogue to be an
integral part of the poem, and that it grows gradually out of the
poem itself and is not merely tacked on. I do not, however, find
Shanley's view acceptable, at least as he states it. It is, perhaps,
rather an over-simplification of the truth than an untruth. As it is,
it will not fit this complex poem. If this were all that Chaucer meant
us to see in his poem, why does he expend so much of his powers in
making the love of Troilus and Criseyde a beautiful thing, and
what is the point of the long wooing?

To explain the relation of the epilogue to the poem I must go
back to Chaucer's portrayal of Criseyde. Chaucer re-created
Boccaccio's heroine so that she should approximate as nearly as
possible to the ideal of the courtly code. But, one might ask, was
this not an odd thing to do, knowing, as he did, that he was going
to make her commit the worst sin a courtly lady could commit—
that of infidelity to her lover? One might also ask how it could
come about that a lady perfect according to the canons of Courtly
Love, did commit that sin. Yet Chaucer has made it credible to
us that Criseyde should act as she does towards Troilus: he has
drawn her in such a way that we do not feel any inconsistency
between the charming woman of the earlier part of the poem and
the woman who betrays Troilus. Mr. Lewis has pointed out how,
from the beginning, her timidity and fearfulness are emphasized,

[1] *E.L.H.*, 1939, 'The *Troilus* and Christian Doctrine'.

and because of this, when she is alone, she has to find support in the strength and self-assurance of Diomede.

But this quality of timidity, which has been so stressed by the critics, is not peculiar to Criseyde among courtly ladies. It is natural to the type. Fear is one of the things which the Dreamer of the *Roman de la Rose* has to overcome. Thus, for the poet who sets out to create an ideal courtly lady, this quality will be as much 'given' as the qualities of Shame, or Modesty, or Bel Acueil. Perhaps it is now clear what Chaucer has done. He has, as I see it, taken the three central figures of the love convention, the Lady, the Lover, and the Friend, and has endowed them with the qualities which conventionally belong to them; but at the same time he has made of them three consistent and credible human beings. These three beings he sets in action *in real life*—or at least what his genius contrives to make us accept as real life—and he leaves events to work out as they must. The very qualities demanded of an ideal courtly lady are the cause of Criseyde's downfall. She could not have returned to Troilus, nor could he, as we have seen, have taken action to bring her back. True, Criseyde need not actually have been false to Troilus, even if she did not return, but it is entirely credible that one of her temperament should find support where she could. By their very natures, then, the natures given them in accordance with the idea of Courtly Love, the charming figures which Chaucer has created were not strong enough for the situation in which they found themselves. This love of theirs, which Chaucer hymns so beautifully, and for which he feels so much sympathy, *must* fail when it is put to the test. We may note that the reward of the faithful lover is that he is at least allowed to see his love as the thing it is. It is the frailty of human love, in that form of it which was the ideal of the age, which is the theme of the poem.

Here, to some extent, I agree with Shanley, but I do not feel that it is Troilus who is condemned. If anything is condemned (but the word is too harsh), it is the ideal which the characters represent. The words of the Epilogue

'For he nyl falsen no wight, dar I sey' (v. 1845)

are, of course, directly related to this failure of human love. And the sorrow which one feels at the end of the poem seems to me more for the failure of an ideal whose beauty Chaucer had felt, than for the fate of his characters. He shows his regret in the lines:

> And gladlier I wol write, if you leste,
> Penelopes trouthe and good Alceste. (v. 1778–9)

That this theme of the failure of human love in its most ideal form was one sufficiently great and moving to be fittingly handled in the grand manner, needs no demonstration. Nor that to Chaucer, living in an age of faith, the only possible end was the one he gave it. The Epilogue is certainly no repudiation of what had gone before, but neither is it, in any narrow sense, the moral of the story. It is the end to which the whole story inevitably moves.

VI

CHAUCER'S 'GOOD EAR'

Flemer(e) of feendes // out of hym and here (*Man of Law's Tale*, B 460).[1]

I F this line were met with out of its context, one's first thought would probably be that it came from some Middle English poem in alliterative verse. Its movement,[2] marked by the alliteration, is like that of

Strakande ful stoutly // in hor store horne3 (*Sir Gawain and the Green Knight*, 1923).

Daw(e) the dyker(e) // and a dozeine other (*Piers Plowman*, B Text, v. 320).

Marchauntz in the margyne // hadden many 3eres (ibid. vii. 18).

Gracyously umbegrouen // al wyth grene leue3 (*Purity*, 488).

Alternatively, one might think that it came from some passage of religious alliterative prose, for the same movement can be found in several works of this kind. For example:

swotest 3 swetest // alre schefte schuppent (*Seinte Marherete*).[3]

(þis) blinde beholdyng // of þi nakid beyng[4] (*Book of Privy Counselling*).[5]

fleschy felynges // 3 vnskilful stirynges[6] (Hilton, *Scale of Perfection*, Bk. 2, ch. 12).

[1] *The Complete Works of Geoffrey Chaucer*, ed. F. N. Robinson (London, 1933).
[2] I assume that *here* is disyllabic since it rhymes with the infinitive *bere* in the phrase *for to bere*, and with *spere* (dative). But even if it was not, the movement of Chaucer's line can be paralleled in alliterative verse. Cf. 'Dubbed in a dublet of a dere tars' (*Sir Gawain*, 571).
[3] Ed. F. M. Mack, *E.E.T.S.* o.s. 193 (1933), p. 26, l. 25.
[4] In *beholdyng*, the alliteration, falling on the prefix, probably does not coincide with the stress.
[5] Ed. P. Hodgson, *E.E.T.S.* o.s. 218 (1944), p. 147, l. 17.
[6] This reading has been kindly supplied by Miss Helen Gardner from

Chaucer's line occurs in a prayer—the prayer of Constance set adrift in her 'steerelees' boat; and I suggest that this is not mere accident. Even outside works written in alliterative verse, alliteration is so prevalent in Middle English religious works, whether they be in verse or in prose, that one can hardly avoid the conclusion that many writers felt it to be an ornament proper to their subject;[1] and, naturally enough, their alliterative phrases often preserve rhythms which are descended from Old English verse, and from such alliterative prose as Ælfric's. It is likely, then, that Chaucer, bent on conveying the mood of Constance, fell into a familiar 'tune', one that was right for a prayer. That he was not deliberately introducing it, of set purpose, is suggested by the fact that this rhythm combined with alliteration is not found elsewhere in Constance's prayer, nor elsewhere in her tale.[2] On the other hand, similar lines (that is, lines containing the rhythms of alliterative verse, marked by alliteration) occasionally occur in other works of Chaucer in which echoes of some religious writing, or writings, are possible. For example, there is the line from the description of the Parson, 'A shiten shepherde and a clene shepe' (*Prologue*, A 504), or the (less striking) one in the Friar's sermon in the *Summoner's Tale*, 'To been yclawed or to brenne or bake' (D 1731).[3]

Chaucer's use of alliteration in two passages of battle description has often been remarked. Of the description in the *Knight's Tale* (A 2602 ff.) Professor F. N. Robinson writes that 'Chaucer skilfully suggests the effect of the meter, without reproducing its structure or conforming strictly to the rules of alliteration'.[4] This

MS. Harleian 6579 (cf. Orchard edn., p. 211). A later hand has altered *fleschy* to *fleschly*. This example, like Chaucer's line, has *a a* | *b b* alliteration which is rare in good alliterative verse.

[1] This may account for sentences in Chaucer's *Parson's Tale* like 'For soothly oure sweete Lord Jhesu Crist hath spared us so debonairly in oure folies, that if he ne hadde pitee of mannes soule, a sory songe we myghten alle synge' (Robinson, p. 281). There seems to be no marked use of alliteration in St. Raymund of Pennaforte's *Summa*, which is the nearest we can get to the work from which Chaucer adapted the first part of the *Parson's Tale*.

[2] There is a good deal of alliteration in the *Man of Law's Tale*, and lines that really have four stresses (instead of the normal five) are common in Chaucer's works. But it is the four-stressed movement pointed by the alliteration which makes this line remarkable.

[3] The Prioress's Prologue (B 1643 ff.) contains a number of alliterative phrases, but the four-stressed movement is not present.   [4] Op. cit., p. 783.

rather understates the case, for, while it is true that the passage as a whole is not written in alliterative verse, there are lines in it (e.g. 2605, 2610, 2611) which could have come straight from a poem in that metre. Professor R. M. Smith[1] has suggested that Chaucer's description 'owes some of its lines to borrowings from English romances', and he refers to the account of the battle between Ipomadon and Lyolyne in *Ipomadon A*[2] (especially 7989–95), and to 11128–45 in *Partonope of Blois*.[3] Both these passages have some similarity to Chaucer's. In the one from *Partonope* there is a number of the same or similar phrases, and its method of description is rather like Chaucer's;[4] the passage from *Ipomadon A* also provides some verbal parallels and (unlike *Partonope*) is at least as alliterative as his. That there is some connexion between both of them and Chaucer's lines is very likely. Yet it seems to me that the similarities between them and the *Knight's Tale* do not, in themselves, account for the most striking thing in Chaucer's description, the 'feel' of alliterative verse which he conveys in it.[5] The other Chaucerian passage, the description of the sea-fight in the *Legend of Cleopatra* (635 ff.), shares this quality, though perhaps in a lesser degree, for none of its lines are regular 'alliterative long lines'. There are, however, several that would probably pass unnoticed in many an alliterative poem (e.g. 637, 638, 642); and, if there were any doubt that Chaucer had that kind of verse in his head, his use of the word 'heterly' (638) should help to dispose of it, for this word belongs to the special vocabulary of alliterative writings.[6] One

---

[1] 'Three Notes on the *Knight's Tale*', *M.L.N.* 51 (1936).

[2] Ed. E. Kölbing.

[3] Ed. A. T. Bödtker, p. 109 (*E.E.T.S.*, *E.S.*, cix). Robinson had already suggested that 'for the striking use of alliteration' the passage might be compared with *Ywain and Gawain*, 3525 ff. But, as Smith indicates, *Ywain* provides no parallels as striking as those in the two romances mentioned above.

[4] It is not certain, however, that *Partonope* was written early enough to be known to Chaucer, and to me its lines read like an imitation of the *Knight's Tale*, rather than the other way round. This is also the view expressed by Johnstone Parr in 'Chaucer and *Partonope of Blois*', *M.L.N.* 60 (1945).

[5] It is, I suppose, possible that the writer of *Ipomadon A* and Chaucer both knew and were echoing the same passage in alliterative verse. If *Partonope* later imitated Chaucer, there might be just such similarities as we find.

[6] All the references given in the *O.E.D.* to this word in works between 1200 and 1450 come from alliterative verse or from religious alliterative prose, with

could, in fact, say of these two descriptions, as of the first line quoted in this paper, that Chaucer has fallen into the 'tune' appropriate to his subject—for, from Old English times onwards, 'alliterative' poets excelled in descriptions of battle. In view of the length of these passages, it seems likely that he may have done so more deliberately than when he wrote the single line from the *Man of Law's Tale*.

If I am right, we have two instances of Chaucer's ear for a 'tune'. My third instance has been widely recognized as such, and here there is no doubt at all that he was making conscious use of it. His mockery in *Sir Thopas* of the tail-rhyme romances glances at almost every feature that is characteristic of them, but perhaps its subtlest manifestation is in his mimicry of their metre.[1] One particular feature of his practice (and theirs) illustrates well the sensitiveness of his ear. In reading aloud a tail-rhyme stanza, one naturally emphasizes the tail-line, and, in particular, its rhyme-word; and, in a poem of any length, poets do not find it easy to ensure that this natural emphasis shall always fall on a phrase or word that needs it.[2] It is clear that Chaucer recognized the emphatic quality of the tail-line (and the attendant dangers), for into it he puts some of his most successful anticlimaxes:

> His rode is lyk scarlet in grayn,
> And I yow telle in good certayn,
>   He hadde a semely nose. (B 1917–19)
> Ful many a mayde, bright in bour,
> They moorne for hym paramour, .
>   Whan hem were bet to slepe. (B 1932–4)

Another piece of mimicry in *Sir Thopas* is of the same kind, and is equally telling. It is to be heard in the bathetic slowing down of the pace which comes with the single-stressed line; for example:

> He seyde, 'Child, by Termagaunt!
> But if thou prike out of myn haunt,

the single exception of this line of Chaucer's. Its significance in Chaucer's verse is emphasized by J. R. R. Tolkien in 'Chaucer as a Philologist', *Trans. of the Philol. Soc.* (1934), p. 47.

[1] The fullest account of this is given by A. McI. Trounce in 'The English Tail-rhyme Romances', *Med. Aev.* i–iii (1932–4), see especially i, pp. 168 ff.

[2] Mr. Trounce has shown that skilful writers do avoid this difficulty (op. cit. i, pp. 174, 180).

Anon I sle thy steede
With mace.' (B 2000–3)

Such lines are not to be found in the tail-rhyme romances, but
they are a regular feature of the metre of *Sir Tristrem*, where they
often have the same effect of bathos;[1] and, since this romance is in
the Auchinleck MS., it is likely to have been read by Chaucer.[2]

There are, probably, other rhythmic echoes from works known
to Chaucer which will occur to learned readers, and others still
which, at this distance of time, can no longer be detected. One
more may be suggested, this time from a foreign poet. In connexion
with the passage in *The Parlement of Foules* which runs,

'Thorgh me men gon into that blysful place
'Of hertes hele and dedly woundes cure. . . .'
'Thorgh me men gon' than spak that other side,
'Unto the mortal strokes of the spere. . . .' (127 ff.)

Annotators usually refer to Dante's *Inferno* (iii. 1 ff.). Yet, though
there is an obvious similarity in that both passages record inscriptions over gates leading to non-earthly regions, the two passages
are poles apart in true significance, and even more in feeling. The
only other link between them is the similarity of their rhythm.
I believe that what haunted Chaucer's mind was the repeated 'Per
me si va . . .' of Dante's lines, and that it is this, perhaps more than
anything else, that constitutes his 'debt' to the Italian poet. In this
instance it is not easy to say whether Chaucer is deliberately
reproducing Dante's rhythm, or whether this is an unintended
echo of his reading. His 'borrowed' rhythms, as I have suggested,
may be of both kinds; and it is likely that there are some that are
not wholly one or the other.

Of whatever kind they are, they are all evidence of Chaucer's
'good ear'; and they are by no means the only manifestation of it.

[1] Cf., for instance,

Y-hated also þou be
Of alle þat drink wine!
Hennes ȝern þou fle
Out of siȝt mine
In lede! (3063–7)

[2] For evidence that Chaucer knew this manuscript, see Mrs. L. H. Loomis,
'Chaucer and the Auchinleck MS.', in *Studies in Honor of Carleton Brown* (1940),
pp. 111 ff.; also other recent publications by the same author.

He has, of course, an ear for the right word in the right context, as witness the 'oules' with which the Friar threatens his congregation,[1] and the words and phrases from romances which he uses in *Sir Thopas* and nowhere else.[2] He was, too, keenly aware of the sounds made by living creatures, whether man or beast. Instances that are almost too obvious to mention are his reproductions of the noises made by birds and animals, the 'Kek, kek! kokkow! quek, quek' of the vulgar birds in the *Parlement of Foules*, and the triumphant 'wehee' of the clerk's horse as he gallops towards the fen.[3] His humans, too, make appropriate noises, some more and some less articulate. There is Alysoun's malicious giggle 'Tehee!',[4] the carter's 'Hayt, Brok! hayt, Scot' shouted to his pair of horses,[5] and the clerks' 'Keep! keep! stand! stand! jossa, warderere' yelled at theirs.[6] The drunkard is apostrophized by the Pardoner as one who breathes through his 'dronke nose . . . As though thou seydest ay "Sampsoun, Sampsoun!"' [7]

Far more important, as vitally affecting the quality of Chaucer's poetry, are the idiosyncrasies which mark the speech of some of his characters, and are one of his chief means of individualizing them. The instance that springs to the mind is the dialect of the clerks, John and Aleyn, which gives dramatic expression to the statement that they were born in a 'toun . . . that highte Strother, Fer in the north'.[8] Professor Tolkien has shown that, though the clerks do not speak 'pure Northern' throughout their lines, Chaucer's representation of their speech is more than merely impressionistic.[9] There are reasons for thinking that Chaucer's knowledge of their dialect came in part from written sources, but Professor Tolkien notes that it would also have been possible for him to acquire it from living speakers; and the exactness with which some of the

---

[1] D 1730. Compare *Sawles Warde*, ed. R. M. Wilson, 136, and *Ancren Riwle*, ed. J. Morton, p. 212, in both of which the devils toss the souls in hell with 'eawles' ('flesh-hooks').

[2] Cf. Mrs. Loomis's list of words in *Sources and Analogues of Chaucer's Canterbury Tales* (1941), p. 491 n.

[3] *Reeve's Tale*, A 4066.   [4] *Miller's Tale*, A 3740.

[5] *Friar's Tale*, D 1543.   [6] *Reeve's Tale*, A 4101.

[7] *Pardoner's Tale*, C 553–4.   [8] *Reeve's Tale*, A 4014–15.

[9] Op. cit., p. 54: 'The evidence . . . is sufficient to establish the claim of the dialect of the northern clerks to be something quite different from conventional literary representations of rustic speech.'

details of their speeches can be localized[1] seems to suggest some
direct contact with speakers, if not from Strother itself, at least
from the far north of England, beyond the Tees. Here, then, there
is a possibility, and perhaps one might almost say a probability,
that Chaucer is mimicking living speech. Of the other passages in
Chaucer's works which give the same impression it would not be
safe to say anything like as much as this. All that can be said is
that, in them, an individual manner of speaking is indicated by
certain stylistic or linguistic features which are not—or, at any
rate, not in the same degree—features of Chaucer's style elsewhere.
For instance, the wheedling tone of the begging Friar in the
Summoner's Tale (D 1746–53) is conveyed by the grammatical
construction of his speech, which, after the opening 'Yif us' (repeated in 1750), consists almost entirely of a string of nouns or
noun clauses (naming what he wants), broken by parentheses
intended to suggest disparagement of himself or his kind, or
flattery of his victim:

> Yif us a busshel whete, malt, or reye,
> A Goddes kechyl, or a trype of chese,
> Or elles what yow lyst—we may nat cheese—
> A Goddes halfpenny, or a masse peny,
> Or yif us of youre brawn, if ye have eny,
> A dagon of youre blanket—leeve dame,
> Our suster deere,—lo! heere I write your name—
> Bacon or beef, or swich thyng as ye fynde.[2]

This offers a considerable contrast to the more normal construction
of the lines which follow.

Of all Chaucer's characters it is, of course, the Wife of Bath who
gives the strongest impression of an individual actually talking,
and examination of her Prologue shows that here, too, there are

---

[1] Op. cit., pp. 56–59.

[2] This is quoted from Robinson's edition, but I have altered the punctuation
slightly in order to make the construction of the sentence clearer. It may be noted
that the Friar's assumed respect is conveyed, not only by the parenthetic 'leeve
dame, Our suster deere' but also by the exclusive use of the plural pronouns.
Contrast the Friar's speeches to Thomas in which he sometimes uses the plural
pronouns and sometimes the singular, the latter indicating familiarity or (in
2154–5) rage. In the *Wife of Bath's Tale*, the knight addresses 'his olde wyf' as
'Thou' until he has been subdued to the point of saying 'I put me in *youre* wise
governance'.

oddities of construction. Like many great talkers, the Wife evidently speaks at such speed that her words outrun her power to control them. She utters her ideas just as they come into her head and cannot develop her thought logically or keep distinctions clear in argument. Frequent parentheses and repetitions mark the points at which she goes off at a tangent and then hauls herself back to the point from which she started.[1] Some of these characteristics of her speech are exemplified almost at the beginning of her Prologue. In five lines (D 4–8) she has two parentheses, and the following 140 lines or so proceed, not from the statement in 8, but from the doubt expressed in parenthesis in 7 ('If I so ofte myghte have ywedded bee'); and, though she begins these lines with the intention of answering the objection that she should not have been wedded more than once, she keeps on sliding into a general defence of marriage as against virginity. Naturally, the longer she talks the less she is able to exercise rational control, and the account of her fourth husband (453–502), and of how she caught her fifth, illustrates even better these features of her 'style'. In 543–86, for instance, she allows herself to be side-tracked so often that her actual narrative occupies only about fifteen lines out of the forty-three (and even in these fifteen there is repetition); and finally she loses the thread altogether, and gasps,

> But now, sire, lat me se, what shal I seyn?
> A ha! by God, I have my tale ageyn.

Her mechanical repetition of some particular form of expression is another sign that she is not using her mind.[2] When she is telling how she baited her old husbands, she uses the introductory formula 'Thow seist (that)', with the slight variation 'seistow', some fifteen times in just over fifty lines (248–302); and even though

---

[1] This is not, of course, the only reason for the use of parenthesis and repetition, either in real life or in Chaucer's verse. I have suggested quite other reasons for the parentheses in the Friar's speech (see above); and those in the speech of the Host, musing on the tale of Virginia (C 288–319), are different again. For an instance of repetition used in a manner very different from the Wife's, see following note.

[2] This kind of repetition is not, of course, always mechanical. It can be deliberately used for some end, or it may express some attitude of mind. Cf. the Friar's would-be persuasive and, at the same time, patronizing reiteration of the sick man's name—'Thomas, Thomas' (*Summoner's Tale*).

she succeeds in escaping from it for a short time, she returns to it, or the variant 'Thow seydest', a little later (337–78). A passage in her *Tale* subtly conveys, by a change of pronouns and tense, the curious mixture of self-consciousness and lack of self-criticism which is characteristic of many 'talkers'. In the first answers to the question 'What thyng wommen loven moost', the Wife uses the pronouns of the third person and the past tense. ('Somme seyde wommen loven best richesse, Somme seyde honour, somme seyde . . .') She is well inside her tale, and is thinking objectively. But, gradually forgetting that she is telling a tale, she continues, 'Somme seyde that *oure* hertes been moost esed Whan that *we* been yflatered and yplesed'; and finally, conscious only of herself, she is saying 'And somme *seyen* that *we* loven best For to be free . . .'.

It is hard to believe that such idiosyncrasies are not echoes of some living voice to which Chaucer had listened with delight and critical intentness;[1] but there is no way of proving that they are. Yet, since we know that, in some passages in which Chaucer's style, or language, differs from that of the surrounding lines, he is in fact mimicking or echoing something, we can at least say that there is a fair likelihood that here, too, we have a manifestation of Chaucer's 'good ear'. And the same might be said of other passages in his works in which speakers display an individual style—for instance, the Host's muddled repetition of the Monk's definition of tragedy (he has been half-asleep and has only caught part of it),[2] or the exchange of polite nothings between the Black Knight and the dreamer at their first meeting.[3] It need hardly be remarked that, whatever reproductions of the living voice and whatever literary echoes there may be in Chaucer's works, none of them will have been presented to us 'neat'. Just as Chaucer conveys the 'feel' of alliterative verse in the Knight's Tale without writing the whole passage in that metre, or the 'feel' of the Northern dialect without making the clerks speak nothing but 'pure Northern', so in every other instance his aural impressions will merely have provided him with material for his art to work upon.

[1] The same critical intentness that noted the Friar's lisp (*Prologue*, A 264–5), or the Prioress's accent when she spoke French, and her manner of singing 'the service dyvyne' (A 122 ff.).

[2] *Canterbury Tales*, B 3972–7.   [3] *Book of the Duchess*, 519–28.

In conclusion, there are two general observations which are perhaps worth making. The first is that if—as many believe—Chaucer's poetry was read aloud (perhaps by himself) to an audience, all these echoes would have been more effective than they can ever be to those who merely read them in a book. The second is that Chaucer's 'good ear' may account for a great deal more in his poetry than the passages I have mentioned. It is possible that his easy mastery of a variety of metres and styles is in part due to it, and that it manifests itself in the lyrical note he captures from time to time (for example, in the *Prioress's Tale* and in the song of the birds at the end of the *Parlement of Foules*,) in passages in the grand style in *Troilus* as well as in those which have the tone of familiar conversation.

VII

SOME REFLECTIONS ON CHAUCER'S 'ART POETICAL'

WHEN the British Academy did me the honour of inviting me to give the Gollancz Memorial Lecture, I recalled a day long ago on which I had the privilege of visiting Sir Israel Gollancz at King's College, and of consulting him about a piece of work I was hoping to undertake. This seems the fitting occasion to record my gratitude for the kindly help and encouragement he then gave to a mere beginner, who had no claim upon him other than an interest in the Middle English writings to which he devoted so much of his life.

The third book of Chaucer's *House of Fame* opens with the poet's plea to Apollo to guide him in what he is about to write, a plea that echoes Dante's at the beginning of the *Paradiso*; but, instead of continuing as Dante does, Chaucer adds:

> Nat that I wilne, for maistrye,
> Here art poetical be showed.[1]

I am not going to consider in detail what precisely Chaucer meant by 'art poetical'; I shall assume that, in this context, the expression, like the word 'craft', which seems to be used as a synonym a few lines later, implies knowledge of how to write poetry (or skill in writing it) according to established rules. This is, I think, in line with what many medieval writers understood by 'art'.[2]

---

[1] *House of Fame*, 1094–5. Quotations are from *The Complete Works of Geoffrey Chaucer*, ed. F. N. Robinson.

[2] Several medieval definitions of art are given by E. de Bruyne, *Études d'esthétique médiévale*, ii (1946), pp. 371 ff. He sums up as follows: '. . . le Moyen-Âge . . . distingue nettement le théoricien (artifex theorice) de celui que nous appelons le créateur (artifex practice). Le premier parle de l'art, le second agit par art. Mais chez l'un comme chez l'autre, la dignité de l'art vient de sa participation à un savoir organisé. Le Moyen-Âge ne s'imagine pas un artiste qui "ignore" les règles de son métier' (p. 374).

Chaucer's statement in the *House of Fame* that he does not wish to manifest such knowledge or skill reminds one of other passages in which he, or sometimes one of his characters, disclaims any power as a writer or speaker but that of plain speech. More than once what is specifically disclaimed is a knowledge of the 'colours' of rhetoric.[1] 'Thyng that I speke, it moot be bare and pleyn', says the Franklin, and adds, 'Colours ne knowe I none.' It can therefore, I think, be assumed that, to Chaucer, 'art poetical' could mean, more particularly, knowledge of poetic art (or, as we might call it, technique) as set out in such medieval treatises as Geoffroi de Vinsauf's *Nova Poetria* (which Chaucer certainly knew) and the *Ars versificatoria* of Matthieu de Vendôme—treatises in which certain parts of the old doctrine of *rhetorica* are applied to poetry. Whatever be the reason for Chaucer's disclaimers—and it should be remarked that they usually occur in works which are by no means devoid of poetic art in the sense in which I am thinking of it—they suggest a consciousness on his part, perhaps even an acute consciousness, of the kind of thing they disclaim.

The effect which the teaching of the so-called rhetoricians (Geoffroi de Vinsauf, Matthieu de Vendôme, and the rest) had on Chaucer's writing has been discussed by a number of scholars, notably by the late Professor Manly.[2] Attention has been drawn to Chaucer's artificial beginnings, his use of some of the means of amplification described in the treatises, and his frequent introduction of certain rhetorical tropes and figures. The tendency in several

---

[1] See *Canterbury Tales, Franklin's Prologue*, F 716–27, *Squire's Tale*, F 34–41, 102–8. The eagle in the *House of Fame* (853 ff.) is proud of his power to explain things simply. Pandarus deliberately eschews 'subtyl art' (*Troilus and Criseyde*, ii. 255 ff.).

[2] See J. M. Manly, *Chaucer and the Rhetoricians* (Warton Lecture on English Poetry, xvii, 1926); T. Naunin, *Der Einfluss der mittelalterlichen Rhetorik auf Chaucers Dichtung* (Bonn, 1929); F. E. Teager, 'Chaucer's Eagle and the Rhetorical Colors', *P.M.L.A.* xlvii (1932); M. P. Hamilton, 'Notes on Chaucer and the Rhetoricians', ibid. The following also deal, in various ways, with the relations between Chaucer's writings and rhetorical teaching: R. C. Goffin, 'Chaucer and "Reason"', *M.L.R.* xxi (1926) and 'Chaucer and Elocution', *Med. Aev.* iv (1935); C. S. Baldwin, 'Cicero on Parnassus', *P.M.L.A.* xlii (1927) and *Medieval Rhetoric and Poetic* (1928); B. S. Harrison, 'Medieval Rhetoric in the "Book of the Duchess"', *P.M.L.A.* xlix (1934) and 'The Rhetorical Inconsistency of Chaucer's Franklin', *S. in Ph.* xxxii (1935); J. W. H. Atkins, *English Literary Criticism: The Medieval Phase* (1943).

of these discussions has been to consider such features in Chaucer's poetry more or less in isolation, and to look upon them as mere ornaments, appendages to something which could have existed without them[1] and which, it is sometimes implied, would have been the better for their absence. This attitude is natural enough, for as one reads the late twelfth- and early thirteenth-century Arts of Poetry which have been mainly considered in relation to Chaucer, they do suggest a purely mechanical conception of poetry. But to understand fully the influence which these treatises had on medieval poets I think it is necessary to keep in mind the purpose for which they were written. Several of them were school-books, written either by school-masters or for them.[2] They were intended for use in teaching boys who had already received instruction in *grammatica*, that is (to paraphrase one of the well-known defini-tions), who had been taught how to interpret authors (including poets) and how to write and speak correctly.[3] The treatises of the so-called rhetoricians seem to have been designed to carry this elementary study farther by directing attention to certain aspects of poetical composition not already considered, including the use of rhetorical tropes and 'colours'. It is likely that, as in the earlier study of *grammatica*, a boy was expected to learn both by analysis and by composition (of course in Latin).[4] Inevitably, those so

[1] An exception is G. Plessow's discussion of the *Manciple's Tale* (*Des Haushälters Erzählung*, Berlin and Leipzig, 1929), in which he shows that the tale is largely built up by means of rhetorical devices (see especially pp. 17 ff., pp. 126 ff.).
It is not, of course, to be denied that some of Chaucer's rhetorical devices are mere 'appendages'. Many of those in the *Man of Law's Tale*, for instance, are obviously so. This tale, indeed, appears to be an experiment in the application of rhetorical ornament to a simple story. If the experiment is not, on the whole, to the taste of the modern reader, yet it has to be granted that the best thing in the tale, the simile beginning 'Have ye nat seyn somtyme a pale face . . .' (645–51), is, equally with the apostrophes and *exempla*, a rhetorical ornament.

[2] Matthieu de Vendôme taught grammar at Orléans. Évrard the German, whose *Laborintus* was written as a guide to the teacher of Grammar and Poetry, mentions Geoffroi de Vinsauf's *Nova Poetria* and Matthieu de Vendôme's *Ars versificatoria* in his list of authors suitable for boys to study (see *Laborintus*, 665 ff., in *Les Arts poétiques du XIIᵉ et du XIIIᵉ siècle*, by E. Faral). Évrard himself probably taught at Bremen (see Faral, pp. 38–39).

[3] 'Grammatica est scientia interpretandi poetas atque historicos et recte scribendi loquendique' (Rabanus Maurus, *De institutione clericorum*, iii. 18).

[4] The practice in England at the time when Chaucer was educated can only be conjectured. John of Salisbury's famous description of the teaching of

trained (which means, I suppose, the majority of educated men)
would come to think of poetry largely in terms of the statements
and descriptions they had been taught, and if a man were himself
a poet, he would, both consciously and unconsciously, apply what
he had learnt to his own writing.[1] That this resulted in some
excessively ornate verse, we know; but it has of late years been
recognized that there were also other, quite different, results, of
more fundamental importance for literature. Professor Vinaver
has claimed that it was from the study of *rhetorica* (at least partly
as presented in treatises of the kind I have mentioned) that
medieval French writers of romance learnt how to organize their
stories so as to express a particular point of view; and he has shown
that the form of, for instance, the *Suite du Merlin* is the result of
using the device of *digressio* to explain the story. Writing of the
general significance of the study of rhetoric in the earlier Middle
Ages, Professor Vinaver says :

The discipline which in the later Middle Ages was to be largely
reduced to mere stylistic ornamentation had not at that time lost its
original composing function. In a number of important works embody-
ing the doctrine of the rhetoricians from Quintilian onwards the term
colores rhetoricae refers, as in Cicero, not so much to formal elaboration
as to the 'treatment of the matter' from the speaker's or writer's point of
view.[2]

Bernard shows how authors were studied at Chartres in the twelfth century.
He refers to composition in prose and verse (*Metalogicon*, ed. Webb, I. xxiv).
Gervais of Melkley, who must have written his *Ars versificaria* in the early
years of the thirteenth century, also speaks of composition (see résumé by Faral,
op. cit., pp. 328 ff.; on Gervais of Melkley, see Faral, pp. 34 ff.). For an early
fourteenth-century reference to the practice of composition in England, see
A. F. Leach, *The Schools of Medieval England*, pp. 180–1. The Oxford statute
to which Leach refers suggests that composition must have been practised by
intending schoolmasters as well as by boys learning grammar, and the statutes
made for St. Albans Grammar School (1309) also indicate that it was practised
by older pupils (see Leach, p. 186).
    [1] The unconscious application of rhetorical rules is recognized by Gervais of
Melkley, who (according to Faral, p. 328), speaks of 'un sens naturel, d'où
vient que, même sans penser à la théorie, le génie des écrivains applique les
règles d'instinct et fait spontanément des trouvailles heureuses'.
    [2] See *The Works of Sir Thomas Malory*, ed. E. Vinaver, i, pp. xlviii–lxvii.
For Professor Vinaver's discussion of the *Suite du Merlin*, see his introduction
to *Le Roman de Balain*, ed. M. D. Legge, especially pp. xii ff. Reference is made
here to Professor Vinaver, because his statements appear most relevant to the

Professor Vinaver then goes on to show that there is 'a significant agreement in this respect' between Quintilian and certain medieval writers, even as late as John of Salisbury.

There is one point in this passage to which I would object—the assumption that it was no longer possible to regard rhetoric in this way in the later Middle Ages. I believe that, for a number of English poets of the late fourteenth century, *rhetorica* still had some of its old 'composing function'. In particular, I think that it can be shown that Chaucer dealt with certain problems of presentation and organization in ways which are traceable, though certainly not always directly, to rhetorical teaching.[1]

I shall begin with a simple example, the opening stanza of the *Parlement of Foules*. The first line, 'The lyf so short, the craft so long to lerne', has often been remarked on as an instance of one of the artificial ways of beginning a poem—the beginning with a *sententia*—and there are several other rhetorical devices in the stanza. But what is interesting is the way the devices are used. Chaucer's subject in the *Parlement* was to be love, a subject familiar enough in the courtly poetry of his day. His problem was to intro-duce it so as immediately to arrest the attention of his hearers

present discussion; but it is not possible to write on the influence of rhetoric on medieval literature without being indebted to the work of H. Brinkmann (in *Zu Wesen und Form mittelalterlicher Dichtung*, 1928) and of E. R. Curtius (in *Europäische Literatur und lateinisches Mittelalter*, 1948, and in many articles).

[1] I am assuming that Chaucer was trained in *grammatica* and *rhetorica* (or perhaps *poetria*) in his youth. In fact, of course, we know nothing about his education except what can be deduced from his works. His service in the house-hold of the Countess of Ulster need not, I take it, preclude his having been so trained, either previous to it or during it (possibly by a *grammaticus* especially hired for him and other youths in her service). His earliest extant works (or what are generally taken to be such), the *A B C* and the *Book of the Duchess*, reveal the influence of rhetorical teaching; and his knowledge of the standard medieval school-reader, the *Liber Catonianus*, is some slight indication that he had received instruction in grammar. For information about this book and Chaucer's know-ledge of it, see R. A. Pratt, 'Chaucer's Claudian', *Speculum*, xxii (1947), *A Memoir of Karl Young*, pp. 45 ff. (privately printed, New Haven, 1946), and 'The Importance of Manuscripts for the study of Medieval Education as Revealed by the Learning of Chaucer', *Progress of Medieval and Renaissance Studies*, Bulletin No. 20 (1949). It may be worth recalling that a copy of the *Liber Catonianus* was left in 1358 by William Ravenstone, a former master, to the Almonry School of St. Paul's Cathedral, the school which, it is held, Chaucer is most likely to have attended (see E. Rickert, *Chaucer's World*, p. 123, and n. 51).

or readers.[1] What he does is to take the well-known *sententia* 'Ars longa, vita brevis' and use it as a circumlocutory description of his subject. Its form, that of a *contentio* (two contrasted phrases, here applied to the same thing) is arresting, and Chaucer emphasizes it by adding a second circumlocution in the same form:

> Th'assay so hard, so sharp the conquerynge.

The third line repeats the pattern with a difference, the phrase 'the dredful joye' itself containing a contrast, and being amplified by a descriptive phrase, 'alwey that slit so yerne'. Then comes the point to which Chaucer has been leading—'Al this mene I by love'. Having thus given great stress to the idea of love, and at the same time provided some indication of the kind of love he is going to write of, Chaucer amplifies the idea by another descriptive phrase suggesting love's mysterious power and something of his own attitude towards it:

> Al this mene I by love, that my felynge
> Astonyeth with his wonderful werkynge
> So sore iwis, that whan I on hym thynke,
> Nat wot I wel wher that I flete or synke.

This analysis, I hope, makes it clear that the rhetorical devices used here are not, as it were, appended to the fabric of the stanza: they are themselves the fabric. The problem of how to present the subject effectively has been solved entirely by rhetorical methods.

It may be objected that the *Parlement* is a comparatively early work, written when Chaucer was most under the influence of the rhetoricians. In answer to this, I would suggest that the opening of the *Prologue* to the *Canterbury Tales*, though more complex, is

---

[1] The importance of engaging the hearer's attention and goodwill at the beginning of a speech is stressed by Quintilian and the writer of *Ad Herennium*. See Quintilian on the *exordium* (principium), 'Causa principii nulla alia est, quam ut auditorem, quo sit nobis in ceteris partibus accommodatior, prae-paremus' (*Institutio Oratoria*, IV. i. 5); see also *Ad Herennium* (ed. F. Marx, p. 4): 'Exordiorum duo sunt genera: principium, quod Graece prohemium appellatur, et insinuatio. . . . Principium est, cum statim auditoris animum nobis idoneum reddimus ad audiendum. Id ita sumitur, ut attentos, ut dociles, ut benivolos auditores habere possimus.' While most of the twelfth- and thirteenth-century rhetoricians are interested in ways of beginning, they do not consider why an author should take special pains with this part of his work.

organized on lines which are not dissimilar. To present the idea of
spring which, as it revivifies all things, fires men with the desire
to go on pilgrimages, Chaucer once again begins with several
circumlocutory descriptive phrases (each, it may incidentally be
noted, displaying some 'colour' of rhetoric):

> Whan that Aprille with his shoures soote
> The droghte of March hath perced to the roote . . .
> Whan Zephirus eek with his sweete breeth
> Inspired hath in every holt and heeth
> The tendre croppes, and the yonge sonne
> Hath in the Ram his halve cours yronne . . .

Finally he comes to his point:

> Thanne longen folk to goon on pilgrimages.

From *Troilus and Criseyde* one other example may be quoted
which is not, like these two, from the beginning of a work. Chaucer
has told how Troilus was struck 'atte fulle' by the god of love, and
he wishes us to see his case in wider perspective. We are to understand that, for all his pride, Troilus could not hope to escape love.
It was his destiny, as it is every man's. Chaucer begins with the
apostrophe:

> O blynde world, O blynde entencioun!
> How often falleth al the effect contraire
> Of surquidrie and foul presumpcioun;
> For kaught is proud, and kaught is debonaire.
> This Troilus is clomben on the staire,
> And litel weneth that he moot descenden;
> But alday faileth thing that fooles wenden.[1]

The *sententia* which forms the last line of this stanza is followed
by the comparison of Troilus to 'proude Bayard', kept in check
by the whip, and this in turn by an apostrophe to 'worthi folkes
alle' to take example from Troilus not to scorn love, 'For may no
man fordon the lawe of kynde'.

---

[1] *Troilus and Criseyde*, i. 211 ff. The apostrophe and the reference to Troilus's
ignorance of his fate are in Boccaccio's *Il Filostrato* (i, st. 25), but not the
metaphor of Troilus climbing the stair, nor the *sententia* with which Chaucer's
stanza ends. The following three stanzas (218–38) have no parallel in *Il
Filostrato*.

I have chosen to illustrate the rhetorical presentation of an idea, but Chaucer uses similar methods for other purposes, for the presentation of an argument, for instance, as when the old hag in the *Wife of Bath's Tale* discourses to her husband on the true nature of 'gentillesse' and the virtues of poverty, or when Pluto and Proserpyne, in the *Merchant's Tale*, dispute about January's predicament.[1] Most of all he uses these methods in description; but instances of descriptions rhetorically presented are so common in his work at all periods that there is no need for me to 'sermoun of it more'.

To catch the hearer's or the reader's attention and fix it on an idea is one thing; it is a different matter to ensure that his mind will retain that idea for just as long as the poet wishes. In the early *Book of the Duchess*, Chaucer employs for this end a means which, in our day, Mr. T. S. Eliot has found effective—that of verbal repetition.[2] The opening lines of the poem, in which the poet complains that he cannot sleep, contain a succession of phrases expressing the main idea, 'withoute slep', 'I may nat slepe', 'defaute of slep', the last two of which occur more than once. This might be thought accidental, but further examination of the poem shows that it is not. There is an echo of these phrases a little later when Chaucer is about to relate how he took a book to 'drive the night away'; and, when he has finished reading about Ceys and Alcyone, and is telling how this story gave him the idea of praying

---

[1] See *Wife of Bath's Tale*, D 1109–1206 (1177–206 provide a particularly good example of rhetorical presentation) and *Merchant's Tale*, E 2237 ff., especially Proserpyne's reply (2264–304). The argument by which Pandarus persuades Troilus to tell him who it is he loves (*Troilus*, i. 624–714) is another example. Comparison of this passage with *Il Filostrato*, ii, sts. 10–13, shows that, while most of the main points of the argument were taken by Chaucer from the earlier poem, he added almost all the rhetorical amplification. The odd thing is that Pandarus's argument, for all its rhetorical devices, does not sound less 'natural' than Pandaro's, but rather more so. Boccaccio's passage is perhaps too straightforward to be quite convincing as the speech of one friend to another at a time when both are under the stress of emotion.

[2] See Helen Gardner, *The Art of T. S. Eliot* (1949), pp. 51 ff. As Miss Gardner points out, however, the meaning of Mr. Eliot's repeated words does not remain constant, as with Chaucer; 'it is deepened or expanded by each fresh use'. In aim and effect Mr. Eliot's use is rather nearer to the *Pearl* poet's practice of ringing the changes on the various meanings of some of his refrain words (*cortaysye*, *ry3t*, for instance), though close analysis would reveal some interesting differences between them.

to the god of sleep for help,[1] his lines echo and re-echo with phrases containing the words 'sleep' or 'sleeping', in the following order : 'defaute of slep', 'For I ne myghte, for bote ne bale, Slepe', 'goddes of slepyng', 'goddes that koude make Men to slepe', 'defaute of slepynge', 'make me slepe', 'make me slepe a lyte', 'to slepe softe', 'make me slepe sone'. These all occur in about forty lines; they culminate, some ten lines farther on, in the statement:

> Such a lust anoon me took
> To slepe, that ryght upon my book
> Y fil aslepe.

Other parts of the *Book of the Duchess* show a similar, though usually less frequent and less effective, repetition of what one may call a key-word or key-phrase. In the passage describing the hunt, the words 'hunt', 'hunting', 'huntes' ('hunters'), 'hunten' recur, and a little later the changes are rung on the words 'floury', 'floures'. It would, I think, be possible to show that in the first part of the description of the poet's dream almost every paragraph has its own key-word or phrase, and, though the practice is less marked later, there are still signs of it, for example in 617-54, where the word 'fals', first introduced in the phrase 'fals Fortune', appears again and again.

This kind of verbal repetition is not confined to Chaucer's early work. There is a more restrained and more subtle use of it in the *Prioress's Tale*. The word 'litel', several times repeated in the opening stanzas ('A litel scole', 'A litel clergeon', 'This litel child, his litel book lernynge'), is caught up from time to time, later in the tale, in the phrases 'this litel child', 'hir litel child', 'My litel child'. The reiteration of this word is doubly effective, as recalling the boy martyr who 'so yong and tendre was of age', and as a reminder of the teller of the tale, with whose nature it is so perfectly in keeping. With the line, 'He Alma redemptoris herde synge', a second *motif* is introduced, which is reflected by the repetition, at intervals throughout the rest of the tale, both of word 'synge' (or 'song') and of some part of the phrase 'O Alma redemptoris mater'. The two

---

[1] *Book of the Duchess*, 221 ff.

combine in a triumphant line when the martyred child is lying on
his bier before the high altar:

> Yet spak this child, whan spreynd was hooly water,
> And song O Alma redemptoris mater.[1]

The opening sections of the *Book of the Duchess* also provide the
first hints for another use of repetition. The repeated word 'slepe',
besides sounding the key-note of a passage, serves as a link between
one paragraph and another some distance from it. This use of
repetition, as a device to link different parts of a work, is also to be
found in Chaucer's later poems. An instance of it in the *Canterbury Tales*, the echo in the Merchant's Prologue of the last line of
the Clerk's Envoy, is well known; but it is, I think, worth while
to look at it again. The Clerk has followed up his tale of Griselda
with the warning that 'Grisilde is deed and eek hire pacience', and
then, addressing wives, he ironically bids them 'sharply taak on
yow the governaille'. He concludes:

> Be ay of chiere as light as leef on lynde,
> And lat hym [the husband] care, and wepe, and wrynge and waille.

This is too much for the Merchant, who bursts out,

> Wepyng and waylyng, care and oother sorwe
> I knowe ynogh . . .,

and he explains that he has a wife, 'the worste that may be', to

---

[1] There are also in the *Prioress's Tale* some slight traces of stanza linking by
repetition, notably in 1838–9, but see also 1691–2, 1726–7, 1866–7.

A study of the various kinds of verbal repetition in Chaucer's works (both
those which are recognized by the rhetoricians and those which are not), and
of their effects, might give interesting results. Even when the practice is tech-
nically the same, the results are often different. For instance, the repetition
noted in the *Book of the Duchess* and the *Prioress's Tale* makes its appeal to the
emotions, but the repetition in the *Wife of Bath's Tale* of the words *gentillesse,
gentil, gent(e)rye* (D 1109–76) and of the word *poverte* (1177–1206) helps to drive
home the arguments, that is, its appeal is to the intellect. In the latter part of this
argument Chaucer is using the rhetorical device of *repetitio* (the repetition of the
first word of a clause), which he also frequently employs elsewhere, again with
varying effects. Compare, for instance, the repetition in *Manciple's Tale*, H 318 ff.
with that in *Knight's Tale*, A 2918 ff. or that of the words 'Thou seist' ('seistow')
in the *Wife of Bath's Prologue*. (Incidentally, it may be remarked that *Manciple's
Tale*, 318 ff. exemplifies the difficulty of making clear-cut distinctions between
some of the rhetoricians' terms. Naunin, op. cit., p. 45, calls the figure here
used *repetitio*, while Plessow labels it *conduplicatio*. In fact, Geoffroi's definition
of either term could cover it.)

whom he has been wedded just two months. Here the Merchant's
repetition of the Clerk's words acts as a mechanical link between
two tales; but it does much more than this. It reveals at once the
overcharged heart of the Merchant and so prepares us for the
bitter tone of the tale that follows.

A rather different effect is produced by the same device in the
Parlement of Foules. In Chaucer's account of the *Somnium Scipionis*,
Africanus tells Scipio that

> what man, lered other lewed,
> That lovede commune profyt, wel ithewed,
> He shulde into a blysful place wende,
> There as joye is that last withouten ende.

The words 'blysful place' are again used by Africanus at the end of
the dream, and are kept in mind during the course of it by the phrases
'hevene blisse' and 'that ful of blysse is'. When Chaucer has ceased
his reading, which has given him a hint of celestial bliss, he falls
asleep and is himself led by Africanus to a gate which we shall
presently know to be the entrance to the Garden of Love. The first
inscription he reads over the gate runs:

> Thorgh me men gon into that blysful place
> Of hertes hele and deadly woundes cure.

So, at the moment of entering the Garden of Love, we are made to
recall that other 'blysful place'.[1]

One more instance, from the *Merchant's Tale*. Chaucer tells us
that the young wife May is so moved by pity for the squire Damyan
that she decides to grant him her grace. 'Whom that this thyng
displese, I rekke noght', she says to herself. This is the prelude to
her deception of her old husband, and at this point Chaucer slips
in the words which he twice uses elsewhere in the *Canterbury Tales*:

> Lo, pitee renneth soone in gentil herte!

The repetition reveals, as nothing else could, the gulf between
May's pity for Damyan, and the pity of Duke Theseus for the rival
lovers or of the innocent Canacee for the deserted falcon.[2]

---

[1] Another slight verbal link between these two passages (compare 62 'welle
of musik and melodye' and 129 'welle of grace') may or may not be intentional.

[2] See *Merchant's Tale*, E 1986, *Knight's Tale*, A 1761, *Squire's Tale*, F 479.
The line, as used of Canacee, comes after the *Merchant's Tale* in our modern

It would be well to consider at this point how Chaucer's practice in this matter of verbal repetition is related to the teaching of the rhetoricians. They recognize, among the 'colours' of rhetoric, seven or eight varieties of verbal repetition, minutely distinguished by such characteristics as the position of the repeated words in the sentence (*repetitio, conversio, complexio*), whether the repetition is of identical or similar sounds, either in related forms or otherwise (*annominatio*), or of words with the same sound but different meanings (a species of *traductio*). Some of these rigidly defined varieties of repetition are to be found in Chaucer's writings, but most of the instances I have just been considering could not, I believe, be classified under any of the types mentioned in the treatises. Moreover, the rhetoricians do not as a rule make any suggestion as to how or why repetition should be used. It is not possible, therefore, to claim that Chaucer learnt the kind of practice which I have illustrated directly from the precepts of the rhetoricians.[1] This, however, is not what I am trying to show; but rather —to repeat what I said earlier—that in certain problems of presentation or organization he used methods adapted from the teaching of the rhetoricians or in some way traceable to its influence. Sometimes he combined a number of devices actually described in the treatises known to us, as he does at the beginning of the *Parlement of Foules* or of the *General Prologue*. Sometimes he adapted devices (that is, either devices actually mentioned by the rhetoricians or others like them) to special purposes which the rhetoricians themselves need not have considered. Here his use of

editions; but uncertainty about the chronology of the tales and about their order (particularly the order of those in Groups E and F), combined with what can now be called the certainty that Chaucer never finally arranged them, leaves it an open question whether Chaucer wrote the *Merchant's Tale* before or after the *Squire's*, and how he would ultimately have placed them in relation to one another.

[1] Some of Geoffroi de Vinsauf's own verses in *Nova Poetria*, especially those composed to illustrate *gradatio* (1145 ff.) and *conduplicatio* (1169–72), might have provided some suggestion for the kind of repetition found in the *Book of the Duchess*, however.

An exception to the statement that the rhetoricians do not indicate why repetition should be used is to be found in Geoffroi's definition of *conduplicatio* —'*Conduplicatio* est quando motu irae vel indignationis idem conduplicamus verbum' (*Summa de Coloribus Rhetoricis*, ed. Faral, p. 324). See also Geoffroi's remarks under *interpretatio* (Faral, p. 325).

verbal repetition as a linking device may possibly be included, though I think that even this is likely to be an over-simplification of the facts. This particular use of repetition is not confined to Chaucer; it appears elsewhere in medieval poetry, particularly perhaps in Middle English alliterative poetry. There are traces of it in Laȝamon's *Brut* and the alliterative *Morte Arthure*; and in *Purity (Cleanness)* the repetition of part, or the whole, of the text of the homily helps to link the several Biblical stories which illustrate it.[1] Chaucer may have known in earlier or contemporary poetry something which gave him a hint of the possibilities of repetition as a linking device, and he may have been consciously influenced by that. In that case his use of the device is traceable to the teaching of the rhetoricians only in the widest possible sense—that a poet trained in that teaching could hardly have failed to observe it and to consider its value for purposes of presentation.

It was necessary to make a distinction between a slavish imitation of the devices which the rhetoricians describe, and the adaptation of these devices, or others like them, to individual ends,

---

[1] In the story of Lear as told by Laȝamon the phrases 'hauekes & hundes' and 'feowerti hired cnihtes' (or slight variations of them) provide a link between some important stages of the story (see *The Brut,* ed. F. Madden, 3256–8, 3274–5, 3295–9, 3560–3). See pp. 40 ff. above.

Verbal repetition, though very common in the alliterative *Morte Arthure*, is not generally used there as a linking device, at least not in the way Chaucer uses it. In 3523–78, however, it does act as a link between Sir Cradok's news of Modred's treachery and Arthur's recital of the news to his council and it is effective as suggesting Arthur's state of mind, his stunned horror at what he has been told.

In *Purity*, the text which forms the theme of the whole poem, 'Beati mundo corde, quoniam ipsi Deum videbunt', is paraphrased in 27–28, and immediately after (29–30) the converse is stated,

'As so saytz, to þat syȝt seche schal he never
Þat any unclannesse hatz on, auwhere abowte.'

The second part of the text (Vulgate 'Deum videbunt') is echoed in varying forms throughout the poem, often in the transitional passages from one part of the matter to another, but also elsewhere. At the end of the parable of the man without a wedding garment, comes the phrase 'Þenne may þou se þy Savior' (176); the words 'Ne never see hym with syȝt' (192) come at the end of section ii, and 'þe syȝte of þe Soverayn' just after the story of the Flood (552), and so on (see 576, 595, 1055, 1112). The words 'clannesse', 'clene', and their opposites 'unclannesse', 'fylþe', representing the first part of the text, also echo through the poem, and the two parts are once more combined at the end:

'Ande clannes is his comfort, and coyntyse he lovyes,
And þose þat seme arn and swete schyn se his face.' (1809–10)

because most of the examples of Chaucer's methods which I am
going to consider next may not seem to have any connexion with
the Arts of Poetry. All these examples have to do with a major
problem of organization, the layout (or *dispositio*) of a poem as a
whole, or of a large part of it; and more than one critic has pointed
out that the rhetoricians have little to say about this.

For my first example I turn once again to the *Book of the
Duchess*. We have here the unusual advantage of knowing the
occasion for which it was written. We can say with certainty that,
in the poet's dream of the Black Knight who is grieving for the
loss of his dead lady, Chaucer figures the loss which John of Gaunt
suffered in the death of his wife Blanche. Before this dream begins,
however, there is a long introductory passage which includes the
story of Ceys and Alcyone. Chaucer gives a reason for the inclusion
of this story when he tells us that the reading of it gave him the
idea of praying to Morpheus for sleep. But there is another,
unstated reason, of much more significance for the poem as a whole.
The real point of the story for Chaucer was that it told of a wife's
grief for the loss of her husband, and thus provided a parallel,
with a difference, to the main theme of the poem. (That Chaucer
meant it to be so understood is clear from his omission of the
beautiful end of Ovid's story; for the transformation of Ceys and
Alcyone into birds and their happy reunion have no part in the
parallel.)[1] To the medieval mind, accustomed to look behind
appearances to the inner meaning, this story and the dream of the
Black Knight could be two examples of the same theme—the loss
of a loved one and the grief of the one who is left. Looked at in this
way, Chaucer's organization of this poem could, I think, be
regarded as a special application of Geoffroi de Vinsauf's first means
of amplification, *interpretatio*, of which he writes, 'let the same
thing be covered in many forms; be various and yet the same'
('multiplice forma Dissimuletur idem; varius sis et tamen idem').[2]

[1] It is for the same reason that the death of Alcyone is dismissed so abruptly
(see *Book of the Duchess*, 212–17).

[2] I am not suggesting that Geoffroi de Vinsauf himself had anything like the
organization of the *Book of the Duchess* in mind when he used these words.
In part of what he says about *interpretatio* in the *Nova Poetria* (ed. Faral, pp.
220–5) he is almost certainly thinking only of verbal variation (cf. 'Sub verbis
aliis praesumpta resume; repone Pluribus in clausis unum'); and this seems to

There is an obvious similarity between the layout of the *Book of the Duchess* and that of the earlier part of the *Parlement of Foules*. In the *Parlement* the poet places side by side two visions, the one read in a book and concerned with the blissful place that awaits the righteous who work for common profit, the other concerned with that blissful place which, to some, is the 'wey to al good aventure', but brings others to the 'mortal strokes of the spere'— that is, the Garden of Love. The two visions are linked not merely verbally but by the fact that Africanus is the guide in both.[1] But the similarity of this arrangement to that of the *Book of the Duchess* is only partial, for the two stories in the earlier poem are parallels, but the two visions in the *Parlement* are parallel only in form; in significance they present a contrast. This is never stated, for the contrast between heavenly and earthly bliss, which Chaucer makes explicitly at the end of *Troilus and Criseyde*, would be too weighty a matter for this much lighter poem. Yet I think it is just hinted at in the lines at the end of the first vision, where the poet tells us that, on finishing his book, he went to bed

> Fulfyld of thought and busy hevynesse;
> For bothe I hadde thyng which that I nolde,
> And ek I nadde that thyng that I wolde.[2]

Later in this poem another contrast is suggested by the descriptions of the two goddesses, Venus and Nature. Chaucer first describes Venus lying in a dark corner of the temple which, he has told us, is filled with the sound of 'sykes [sighs] hoote as fyr. . . . Whiche sikes were engendered with desyr'. Then he presents

---

be all that is in his mind in the *Documentum de arte versificandi* (Faral, p. 277). Even so, a creative mind, occupied with problems of organization, might have found in his words a hint for variation on a larger scale.

The parallelism between the story of Ceys and Alcyone and the theme of the poet's dream is pointed out by W. Clemen in *Der Junge Chaucer* (1938), pp. 39 ff., but his interpretation of it differs from mine.

[1] Chaucer twice draws attention to this connecting link, see pp. 96 ff., 106–8.

[2] The significance of these lines is made clearer by reference to their source in Boethius's *Consolation*. They echo a speech made by Philosophy in the course of her discussion of true and false 'blisfulnesse' (see *Boece*, iii, pr. 3).

On the similarity between *Parlement*, 50–70 and *Troilus*, v. 1807–20, and the implied contrast in the *Parlement* between heavenly and earthly bliss, see B. H. Bronson, *In Appreciation of Chaucer's Parlement of Foules* (University of California Publications in English, iii, 1935). See also pp. 109 ff. above.

Nature, the deputy of that almighty Lord who knits the discordant elements into a harmony. Nature sits, surrounded by the birds, on a hill of flowers, and Chaucer remarks that her halls and bowers were made of branches. Again no explicit contrast is made; the two juxtaposed descriptions merely hint at the difference between Courtly Love and the natural love of creature for creature which will culminate in the unions of the lesser birds.

This method of presenting, in more or less parallel forms, two things which are essentially to be contrasted cannot be directly related to anything recommended by the rhetoricians, though Matthieu de Vendôme's portraits of Helen and Beroe, which present the antithesis of beauty and ugliness, could possibly have provided some suggestion for it.[1] But it may well have been developed by Chaucer himself from his use of parallels in the *Book of the Duchess*. The more complex scheme was perhaps more after Chaucer's mind. Certainly he makes a masterly use of it in the *Canterbury Tales*, when the Miller 'quits' the Knight's noble tale of the rivalry of Palamon and Arcite for Emelye with the low comedy of the rivalry of the two Oxford clerks for the carpenter's wife. Here, too, there is a verbal link, when the line spoken by the dying Arcite is applied to Nicholas in his neat chamber—'Allone, withouten any compaignye'.

I turn next to some of Chaucer's tales, and I shall begin with the *Knight's Tale*, the presentation of which has, perhaps, something in common with what I have been describing, though it is, of course, far more complex. But, before I can go 'streght to my matere', I must digress a little to consider, though very sketchily,

---

[1] See *Ars versificatoria*, ed. Faral, pp. 129–32. Faral (p. 77) remarks that Matthieu treats these two portraits 'en manière de pendants antithétiques' and he notes other medieval examples of 'opposed' descriptions. Nearly related to these is the passage in *Sir Gawain and the Green Knight*, 943 ff., which describes Morgan le Fay and the lady of the castle antithetically. What Chaucer does in the *Parlement* is obviously much farther removed from Matthieu.

It is perhaps worth noting that Chaucer's presentation of the two visions has a good deal in common with the presentation of ideas in the rhetorical figure of thought known as *contentio*, of which Geoffroi de Vinsauf writes 'quando res comparo, secum Contendunt positae rationes' (*Nova Poetria*, 1253–4). Chaucer uses *contentio* (both the figure of thought and the figure of words) rather frequently in the *Parlement*, and it seems possible that these figures, and the layout of the poem, reflect his state of mind at the time the poem was written.

some of the ways in which parallels are used by other medieval
story-tellers. Parallelism, of one kind or another, is, of course, a
marked feature of medieval story-telling. In its simplest form it
consists in a repetition of the same incident with some variation in
detail. This is what we often find in folk-tales, and in many
medieval romances which are derived from them. There is an
instance of it in Chaucer's *Man of Law's Tale* where, as in other
versions of the Constance story known to us, the heroine is twice
set adrift in an open boat. In this form the parallelism can have
nothing to do with rhetorical teaching, though it witnesses, I
suppose, to some primitive feeling for an ordered narrative. But
this simple device was developed in various ways by story-tellers
who had something of their own to express. One development has
been explained by Professor Vinaver in his Introduction to the
French romance of *Balain*. In this romance, Balain has many and
various adventures which appear to be quite unconnected with one
another, but, as Professor Vinaver has shown, they are actually
'parallels' in the sense that they all illustrate the same thing; the
mescheance ('ill fortune') which finally overwhelms Balain.[1] (It may
be remarked, incidentally, that this seems to have something in
common with Chaucer's method in the *Book of the Duchess*. To it,
too, one could apply Geoffroi de Vinsauf's words, 'multiplice
forma Dissimuletur idem'.) This way of presenting a story does, as
Professor Vinaver claims, render it coherent and emotionally
satisfying; but it has the obvious disadvantage of leaving it shapeless. Yet in parallelism itself there are the beginnings of design,
as we can see from folk-tales; and this potentiality was also
developed in medieval poetry. The Middle English romance of
Sir Gawain and the Green Knight is an outstanding example of
how, by means of parallel incidents and descriptions, a narrative
can be fashioned into a comprehensive pattern. The poet of *Gawain*
was not, however, content merely to produce a formal order.
His interest was in knightly virtue, and particularly the virtue of
'courtesy', as illustrated in the character of Gawain; and the
incidents of the story have meaning and coherence because they
throw light upon the various aspects of Gawain's 'courtesy', just

[1] See the Introduction to *Le Roman de Balain*, especially pp. xxv ff.

as Balain's many adventures are given meaning by the underlying theme of *mescheance*. The *Gawain* poet has, in fact, seen how to use his parallels in two ways at once, so as to produce both an internal and an external order.

Chaucer never wrote anything quite like this, but his *Knight's Tale*, though less completely patterned, is nevertheless an example of a narrative comprehensively organized for a particular end; and again the organization largely depends on a skilful use of parallelism. In a recent article, to which I am very much indebted in what I shall say about this tale, Mr. William Frost remarks that:

> Much of the beauty of the Knight's Tale . . . resides in a certain formal regularity of design. Thus the May-songs of Emelye and Arcite . . . come at two crucial points in the plot; while early May is also the time of the final contest that will make one hero happy and the other glorious. Thus the Tale begins with a wedding, a conquest and a funeral; and ends with a tournament, a funeral and a wedding.[1]

[1] See W. Frost, 'An Interpretation of Chaucer's Knight's Tale', *R.E.S.* xxv (1949). That I am indebted to this article for some fundamental ideas about the *Knight's Tale* is easily apparent; but I cannot accept Mr. Frost's views completely. He appears to me to lay more stress on the *motif* of friendship than Chaucer does, and I do not agree that the 'conflict between love and comradeship in the hearts of the two knights is the emotional focus of the story'. As I understand the story, the 'emotional focus' is their rivalry in love. The fact that they are kinsmen and sworn brothers adds poignancy to the situation, and their final reconciliation helps one to acquiesce in the solution; but these things appear to me to be subordinate in interest to the theme of rivalry in love.

Some of the expressions which Mr. Frost uses of the tale seem unfortunate, as when he writes of its 'theological' interest ('the theological interest attaching to the method by which a just providence fully stabilizes a disintegrating human situation', p. 292) and of its teaching 'a deep acceptance of Christian faith' (p. 302). Chaucer develops the wider issues of the story in the light of Boethian thought, as expounded in the *Consolation of Philosophy*, and its solution is in line with that thought. The general terms used by Mr. Frost, while not actually misleading, do not adequately convey the conceptions that lie behind the tale. As for the term 'tragic' (see pp. 299–301), I doubt whether the word, in any sense in which it is used in serious criticism today, or was understood in the Middle Ages, is properly applicable to this tale.

While it is not to be denied that the tale is sufficiently well suited to the Knight to arouse no questions in the reader's mind, it cannot safely be maintained that it is 'an important function' of the tale 'to present the mind and heart' of the Knight; for what little evidence we have suggests that it was written, substantially as it is, before Chaucer began the *Canterbury Tales*.

It may be noted that the 'symmetry' of the *Knight's Tale* is again emphasized in C. Muscatine's article, 'Form, Texture, and Meaning in Chaucer's "Knight's Tale" ', *P.M.L.A.* lxv (1950), which I did not see until after the delivery of this lecture.

These are, of course, relatively unimportant parts of the design, but they are interesting because they indicate how comprehensive the design is. At the centre of it, so to speak, there are the two knights, Arcite and Palemon, and, in order that our attention may not be distracted from them, Emelye's part in the action is diminished (as compared with that of Boccaccio's Emilia),[1] so that she is little more than the beautiful object of their desire.

Mr. Frost has remarked on the 'systematic and delicately balanced parallelism' of Chaucer's presentation of Arcite and Palemon, and on the fact that this parallelism intensifies the problem of who shall win Emily. It should also be noticed that it throws into relief the one point in which the heroes differ. Though Chaucer makes them similar in age, rank, and fortune, and in general individualizes them little, he does differentiate them in the one point that matters for the story—their behaviour as lovers. Moreover, he remodels Boccaccio's account of their first sight of Emelye so that the impact of love immediately reveals this difference. In Chaucer's story it is Palemon who first sees Emelye, and it is only he who takes her to be the goddess Venus.[2] Arcite knows at once that she is a woman, and is quick to recognize that henceforth he and Palemon are rivals. It is he who casts aside the ties of friendship, declaring:

> Ech man for hymself: ther is noon oother.

The significance of this scene is well brought out by Mr. Frost. It marks the beginning of the conflict and at the same time prepares the way for the resolving of it. For Arcite, who has shown himself to be what is now called a 'realist' in love and in friendship, will pray to Mars for victory in the tournament, believing that thereby he will win Emelye; but Palemon will care nothing for victory and will simply beg Venus, 'Yif me my love, thow blisful lady deere'. So, when Mars and Venus are allowed to grant the two suppliants what they asked for, it follows that Arcite will be victorious, but must die before he can possess Emelye, and that Palemon will be defeated, but will win Emelye in the end.

[1] See *Teseida*, iii, sts. 18–19, 28–31; iv, sts. 56–58, 61; v, sts. 77 ff. There is nothing in the *Knight's Tale* to correspond to any of these passages.
[2] Contrast *Teseida*, iii, st. 13.

Chaucer leaves no loose end; even the broken friendship is re-paired in the dying Arcite's generous words about Palemon. The conclusion is a neat and, one might almost say, logical result of the one difference in the two men who were in so many ways alike.

If this were all there is to the tale, I think one would object that it is too neat and logical to be just. Certainly one might feel this strongly in the case of Arcite, who cannot be thought to have fully deserved his cruel fate. But there is, of course, another aspect of Chaucer's tale. He inherited from Boccaccio's *Teseida* the conflict between Mars and Venus, of which the conflict between the two knights is a reflection on the earthly plane; he also inherited the parallelism between Saturn's function, as arbiter between Mars and Venus, and Theseus's function, as arbiter between the knights. The parallelism between Saturn and Theseus Chaucer developed farther. The story of Palemon and Arcite becomes in his hands an illustration of the power which destiny wields over man. This theme is emphasized at the beginning by the victims themselves. 'Fortune hath yeven us this adversitee', says Arcite, of their im-prisonment: 'We moste endure it; this is the short and playn'; and a little later Palemon is railing at the 'crueel goddes that governe This world with byndyng of youre word eterne'. As they complain, they are the prisoners of Theseus, who at all times in the story has power of life and death over them. So the control which the gods have over man is made manifest in the material world by the power of Theseus; he is (to quote Mr. Frost again) the 'executant of destiny' on earth, and in this respect, too, he parallels the functions of the planetary powers and, more particularly, of Saturn. But, according to the Boethian philosophy, which Chaucer is reflecting in this poem, the planetary powers are not the final arbiters. It is fittingly left to Theseus, who stands outside the conflict and can see a little more than the other human actors, to recall the 'Firste Moevere', 'the prince and cause of alle thyng', who, when he first made the fair chain of love, 'Wel wiste he why, and what thereof he mente'. With this concluding speech Theseus removes the human conflict, and its apparently unjust resolving, to a yet more distant plane where earthly affairs, however they may seem to men, are part of an established order, a plan in which, though he cannot hope to understand it, man should acquiesce.

I have tried to show only the main features of the organization of the *Knight's Tale*, but there is much on a lesser scale which reveals similar methods. I will mention one instance only. It is well known that, in place of Boccaccio's diffuse account of the many champions who come to fight for Palemon and Arcite, Chaucer describes two champions only, Lygurge and Emetreus. Thereby his story obviously gains in brevity, neatness, and vividness. What is more important, it also gains in significance. The two champions stand as representatives of the two opposing forces in the coming tournament, and so, ultimately, as representatives of the two rival knights. The two descriptions, though entirely different in detail, are alike in manner, suggesting the same kind of parallelism as between Palemon and Arcite, between things similar yet dissimilar. In several ways this comparatively minor piece of reorganization could be said to epitomize what Chaucer does in his tale as a whole.

It is a far cry from this finely ordered tale to the treatises of the rhetoricians, and I can produce no logical proof of a connexion between them. I can only hope that the various links which I have tried to establish between the Arts of Poetry and Chaucer's practice are sufficiently strong to support my feeling that this kind of order is the product of a genius which has known the discipline of a training in medieval rhetoric, or, more properly speaking, in the 'art of poetry'.

As my last examples I shall take three tales—the tales of the Pardoner, the Manciple, and the Nun's Priest—in which the methods of presentation are much more directly related to rhetorical teaching. Indeed, it can be said of all three, diverse as they are in subject and mood, that in them Chaucer used rhetorical methods more or less as the rhetoricians themselves intended. Manly remarked of the *Pardoner's Tale* that the story of the three rioters displays Chaucer's 'advanced method' (by which he meant that the rhetorical influence in it is slight) and that 'the long passages of rhetoric, placed between the opening twenty lines, . . . and the narrative itself, are thoroughly explained and justified by their

function as part of the Pardoner's sermon'.[1] This, I think, gives
a false impression. The *Pardoner's Tale* does not consist of a more
or less unadorned story plus some passages of rhetoric. On the
contrary, the whole discourse which is known as the tale of the
Pardoner is a closely integrated unity. In the opening twenty lines
to which Manly refers, the Pardoner provides the setting for a story
by describing a company of 'yonge folk that haunteden folye'. As
he explains, these young folk spent their time whoring, playing at
dice, eating and drinking excessively, and swearing oaths

> so greet and so dampnable
> That it is grisly for to heere hem swere.

The Pardoner then pauses to dilate upon some of these sins, in
particular upon lechery, gluttony, gambling, and swearing. He
uses for this purpose various means of amplification, apostrophe
and *exemplum* being his favourites. When he has finished inveigh-
ing against the sins, he tells the terrible tale of the three rioters.[2]
This is an impressive illustration not only of his favourite theme,
'Radix malorum est cupiditas', but also of what may befall those
who commit the sins he has preached against, and he rounds it off
with a final apostrophe against homicide, gluttony, hazardry, and
swearing. The story and the tirade against the sins are so closely
connected with one another that one can either regard the story
as an *exemplum* illustrating the tirade, or one can consider the
story as the central point and the dilations upon the sins as ampli-
fications of it. Either way, the whole tale is organized according to
rhetorical methods.

But this organization is for a special purpose. By his words at the
end of his Prologue,

> A moral tale yet I yow telle kan
> Which I am wont to preche . . .,

---

[1] See *Chaucer and the Rhetoricians*, p. 20.

[2] Actually, although Chaucer writes, 'Thise riotoures thre of which I telle'
(C 661), he has not previously mentioned them. This has led some critics to
suspect that the tale of the three rioters was not originally connected with the
preceding 'homily on the sins of the tavern' (see Carleton Brown, *The Pardoner's
Tale*, 1935, for an exposition of this view). If Carleton Brown is right, and it is
not a mere oversight that the three rioters are not mentioned in the opening lines
of the *Tale*, one can only marvel at the skill with which two originally distinct
elements have been amalgamated and interrelated.

the Pardoner has led the reader to expect something related to a
sermon. What Chaucer gives him is not a sermon constructed
according to the elaborate rules of the *Artes praedicandi* (which
would, in any case, have been unsuited to the Pardoner's usual
audience, and his present one), but a tale so presented that it will
create the illusion of a sermon. It has some of the regular features
of a sermon. The theme is known, for the Pardoner has said that
he has only one. His final apostrophe against the sins acts as a
peroration, and is followed by a benediction.[1] In his dilations upon
the sins of hazardry and swearing there is a slight suggestion of the
'division' of the theme, so essential a part of the medieval sermon;
for these are branches of avarice, as appears from a passage in the
treatise on the seven deadly sins which forms part of the *Parson's
Tale*—a passage which is actually echoed by the Pardoner.[2] But
for the most part the illusion depends upon the Pardoner's
examples, especially the Scriptural ones at the beginning, and on
his direct attacks upon the sins, or the sinner:

> O glotonye, ful of cursednesse!
> O cause first of oure confusioun!

and

> O dronke man, disfigured is thy face . . .

It depends, that is, on a few common rhetorical devices—devices
fitting for a preacher and appropriate in the mouth of the Pardoner,
who has told us that, as he preaches:

> Myne handes and my tonge goon so yerne,
> That it is joye to se my bisynesse.

So the tale is shaped for its ultimate purpose, the completing of the
portrait of the Pardoner; but that purpose is only fully achieved
by the complex pattern of irony which Chaucer has woven into it.

---

[1] See C 895–903, and 916–18.

[2] See *Parson's Tale, De Avaricia* (Robinson's ed., p. 301): 'Now comth
hasardrie with his apurtenaunces, as tables and rafles, of which comth deceite,
false othes, chidynges and alle ravynes, blasphemynge and reneiynge of God, and
hate of his neighebores, wast of goodes, mysspendynge of tyme, and somtyme
manslaughtre.' Compare with this passage *Pardoner's Tale*, C 591–4. The tale
of the three rioters gathers up most of the sins mentioned in the passage in the
Parson's Tale.

The Pardoner, who feels himself to be so much cleverer than his victims, delights in and confidently exploits the cheap irony of his preaching against his own vice:

> I preche of no thyng but for coveityse.
> Therfore my theme is yet, and evere was,
> Radix malorum est cupiditas.

He is not, however, as clever as he believes himself to be, for the Host is not gulled by him. But this is a small part of his self-deception; its full extent is revealed by his own sermon. In his tale of the three rioters, who went out to seek for death and—after they had given up the search—found it at one another's hands, there is an irony which cuts so much deeper than any the Pardoner shows himself to be conscious of, that we feel him, equally with them, to be the victim of it. He understands no more than they that the wages of sin is death.[1]

It is a descent from this tale to the Manciple's. Yet, in its method, the *Manciple's Tale* resembles the Pardoner's, and even more closely the Nun's Priest's, and I doubt whether it is any more dependent for its form on rhetorical devices than they are. When, therefore, it is condemned as being over-rhetorical, it would seem to be condemned for the wrong reason. The real difference between it and the other two tales is that, in it, Chaucer appears to have been interested in rhetorical devices only for their own sake; there is no motive for the amplification of the story of Phoebus and the crow.

In the *Nun's Priest's Tale* Chaucer uses almost every means of amplification known to the rhetoricians, *interpretatio, comparatio, prosopopoeia*, apostrophe, digression, description; and he uses them precisely as the rhetoricians intended, to amplify, or extend, the little tale of the cock and the fox. It may be objected that this is a different case altogether; that here Chaucer is ridiculing the rhetoricians and is using their own methods to show them up. He is, of course, amusing himself at their expense; this would be clear

---

[1] I am indebted to Miss M. M. Lascelles for some suggestions about Chaucer's handling of the *Pardoner's Tale* and the *Nun's Priest's Tale*, but she is not responsible for any statement made here or any opinion expressed.

if there were no echoes of Geoffroi's *Nova Poetria*[1] and no allusion to his famous apostrophe on the death of Richard I:

O Gaufred, deere maister soverayn . . .
Why ne hadde I now thy sentence and thy loore
The Friday for to chide, as diden ye?

But when this mockery is quoted (as it sometimes is) to prove that Chaucer saw the folly of applying rhetorical methods to poetry, it should be remembered that, if he is here attacking rhetorical methods, he is at the same time attacking much of his own most serious poetry. The apostrophe 'O destinee, that mayst nat been eschewed!' is not in itself more ridiculous than some of Troilus's bitter outcries against Fortune. The joke lies in the incongruity between the high-sounding line and the farmyard birds to whose fate it refers:

O destinee, that mayst nat been eschewed!
Allas, that Chauntecleer fleigh fro the bemes!
Alas, his wyf ne roghte nat of dremes!

The joke is a better one if it is recognized that fine apostrophes and tragic *exempla* have their proper functions. It is the best joke of all for those who, like Chaucer and presumably his readers, had been taught the rhetorical doctrine of the three styles, and knew that the only fitting style for the farmyard was the *stylus humilis*.[2]

I would ask you to consider for a moment what would happen to the *Nun's Priest's Tale* if all traces of rhetorical amplification were to be removed from it. (This means the delightful descriptions of the cock and the hens as well as Chauntecleer's examples of prophetic dreams, the apostrophes, asides, and so on.) There would be nothing left but the bare bones of the story, something utterly different in kind from the subtly humorous poem which Chaucer created for a quick-witted and sophisticated audience. It is inconceivable that Chaucer should not have been aware of the extent

[1] On these echoes, see Marie P. Hamilton, 'Notes on Chaucer and the Rhetoricians', *P.M.L.A.* xlvii (1932), K. Young, 'Chaucer and Geoffrey de Vinsauf', *Modern Philology*, xli (1944), and a brief note by R. A. Pratt, 'The Classical Lamentations in the "Nun's Priest's Tale" ', *M.L.N.* lxiv (1949).
[2] On the doctrine of the three styles see Faral, pp. 86 ff., and, for a more recent discussion, De Bruyne, *Études d'esthétique médiévale*, ii, pp. 41 ff.

to which the structure of his story, and all that gave it its special quality, depended on rhetorical methods. Chaucer often makes fun of things for which he had a serious regard, and particularly in the *Nun's Priest's Tale* he mockingly alludes to many things in which he elsewhere shows deep interest—the significance of dreams, for example, and the question of pre-destination and free will. So it seems to me likely that if, as we read the *Nun's Priest's Tale*, we laugh too heartily and unthinkingly at the rhetoricians, there is a danger that Chaucer may be laughing at us.

BIBLIOGRAPHY OF
WRITINGS BY DOROTHY EVERETT

Only the more important of the author's many reviews are included in this list

Articles

'The Middle English Prose Psalter of Richard Rolle of Hampole', *M.L.R.* xvii (1922), pp. 217 ff. and 337 ff.; xviii (1923), pp. 381 ff.

'A Characterisation of the English Medieval Romances', *E. and S.* xv (1929), pp. 98 ff.

'Another Collation of the Ellesmere Manuscript of the *Canterbury Tales*', *M.Æv.* i (1932), pp. 42 ff.

'The Relationship of Chestre's *Launfal* and *Lybeaus Desconus*', *M.Æv.* vii (1938), pp. 29 ff.

'Legal Phraseology in a passage in *Pearl*' (with Naomi D. Hurnard), *M.Æv.* xvi (1947), pp. 9 ff.

'Chaucer's "Good Ear"', *R.E.S.* xxiii (1947), pp. 201 ff.

'Some Reflections on Chaucer's "Art Poetical"', *Sir Israel Gollancz Memorial Lecture*, British Academy (1950).

Contributions to The Year's Work in English Studies

Chapter on Middle English, vi–xv (1925–34).

Chapter on Chaucer, Lydgate, and Gower, xvi (1935).

Chapter on Chaucer, xvii–xxxii (1936–51).

Reviews

Floris and Blancheflur, ed. A. B. Taylor, *R.E.S.* iv (1928), pp. 220 ff.

Writings ascribed to Richard Rolle, Hermit of Hampole, and Materials for his Biography, Hope Emily Allen, *R.E.S.* v (1929), pp. 79 ff.

Valentine and Orson: a study in Late Medieval Romance, Arthur Dickson, *R.E.S.* vi (1930), pp. 331 ff.

The Gests of King Alexander of Macedon, F. P. Magoun Jr., *R.E.S.* vi (1930), pp. 329 ff.

Winner and Waster and *Death and Liffe*, ed. Sir Israel Gollancz, *R.E.S.* ix (1933), pp. 213 ff.

Eger and Grime, ed. James Ralston Caldwell, *M.L.R.* xxix (1934), pp. 446 ff.

Athelston. A Middle English Romance, ed. A. McI. Trounce, *R.E.S.* xi (1935), pp. 112 ff.

Seinte Marharete þe Meiden ant Martyr, ed. Frances M. Mack, *R.E.S.* xi (1935), pp. 337 ff.

The Manuscripts of Chaucer's Canterbury Tales, Sir William McCormick, *R.E.S.* xi (1935), pp. 342 ff.

Chaucer's Canterbury Tales und das Decameron, Lorenz Morsbach, *M.Æv.* iv (1935), pp. 54 ff.

Chaucer: Troilus and Criseyde, abridged and ed. R. C. Goffin; *Chaucer: the Pardoner's Tale*, ed. Carleton Brown, *M.Æv.* vi (1937), pp. 144 ff.

The Complete Works of Geoffrey Chaucer, ed. F. N. Robinson, *M.Æv.* vii (1938), pp. 204 ff.

The Battle of Maldon, ed. E. V. Gordon, *M.Æv.* viii (1939), pp. 156 ff.

Sawles Warde, ed. R. M. Wilson; *The Conflict of Wit and Will*, ed. Bruce Dickins, *R.E.S.* xvi (1940), pp. 72 ff.

The Battle of Brunanburh, ed. Alistair Campbell, *M.Æv.* ix (1940), pp. 35 ff.

Early Middle English Literature, R. M. Wilson, *M.Æv.* x (1941), pp. 47 ff.

Hali Meiðhad, ed. A. F. Colborn, *R.E.S.* xvii (1941), pp. 117 ff.

The Text of the Canterbury Tales, John M. Manly and Edith Rickert, *R.E.S.* xviii (1942), pp. 93 ff.

Essays on King Horn, Walter H. French, *R.E.S.* xviii (1942), pp. 330 ff.

Sources and Analogues of Chaucer's 'Canterbury Tales', ed. W. F. Bryan and Germaine Dempster, *M.Æv.* xii (1943), pp. 78 ff.

The Literary Relationships of Chaucer's 'Clerkes Tale', J. Burke Severs, *M.Æv.* xiii (1944), pp. 47 ff.

Chaucer's World, compiled by Edith Rickert, ed. Clair C. Olson and Martin M. Crow, *R.E.S.* N.S. i (1950), pp. 156 ff.

The Poet Chaucer, Nevill Coghill, *R.E.S.* N.S. ii (1951), pp. 159 ff.

Chaucer and the Canterbury Tales, W. W. Lawrence; *Chaucer the Maker*, J. Speirs, *R.E.S.* N.S. iii (1952), pp. 377 ff.

The Lost Literature of Medieval England, R. M. Wilson, *M.Æv.* xxii (1953), pp. 31 ff.

INDEX

Ælfric, 140.
Against a Wen, Charm, 24.
Alanus de Insulis, De Planctu Naturae, 107, 112.
Alexander A, 54 ff.
Alexander B (Alexander and Dindimus), 54 ff.
Alexander C (Wars of Alexander), 54 ff.
alliterative prose, 139–40.
alliterative verse: style and diction, 23–24, 26, 47; 'popular' and 'classical', 26 ff., 37–38; audience of, 47 ff.; echoed by Chaucer, 139 ff.
Amis and Amiloun, 9.
Ancient Mariner, 11, 13, 14.
Ancren Riwle, 144.
Ancrene Riwle, 25.
Anglo Saxon Chronicle, 37; poem on the death of Edgar, 26; Alfred and Godwin, 26, 28.
Artes prædicandi, 171.
Art of Poetry, see Rhetoric.
Athelston, 9.
Augustine, St., 94.

Ballads, 16.
Battle of Maldon, 62.
Bede, Ecclesiastical History, 30.
Bennett, Arnold, 8.
Beowulf, 10, 23, 36, 37, 62, 74.
Bestiary, 26.
Boccaccio: Il Filostrato, 116 ff., 155, 156; Olympia, 69; Teseida, 107, 128, 167–9.
Boethius, De Consolatione Philosophiae, 107, 110, 128, 132–3, 135, 163, 166, 168.
Bonaventura, St., 93.
Book of Privy Counselling, 139.
Bradwardine, Thomas, 94–95.
Breton lais, 14, 16, 21–22.

Chansons de geste, 5, 19–21.
Chanson de Roland, 9, 19–20 ff.
Chaucer, Geoffrey, 1, 4, 7, 15, 47–48, 81, 85, 93; ABC, 153; Book of the Duchess, 2, 97, 100 ff., 103, 108, 147, 153, 156–8, 160, 162–5;
Canterbury Tales, 99, 104; Clerk's Tale, 97; Complaint of Venus, 102; Franklin's Prologue, 150; Franklin's Tale, 22; Friar's Tale, 144; House of Fame, 100 ff., 116, 149–50; Knight's Tale, 68, 103, 140, 141, 158, 159, 164–5, 166–9; Legend of Good Women, 98–99, 100 ff., 108, 141; Manciple's Tale, 158, 169, 172; Man of Law's Tale, 21, 139, 140, 142, 151, 165; Merchant's Prologue, 158; Merchant's Tale, 156, 159–60; Miller's Tale, 144, 164; Nun's Priest's Tale, 97, 169, 172–4; Pardoner's Tale, 144, 169–72; Parlement of Foules, 97 ff., 143, 144, 148, 153–4, 159, 160, 163–4; Parson's Tale, 140, 171; Prioress's Prologue, 140; Prioress's Tale, 97, 148, 157–8; Prologue, Canterbury Tales, 8, 98, 140, 154–5, 160; Reeve's Tale, 144; Retractation to, Canterbury Tales, 102, 135; Sir Thopas, 11, 142–3, 144; Squire's Tale, 150, 159, 160; Summoner's Tale, 140, 145, 146; Troilus and Criseyde, 2, 77, 99, 101, 104, 109–10, 114, 115 ff., 148, 150, 155, 156, 163, 173; Wife of Bath's Tale, 11–12, 145, 147, 156, 158; Wife of Bath's Prologue, 145 ff., 158.
Chevalere Assigne, 9.
Chrétien de Troyes, 7, 22, 33; Cleges, 126; Lancelot, 99; Yvain, 99.
Cicero, 152–3; see Macrobius, Somnium Scipionis.
Cleanness, see Purity.
Courtly Love, 77 ff., 99–100, 108, 112–14, 125–7, 129–30, 136–8.

Dante, 69, 95, 107, 111, 135, 143, 149.
Death and Liffe, 52–53.
de Bohun, Humphrey, Earl of Hereford, 48, 53.
Departing Soul's Address to the Body, 24–25, 26, 27, 37–39.
Deschamps, 100.
Description of Durham, 26.
Destruction of Troy, 57–58.

Dryden, *Conquest of Granada*, 9.
Duke Rowlande and Sir Ottuell of Spayne, 20.

Eliot, T. S., 156.
Emaré, 8, 9, 21–22.
Évrard the German, *Laborintus*, 151.

Fabliau, 21.
Fair Annie, ballad of, 16, 17–18.
Fight at Finnsburuh, 28.
Floris and Blauncheflur, 3.
Froissart, 100, 103; *L'Espinette amoureuse*, 101.
Fuerres de Gadres, 55.

Geoffrey of Monmouth, 30–32.
Geoffroi de Vinsauf, *Nova Poetria*, 103, 150, 151, 158, 160, 162, 164, 165, 173.
Gervais of Melkley, 152.
Giraldus Cambrensis, 25.
Gower, *Confessio Amantis*, 21, 22, 99, 100.
Grave, The, 24, 25.
Gregory the Great, St., 92.
Guido della Colonne, *Historia Troiana* (*Historia Destructionis Trojae*) 4, 57–58.
Guillaume de Lorris, see *Roman de la Rose*.
Guy of Warwick, 3, 9, 12.

Havelok, Lay of, 3, 8, 9.
Henry of Huntingdon, 25.
Hind Horn, ballad of, 16, 18.
Historia de Preliis, 54 ff.
Horn Childe and Maiden Rimnild, 16, 19.
Huchoun, 47.
Huon de Bordeaux, 19.

Ipomadon A, 141.

John of Salisbury, 151–2, 153.
John Ball, Letter to the peasants of Essex, 48.
Joseph of Arimathie, 59–61.

Keats, John, 13.
King Horn, 5, 9, 12, 16, 19, 38, 39.
King of Tars, 11.
King Orfeo, 16.
Knight of Courtesy, 9.
Kyng Alysaunder, 82.

Laȝamon's *Brut*, 25, 26, 28 ff., 46, 161.
Lai le Freine, 16–17.
Langland, William, see *Piers Plowman*.
Lestoire del Saint Graal (*Grand Saint Graal*), 59–60.
Liber Catonianus, 153.
Lollius, 115–16.
Lybeaus Desconus, 8, 9, 12, 13.
Lycidas, 85, 96.
Lydgate, *Fall of Princes*, 116; *Troy Book*, 3, 4, 5.
Lyfe of Alisaunder, 3, 4, 9.

Machaut, 100; *Jugement dou Roy de Behaigne*, 103.
Macrobius, *Somnium Scipionis*, 103, 105–7, 159.
Malory, *Morte Darthur*, 61, 65.
Marie de France, 17, 22.
Matthieu de Vendôme, *Ars versificatoria*, 103, 150–1, 164.
Morte Darthur, see Malory.
Morte Arthure, alliterative, 3, 5, 9, 21, 61 ff., 161.

Orosius, *Historia adversus Paganos*, 54.
Oton de Graunson, 108; *Songe sainct Valentin*, 102.
Ovid, 107; *Metamorphoses*, 2.
Owl and Nightingale, 99, 102.

Parliament of the Three Ages, 49, 50–52.
Partonope of Blois, 141.
Patience, 68 ff.
Pearl, 68–70, 73–74, 82, 85 ff., 156.
Petrus Chrysologus, 92.
Piers Plowman, 8, 48, 50, 51, 52, 68, 74, 139.
Proverbs of Alfred, 26, 38.
Proverbs of Hendyng, 25.
Purity (Cleanness), 15, 68 ff., 139, 161.

Quatre Fils d'Aymon, 19.
Quintilian, 152–3, 154.

Rabanus Maurus, 151.
Raymund, St., of Pennaforte, *Summa*, 140.
Rhetoric: used by Chaucer, 103–6, 113, 131–2, 149 ff.; by Machaut and Froissart, 103; by the *Pearl* Poet, 73–74, 84, 93; in Laȝamon's *Brut*, 42–43; in *Joseph of Arimathie*, 60.

Roland and Vernagu, 9.
Romances, 1 ff.; meaning of term, 2 ff.; alliterative 53 ff.; Arthurian, 10, 20, 53; of Charlemagne, 5, 20; tail-rhyme, 142–3; (*see also separate titles*).
Roman d'Alixandre, 55.
Roman de Balain, 152, 165.
Roman de Brut, see Wace.
Roman de la Rose, 69, 90–91, 100–1, 103, 125–6, 130, 137.

Saint's Legends, 15–16.
Sawles Warde, 144.
Scale of Perfection, 139.
Seinte Marherete, 139.
Siege of Jerusalem, 58–59.
Siege of Thebes, 2.
Sir Aldingar, 16, 18.
Sir Eglamour of Artois, 21.
Sir Ferumbras, 3, 20.
Sir Gawain and the Green Knight, 5, 6, 8, 9, 13–14, 23, 48, 51, 52, 68–69, 73, 74 ff., 87, 93, 139, 164, 165–6.
Sir Isumbras, 16.
Sir Launfal, 10.
Sir Orfeo, 6, 9, 10, 13–14, 16.
Sir Perceval of Galles, 12, 13.

Sir Torrent of Portyngale, 21.
Sir Tristrem, 143.
Somnium Scipionis, see Macrobius.
Song of Roland, 9, 20.
South-English Legendary, 15, 16.
Sowdone of Babylone, 20.
Squyr of Lowe Degré, 5–6.
Suite du Merlin, 152.

Trevisa, 48.
Towneley Second Shepherd's Play, 15.

Usk, *Testament of Love*, 92.

Virgil, 115, 134.
Vernon MS., Lyrics of, 88.

Wace, *Roman de Brut*, 30, 36, 40, 42–45.
Wade, Story of, 25.
Weddynge of Sir Gawen, 10.
William of Malmesbury, 25.
William of Palerne, 48, 53 ff.
Winner and Waster, 49 ff.
Worcester Fragments: First, 24, 26; others, see *Departing Soul's Address to the Body.*
Wyntoun, Andrew, *Orygynale Cronykil*, 47.

Ywain and Gawain, 9, 141.

PRINTED IN GREAT BRITAIN
AT THE UNIVERSITY PRESS, OXFORD
BY VIVIAN RIDLER
PRINTER TO THE UNIVERSITY